Celtic Civilization
and
Its Heritage

JAN FILIP

Celtic Civilization and Its Heritage

(Second revised edition)

COLLET'S
Wellingborough

1977

ACADEMIA
Prague

Published in co-edition with ACADEMIA, Publishing House of the Czechoslovak Academy of Sciences, Prague

Sole distributors for the whole world with the exception of Socialist Countries

Collet's Holdings Ltd.
Denington Estate, Wellingborough
Northamptonshire, NN8 2QT

5

Contents

A FEW WORDS OF INTRODUCTION   9—10

I.   THE PREHISTORICAL BACKGROUND OF THE HISTORICAL
     CELTS   11—27
     The role of archaeology in solving the problems of
     the Celtic past – Development from the Early
     Stone Age – The basic components of Celtic ethno-
     genesis

I.   THE ENVIRONMENT OF THE HALLSTATT IRON AGE CHIEF-
     TAINS – THE FORTS OF THE OVERLORDS AND THEIR CON-
     TACTS WITH THE MEDITERRANEAN   28—59
     The importance of the Hallstatt period for the
     culmination of the process of Celtic ethnogenesis –
     Social differentiation. Chamber-graves and chief-
     tains' burials – Centres of development in the 6th
     century. Chieftains' strongholds – Contacts of the
     princely courts with the southern region and the
     rise of an Early La Tène art style

III. ARMED EXPEDITIONS OF THE CELTS INTO THE REST OF
     EUROPE – PERIOD OF CELTIC EXPANSION AND LATER
     CENTRAL EUROPEAN CONCENTRATION   60—80
     The Celts in Italy – Celtic incursions into the
     Carpathians and into the Balkans – Celtic tribes
     in the Czech Lands and in Slovakia – The invasions
     of the Cimbri and of the Teutones – Gaul in the
     La Tène period and in Caesar's time – Historical
     Celts in the British Isles

IV. CELTIC LANGUAGES AND THE OLDEST SURVIVING LITER-
     ATURE   81—85
     Gaelic-Goidel and Gaulish dialects – Our present-

-day knowledge of Gaulish language. Interpretation of place-names – The oldest survivals of Irish literature

V. CELTIC SOCIETY AND ITS STRUCTURE   86—100
Appearance and character of the Celts – Celtic dress – Torcs and their socio-ritual significance in Celtic society – Food and feasts of the Celts – The structure of Celtic society – Kingship and aristocracy – The druids

VI. THE WARRIOR ORGANIZATION OF THE CELTS AND THEIR MODE OF WARFARE   101—108
The leading warrior group and their equipment – Outward marks of social prestige – Methods of warfare

VII. THE ECONOMIC BASIS AND CIVILIZED ACHIEVEMENT OF CELTIC SOCIETY   109—142
House and village – Farming and land ownership – Crafts and trades and the high level of Celtic technology. Iron bloomeries and forges – Domestic production and later mass production. Different branches of manufacture – Celtic oppida and their systems of fortification – Oppida in the Czech Lands – Trade and transport – Celtic coinage – the oldest coinage in Central Europe

VIII. CELTIC ART AND CELTIC RELIGION   143—181
Early La Tène style in Celtic handicrafts and Celtic ornament – Mature La Tène style – Plastic style and Sword style – Insular Celtic Art – Celtic architecture and sculpture – The Celto-Ligurian seabord – Celtic sculpture in Gaul and in Central Europe – Celtic masks – Celtic sacred sites and sanctuaries – Votive deposits and sacrifices – Celtic conceptions of the supernatural – Burial rites

IX. THE CIVILIZATIONAL AND CULTURAL HERITAGE OF THE CELTS   182—199
The Romanization of Gaul and the Celtic heritage – Celtic traditions in Ireland and in Britain – The Neo-Celtic Style and its repercussions on the Continent. Book illumination – The Celtic Heritage in Central and Northern Europe

BIBLIOGRAPHY 200—203

LIST OF THE PRINCIPAL WORKS OF ACADEMICIAN JAN
FILIP 204—205

INDEX OF NAMES 206—212

CULTURAL AND SUBJECT INDEX 213—215

THE PRESENT STATE OF STUDIES IN CELTIC HISTORY AND
FUTURE PROSPECTS 216—000

FIGURES: 1—52 IN TEXT, I—XL PLATES ON ART PAPER

A few words of introduction

It is fascinating to discover how modern archaeological research provides missing pieces in the jig-saw puzzle picture of life in Celtic society where historical and linguistic research left gaps. Rigorous analysis of new finds and of the way they fit together sheds fresh light on hitherto unexplained aspects of ancient societies and dispels mysteries that have daunted researchers for many years. Much spade work, both in literal and metaphoric senses of the word, needs to be done; but we already have before us a credible, all-round picture of Celtic Society and Civilization, so vital in the development of Europe. Archaeology has provided answers to many of the problems confronting the historian—a gratifying reward for the painstaking work of the dedicated archaeologist.

Celtic Civilization and Its Heritage draws on European material available up to 1961 and on my own studies of Czechoslovak and Central European finds, not widely known to foreign researchers. A popular style is chosen to make the subject attractive to a broad public, but I hope that the specialist will also be interested. In fact, some finds are published here for the first time. In certain instances I venture guesswork, but I am careful to indicate this.

I believe this work is the first attempt to present an all-round view of our Celtic past, to survey the full spread of this fascinating people throughout Europe. A knowledge of life, art, language and social order of the Celtic era is shown here to be astonishingly relevant to an understanding of many facets of European culture today. Not in the least surprising to the reader, I am inclined to think, will be the richness of the Celtic heritage in the Czech lands.

J. F.

I

The Prehistoric Background of the Historical Celts

First of the prehistoric peoples to rise from anonymity in the territories north of the Alps were the Celts, whose early written history was marked, to the amazement of the rest of Europe, by bloody clashes and plundering raids on the richest centres of the contemporary world. Previous to this nothing was known of them by the civilized South, especially the Greek and Roman world, to which we owe the first historical testimony about Europe. And yet, there had come into being by the middle of the first millennium B. C., north-west of the Alps, as the outcome of a complex sociological process, this remarkable people, the first of the 'barbarian' peoples, as the civilized South was wont to call them, to become the classic people of the barbarian world. It was they who brought Central Europe into closer contact with the Mediterranean world, and, thanks to their creative powers, carried to its culmination the proto-historical development of civilization in the territories north of the Alps. Trade and commerce were the means of achieving at least a partial contact between the Celtic environment and that of the Mediterranean, at first from the latter end of the 6th century and then with growing intensity throughout the 5th century B. C.

Meanwhile, throughout the Celtic world, an important economic and social transformation had taken place, the latter in the sense of a social differentiation, growing out of native conditions and premises. Outwardly it was documented by the rise of numerous power-centres of native overlords, of whose existence the Mediterranean world learned only very slowly, when it began to prove economically advantageous to trade their products with them and thus help to raise the living standards and prestige of the ruling class. And then, almost without warning, well-armed groups of Celtic warriors, boldly and without scruple, attacked the most important centres of the South, made their way into the North Italian plain, raided

Rome itself, penetrated as far as Sicily, while other groups intruded into the Carpathian Basin, the Balkans and even deep into Asia Minor. The southern world was shocked by the force of their assaults, by their courage, their bravery and their thirst for plunder. Only then did they realize the unpleasant fact that, beyond the Alps, had grown up a conglomerate of peoples who, for another five centuries, were to be an important military and political factor in European history. Indeed, by the 4th century, the Celts were ranked, along with the Scythians and the Persians, among the most numerous barbarian peoples of the known world. And yet this people never formed an absolute ethnical unity, nor even a unified state, an empire which would merge a wide variety of tribal groups in a firm, well-organized and consolidated whole. On the contrary, they were split up into a number of large and small tribal communities, speaking different, though mutually related, dialects, the majority of which were later to die out.

The Greek world called them Keltoi, Celts. It would seem that this designation became widespread in the era when the rise of centres of power of a ruling warrior class was at its height, if not earlier, then at the latest in the 6th century, nor is it ruled out that it was originally the name of a single tribe or even of a ruling family, which was then transferred to the whole people. It would not be correct, however, to presume an ancient Celtic language from which all later dialects derived. There existed a group of various dialects, just as there had earlier existed a tangle of cultures and cultural groups, from which later evolved a unifying Celtic culture and a unified style.

The name Keltoi was the first under which this people was known to the literate world. The Romans, however, called them Gauls (Galli), and from this name various territories occupied by Celts derived their designations; Cisalpine Gaul (Gallia Cisalpina, in present-day North Italy), then Narbonensian Gaul (Gallia Narbonensis in Southern France) and Transalpine Gaul (Gallia Transalpina), the heart of present-day France, well-known for the Gallic Wars waged in the last century before our era by Julius Caesar. Later the name Galatae, Galatians, appears, but also at a time when the old centres of the Hallstatt culture had long since fallen into decay. This name is used in all his universal histories by Polybius, the Greek scholar, familiar with the Roman environment, who had visited among other places Spain and Southern France (d. 120 B. C.), and after him by other Greek writers. This was also the name given to the inner part of Asia Minor into which the Celts or Gauls penetrated. It is claimed that the language spoken by these Celts was related to that of the Treveri, Celts settled in the district of Trier, on the Moselle, as is testified to by St Jerome, writing in the 4th century. All these names, however, are more or less synonyms. Diodorus Siculus, who travelled throughout a greater part of Europe, and Caesar, who fought for some years in Gaul, confirm that Galli and Galatae were different names for the people called Keltoi, Latin Celtae. Diodorus held Celts to be the more correct appellation. Similar explanations are to be found among later historians and geographers. Only in Britain and Ireland this name does not seem to have been current.

The extent of Celtic settlements was originally much smaller. Not even Gaul the main basis of Celtic power and the magnet for Roman conquering interests in the last century B. C., was originally settled entirely by Celts. However, in early times, the original Celtic territory comprised also Southern Germany and a part of Bohemia, and in later centuries new streams of Celts occupied almost the whole of Central Europe, including present-day Czechoslovakia. In mediaeval times the settlement of Bohemia by Celts was forgotten, so that even the earliest Czech chronicler, Kosmas (d. 1125), supposed the first inhabitants of Bohemia to have been the tribe at whose head was Father Čech. This view was maintained into the 15th century. It was Daniel of Veleslavín, a Czech printer, who, in the 16th century, published the Bohemian Chronicles of Aeneas Silvius and Kuthen and noted for the first time in the Introduction to the same that the first historically attested inhabitants of Bohemia were the Gaulish Boii, who gave their name to the country — Boiohemum, Bohemia. This fact was never subsequently lost sight of and, in the 19th century, it was given scholarly confirmation, especially by František Palacký. Another Czech historian, J. E. Vocel, in his *Prehistory of Bohemia*, published in 1868, considers the Celtic settlement of Bohemia to be an accepted fact. Thus the picture of the earliest Celtic past has a special attraction for us, as a substantial part of Celtic history had its setting in Central Europe, and the following ages preserved not a few vestiges of the civilization of the Celts. The present state of knowledge already allows us to focus our attention on the earliest times, the prehistoric background out of which the Celts as a people emerged.

From the 5th century B. C. onwards Celts as the name for this people spread quickly throughout contemporary Europe.

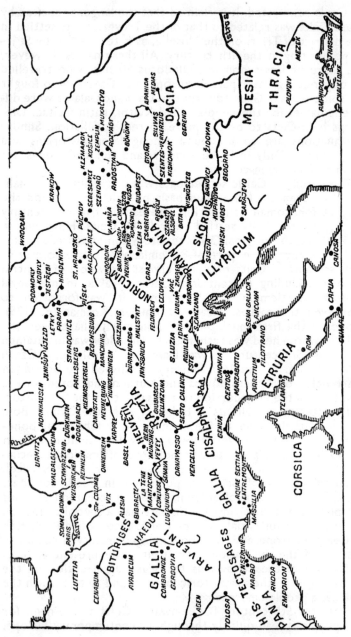

Fig. 1. Important places and find-sites in the Celtic world.

What preceded that time, however, remained a mystery. From the latter end of the 18th century, romanticism stimulated interest in the Celtic past, which had already been awakened in Western Europe. This interest then developed into full-blown Celtomania, which often quite uncritically accumulated true and hypothetical testimony relating to the glorious Celtic past. From the 17th century the view was held that the Celts were the builders on the western coast of France and in England of the megalithic monuments, consisting of immense stone blocks — menhirs, and dolmens (chamber tombs of huge stones, also known as cromlechs), as well as of the long avenues of stones or the circular arrangements of stones (of which Stone-henge is an outstanding example) presumed to be astronom-ical observatories and cult centres. The Romantics considered the Celts to be the oldest nation, identified their beginnings with the descendants of Biblical personages and traced their settlements practically all over Europe, often on the basis of quite arbitrary etymological interpretations. Ideas of the maturity of the Celts were also strengthened by literary fakes. The best-known of these are the epic poems of the Scottish poet, J. Macpherson, from 1760—1763, of which the author affirmed that he had translated them from the Celtic originals of Ossian, a hero-warrior of the 3rd century A. D. The echoes of these unfounded etymologics have continued up to our time, and the most diverse archaeological finds were attrib-uted, on the flimsiest of grounds, to the Celts. At the end of last century pan-Celtic tendencies appeared in opposition to military pan-Germanism and British imperialism, and the Breton folk-songs, describing the resistance of the Druids to Christianity and to Frankish aggression, were held to be genu-ine; actually, they were the work of Hersart de la Villemarqué, published in 1839.

The Celtic tradition was thus very strong in the West and nourished by contributary data based on a wide variety of sources and monuments: the evidence of Classical writers, who testified to the way of life of the Celts and their martial spirit, literary monuments from the Gallo-Roman period, especially inscriptions on tombstones and similar epigraphic material, then the linguistic evidence of place-names, the names of rivers and hills, or other topographical features, Celtic coins, finds of which quickly accumulated, objects of Celtic art and documents of their material culture in the countryside, and, finally, chance anthropological measurements — sources varying greatly in kind and in value and also variously interpreted.

Already in the 19th century comprehensive literary works arose of an historical, philological, numismatic and also archaeological character dealing with the Celts, so that today the specialized literature would fill the shelves of a good-sized library. Nor is it any wonder, for the various stages of the development of a Celtic society and civilization had their setting on the soil of a greater part of Europe, stretching from Ireland and Scotland in the north-west to the Black Sea in the south-east.

The role of archaeology in solving the problems of the Celtic past

Formerly archaeology could not compete on an equal footing with linguistic or historical studies, for it was still struggling to justify its existence and only slowly leaving behind its amateur beginnings and becoming a branch of science, with its own techniques and methods. The more accurate delimitation of the culture of the Celts at the time of their greatest flourishing in Europe (between the 5th and 1st cents. B. C.) dates from the second half of last century. It was named after La Tène (the Swiss find-place beside Lake Neuchâtel) the La Tène Culture (and Age), as the culture of the second Early Iron Age, which followed that of the first Early Iron Age, known also as the Hallstatt Iron Age. Then gradually groping and uncertainty gave way to more systematic study, which deepened our knowledge of the La Tène Age and attempted to trace the development of Celtic society in the Hallstatt Age and even earlier. Fortunate chance discoveries, the results of systematic field excavations and analytical studies of all kinds, carried out with the utmost precision and up-to-date working methods, make it possible today to solve a number of problems of the Celtic past almost definitively, without in any way doing violence to the testimony of the archaeological evidence. It also permits of a critical attitude to different aspects of a number of earlier conclusions based on linguistic studies or on the interpretation of brief or fragmentary allusions in classical writers. One of the modern results of archaeological science, to which Czech scholars have made an important contribution, is the new picture that has been built up of the Hallstatt Age. It is a surprising and exciting picture, for it affords a glimpse of the remarkable birth of the early historical Celts before they entered the European stage as a feared and important factor in the history of our continent. Here archaeology has already taken over the leading role in the investigation of the key tasks of ethnogenesis and soon it will take over the leading role in the study of a still earlier period in the story of the Celts — that dating from the end of the Stone Age and covering the Bronze Age, where the results of research allow only of provisional conclusions being reached.

Development from the Early Stone Age

In the past of these territories, where only in the course of a gradual and complex process the consciousness was born of belonging to a greater whole, later designated the Celts, many cultures and cultural groups entered and left the stage in prehistoric times, and, in the specialized literature, there are many guesses and hypotheses as to their identity and significance. The passage of hunting bands in the Lower and Middle Paleolithic can scarcely have left deeper traces. In the 4th—3rd millennia B. C. we come across, in flatter and more fertile places in the Danube Basin, older agricultural peoples whose earlier homesteads probably formed the substratum on which the relations and ties of later times were formed. At present we are already fairly well informed about their culture, but it is not yet clear to what ethnic group they belonged, nor, with our present resources, is the question soluble. The settlements of this people were dispersed not only throughout the basin of the Middle Danube, but across the Rhine and into Eastern France and Belgium. Further to the south-west and west, this same people was in contact with other Neolithic cultures, such as the Cortaillod in Switzerland, which had affinities with the French Chassey culture; here we have to do again with a larger cultural region extending as far as the British Isles (Windmill Hill). The marginal overlapping between these two extensive cultures, the Central European and the West European, is located in just those territories where later the centres of Celtic power were to arise.

The situation became more complicated in the Late Neolithic, towards the end of the 3rd millennium, with the appearance in the west of the people of the Michelberg culture, who for a number of reasons fortified hill settlements; recently they have been brought into closer connexion with the extensive area settled by the Beaker people, well represented also in Central Europe. In addition, there were a number of other groups of population to which we shall refer later. The incursion of the mobile people with the Bell Beaker pottery, already acquainted with bronze, whose area of origin was the south of Spain and the North African coastal strip, was preceded by an influx of people with stone battle-axes who, in Central Europe, are named the Corded Ware people, after the distinctive decoration of their pottery. Ethnically they seem to have been of eastern origin, to have kept horses and penetrated as far as the Rhine Basin in the west. In some parts of Central Europe, there was direct contact between these two peoples, for they were settled side by side, in the same territories.

For the reader it would be too tedious to give a detailed account of all the connexions, a matter of interest only to the specialist. But yet it is necessary here to pause for several important reasons. First of all, the Battle-Axe people are often assumed to be the first Indo-Europeans to enter the Central European region. Many investigators hold the view that the common lexical stock of several ethnical groups and complexes, among them the Celts and the Germans, go back to the time before the individual languages or dialects became more fully differentiated. The Celtic dialects were originally related, to a considerable extent, to the Germanic and Italian dialects, especially as regards the stock of words. It is presumed that this lexical stock derives from the Neolithic and the Bronze Age. And so, today, many investigators are of the opinion that the dispersion of Indo-European groups can be dated back to the time when a distinction began to be made between copper and bronze, that is, towards the end of the 3rd millennium. The arrival of new Indo-European groups in Asia Minor and India is often dated to the period about 2000 B. C., and, in Greece and Italy, to somewhat later. At the beginning of the Iron Age the period of dispersion is considered to be over, the Celts and Germans alone being possibly still in closer contact round about 1000 B. C.; they have, namely, the same word for iron (Celtic, *isarno*, Gothic, *eisarn*). These are, however, linguistic suppositions, and the latter fact could also be explained as due to the influence of the Celtic world on Germanic peoples.

Archaeology is, naturally, still less able, with the means and methods at its disposal, to build up a picture of the rise and development of language communities towards the end of the Neolithic. The archeological record shows that at this time the whole area under discussion was occupied by a conglomerate of cultures, of different origins, often existing side by side. There is no doubt that the share of the Cord Ware (Battle-Axe) People was considerable in the zone which we later designate the homeland of the Celts. The British scholar Hawkes does not hesitate to call the Bell Beaker People, mingled with the Cord Ware People, Celts (Proto-Celts), and also the Frenchman, H. Hubert (to mention only two of the most distinguished names in this field) seeks the origins of insular Celts as far back as in the Megalithic Period and towards the end of the Neolithic. A definitive solution of this problem is still, however, a matter of the future.

The situation underwent a perceptible change in the 2nd millennium B. C., in the Bronze Age. Instead of a mosaic of independent cultures, larger and more characteristic cultural complexes came into evidence in the whole territory north and north-west of the Alps. Besides the large Central European region of the Únětice (Aunjetitz) culture, in the Early Bronze Age, there arose in Southern Germany the Straubing and Adlerberg cultures. In the south of Britain, the Wessex Culture soon produced a rich flowering, which profited from close contact with Irish sources of the bronze industry. In the territory which was later to form the core of Celtic settlement, there appeared in the course of the developing Bronze Age the Tumulus People, witnesses to whom are everywhere cemeteries, with large or small groups of barrows. They were a people of more pastoral inclinations, who settled on less fertile ground, often hitherto unexploited gravel soil, at higher levels. From Burgundy to Lothringen and to beyond the Bohemian Forest, from Vogelsberg and Rhön north of the Main, beside the sources of the Fulda, to Switzerland, we find this people settled about the middle of the 2nd millennium, with related groups on the Middle Danube, including a part of Moravia. Contracted burials, which had still been prescribed in the Early Bronze Age, had given way to inhumations in the extended attitude and, later, cremation became increasingly common. In the course of time the Tumulus Culture spread considerably, reaching Belgium in the north-west, the Teutonburg Forest and the Harz Mountains.

The Tumulus People undoubtedly grew out of the older Eneolithic and Early Bronze stock und took over many elements from neighbouring cultures, especially on the east, as far as the Carpathians. Their obvious concentration in the territory north-west of the Alps, the historical domain of the Celts, has led many scholars to consider the Tumulus People to be

Celts (Lantier). And, indeed, we are justified in assuming that the homelands of the people with this burial rite, whose settlements extended to a considerable part of Bohemia, was the environment in which, at least in certain regions, the process took place in which the prehistoric complex of related peoples assumed the definitive shape of the historical Celts It seems, however, that one more factor was required for its culmination — the culture of the Urnfields, in the latter part of the 2nd millennium, at the very dawn of the Early Iron Age in Central Europe. In the south-east, the glorious epoch of the Minoan-Mycenaean civilization was on the decline and the power of the rulers of the fortified citadels (Mycenae, Tiryns) approaching its end; in Asia Minor, the great Hittite Empire, whose influence made itself felt as far as South-east Europe and deep into the Carpathian Basin, was breaking up; in Egypt, foreign invaders had appeared on the scene. In certain parts of Europe, especially in Poland, Silesia, Lusatia, Saxony and the adjacent territory of Bohemia, the importance of the people with the Lusatian (Lausitz) Culture greatly increased, a people that consistently cremated their deads and placed the broken bones in urns in extensive urnfields. They were a farming people, but had a good command of bronze-working and the technique of building defensive earthworks and palisades. Their influence soon percolated to the neighbouring regions of Central and South Bohemia, as well as to the region south of the Danube and as far as the Tyrol. Then suddenly the culture of the Urnfielders appeared at the turn of the 2nd and 1st millenniums in the Tumulus Bronze Culture of South Germany and in a considerable part of the Danube Basin, in North-west Switzerland and on the border of France. In its South German-Swiss variant it penetrated ever deeper into France and, in places, even farther afield. Everywhere cremation burials spread and everywhere there is a related cultural inventory. There is something almost incomprehensible in the fact that, in the period formerly called the Early Hallstatt (according to Reinecke's chronology, Hallstatt A and B) and today almost generally called Late Bronze, we come across local groups of Urnfielders throughout a considerable part of Europe, from the Carpathian Basin to Britain in the west and (later) south into Spain.

Attempts to explain this phenomenon have long engaged the attention of European archaeologists. Formerly it was common to talk of a great expansion of the Lusatian Culture, and its consequences were often greatly exaggerated. It must be remembered that the term, the South German (Rhine Basin, North Alpine) Urnfield Culture, is not identical with the term Lusatian Culture, although some features are common to both. The South German urnfields are the outcome of a complex process, in which native elements and eastern influences have an important place. At this time, too, there is a striking increase in the number of weapons, especially swords. Nor is it mere coincidence that these swords appear in graves as part of the equipment of the dead, not only in the Danubian zone, but also in the Alpine region; nor is it by chance that the bronze swords of the Liptov type (Hallstatt A and the beginning of Hallstatt B), originally made in large numbers in the foothills of the Tatras in Slovakia, frequently appear in the South German section of the Danube Basin and there develop their own variant. It must further be borne in mind that many traits of the hybrid Central Bohemian Knovíz and South Bohemian Knovíz-Milaveč cultures are to be found in the culture of the South German urnfields. These are not

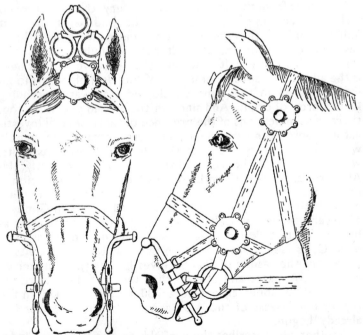

Fig. 2. Horse-trappings of Hallstatt period (7th-6th cents. B. C.) (Reconstruction after Kossack, according to finds).

isolated phenomena, but connected, at least in certain traits, which is all the more understandable when we consider that, throughout the whole Bronze Age, the relations between South Germany and the eastern Danubian region were always extremely lively.

Later on we find the urnfields deep in France, in Aquitania, in the neighbourhood of Arcachon, on the western coast, in the south round about Toulouse (Gascony-Languedoc); then they appear also on the other side of the Pyrenees in Spain, in Catalonia and in Castille. Investigators are of the opinion that these urnfields can be in connection only with those of the North Alpine region and that the area of origin was the valley of the Rhine. From here they apparently advanced directly south to present-day Lyon, and towards Rouen, Tours, Poitiers and the river Dordogne in a westward direction. According to Kimmig, there was a further advance south, from the 8th century, along the Rhone into Provence, Languedoc, Roussillon and across the Pyrenees into Catalonia. The South of France and the Catalonian Urnfield Cultures developed still further; from the end of the 6th century, their inventories include Greek imports, and from the middle of the first millennium B. C. they come more and more under the influences of mature Mediterranean cultures, continuing then into at least the 3rd century. It is evident that what we witness here is the advance of several branches of the Urnfielders, who no longer shared in the same development as was proceeding in the area of origin. And since, in the Iberian peninsula, too, there are indications of the presence of Celts, several investigators (Bosch-Gimpera, Kraft, Navarro) regard the people who were bearers there of the Urnfield Culture as Celts, while others (M. Louis, N. Lamboglia, more recently, M. Almagro) ascribe to them Ligurian character. The situation is not, therefore, perfectly clear, and this must be borne in mind in evaluating the hypothesis put forward by Bosch-Gimpera of several waves of Celts penetrating into Spain as early as in the Hallstatt Period, one of which he designates as Goidelic Celts (see below), and the other as Britonnic Celts. If we accept the results of Spanish investigators (J. Maluquer de Motes, M. Almagro and others), then the Urnfield Culture did not make its appearance before 700, that is, not till, in the region north-west of the Alps, a new historical process had already begun.

Another view ascribes the urnfields to the Veneti, an Indo-European group from the eastern part of Central Europe, who formed a mixed language group in the Rhine-Danube Bronze Culture, within which Celtic character is attributed to at least a part of the people observing urnfield burial.

The view that the Urnfielders belonged to the Celtic group is also maintained in the British Isles. But there too, complete agreement does not exist. We have already seen that several investigators date the first Celtic invasion of the British Isles to the period of transition between the Neolithic and the Bronze Age. But the view that, along with the Urnfielders in the Late Bronze period, Proto-Celts, probably Goidels, reached the British Isles is upheld by some of the foremost British archaeologists; V. Gordon Childe is of the opinion that the people of the Urnfield Culture in England (Early Iron Age A Culture) spoke the form of Q-Celtic that goes by the name of *Goidelic*. Another smaller wave, possibly from the Dutch coast, arrived, in the view of C. and J. Hawkes, about 750 B. C. and, still later, a more numerous incursion from France, across the Channel. T. G. E. Powell is also convinced that the bearers of the Early Iron Age Culture in the British Isles were already Celts and that at least part of them were called Pretani (Preteni). It must be noted that following the great flowering of the Wessex Culture, in the south of England, a period of stagnation set in, which continued till a change was brought about by the arrival of new streams in the period of the Urnfield Cultures.

The basic components of Celtic ethnogenesis

In the present state of our knowledge, two basic components of Celtic ethnogenesis have thus emerged — the Tumulus or Barrow-folk Culture of the Bronze Age, with older roots, and the Urnfield Cultures, based on the older Tumulus Culture. It seems to us highly probable that a new proto-Celtic population-group definitely evolved only after a merging of the people of the urnfields with the barrow-folk, thus amalgamating various pre-Celtic groups in a larger unified whole. The fact that Urnfielders irrupted into the British Isles in the Late Bronze Age, which is archaeologically well attested, and later into Spain, can be interpreted as indicating that ethnogenetically this people was at the stage of transition indicated above. We shall proceed to show how extremely important a factor this process was in the development of prehistoric Europe.

The regrouping of the tumulus region of the Urnfield Cultures had, as its final result, the unifying of various cultural elements and paved the way for further progress. The native cultures were not immediately swallowed up in this inundation, but the gradual merging of the old foundations with the new incoming streams prepared the fertile soil for the new line of development. It was the prelude to what we shortly afterwards observe on the European stage: historically recognizable Illyrians appear in the south-east, Celts in the west and Germans in the north. There can be no doubt that in this decisive period in European pre-history single groups of dialects of the later larger ethnical and language groups had already become differentiated and that in the Hallstatt period (Reinecke C and D), in the 7th and 6th centuries B. C., these dialects were fully evolved. From the time of the rise of the Urnfield Cultures, there are ever increasing signs of the coming into being of a Celtic confederation or even nation. This whole region became the jumping-off ground for a further advance, accompanied by considerable changes in the economic and social structure. The sum total of these indices in the Hallstatt period C and D fully entitles us to speak of a Celtic civilization extending from Eastern France to Bohemia.

Fig. 3. Bronze cauldron on tripod from Sainte Colombe (Côte d'Or), France. Tumulus de la Garenne (R. Joffroy 1958).

Already during the period of ascendancy of the Urnfield Cultures (Hallstatt A—B, according to the earlier division) clear signs of coming change are apparent in the social stratification. The furnishings of the grave in Hart an-der-Alz, in Upper Bavaria, still belong to the Urnfield period; the dead laid out on a four-wheeled chariot and armed with a bronze sword of the Liptov type, a dagger and an arrow, were burned on a funeral pyre and the remains were then placed in a spacious grave chamber (4 m × 2 m), along with a set of pottery vessels and a bronze table service (bucket, cup and sieve). Similar discoveries continue to be made. It would seem that

Period B is especially marked by far-reaching changes. In its later phase (B 2) tumulus burial grounds again come into greater prominence, and in them it is quite possible to distinguish between wealthier and poorer strata. Whereas formerly barrow-graves were rarer, in the later urnfields they became increasingly common. This is also true of the South German region of Ulm, in the neighbourhood of Teutlingen, Sigmaringen, Münsingen, Balingen and other present-day towns, where somewhat later we can locate important centres of Celtic power. The grave furnishings of certain burials are richer; the number of pottery vessels is larger (the barrow-grave in Singen had 63, that in Ihringen 38, and in Ellg 30). Gradually *painted* pottery makes its appearance. And just at this time numerous hillforts appear in an arc stretching from the east of France, through Switzerland to Bavaria, as if a part of the population found itself forced to seek refuge and safety. A number of these hill settlements, with markedly confined dwellings, have been systematically excavated, such as Wittnauer Horn in Switzerland (in the Argau Canton, south of Säckingen). Witness to the uncertain times are also finds of (Phase B) hoards of bronze articles buried in Eastern France and in the Rhine Basin.

Many investigators seek the cause of the disturbances in the east, in the Carpathian Danube Basin, and some presume direct instrusions from this region into South Germany. Certainly it cannot be disputed that about this time there appear in the Hungarian Plain still more easterly elements, from the Thraco-Cimmerian region. It is thought that pressure by the Scythians in the region of South Russia ousted Cimmerians from the steppes north of the Black Sea, forcing them to pull out into Asia Minor, as the direction taken by one stream, and into the Lower Danube, as a second stream, and the one which brought into the eastern part of Central Europe distinctive designs of horse-harness, the 'Thraco-Cimmerian' daggers and other goods. According to some investigators, at the time of Cimmerian pressure in the south-east part of Central Europe, sometime between 775 and 725 B. C., certain ethnical movements were initiated.

Everything we have noted above testifies to substantial changes taking place, at latest, by the end of the 8th century. It is at this time, too, that iron begins to appear more frequently and slowly becomes the main metal used, at least to begin with, by the higher social strata. In economic life, a type of economic unit becomes established, in the form of the enclosed farm-stead (Buchau am Federsee); on the Rhine, the recovery of gold from alluvial deposits had been carried on since the time of the Urnfielders, the gold finding its way, as we shall see below, mainly into the coffers of the leading social groups.

The re-emergence of some of the old Tumulus elements in the 9th and 8th centuries is observable throughout the whole territory of the Tumulus Culture in the Bronze Age, from Eastern France and South Germany to as far as Bohemia, in the east. Often there are successive barrow-grave burials at the same place, from the Bronze Age, from the age of the Urnfielders and from the Hallstatt period. Thus in Bohemia, at Tajanov-Husín, in the Klatovy district, of 50 excavated barrow-graves, 14 are from the Bronze Age, 12 from the period of the Milaveč-Knovíz Culture, 7 from the Hallstatt period and 5 from a still later time. The sequence is similar in Újezd u Sv. Kříže, in the Plzeň district, and elsewhere. Only occasionally are barrow-grave cemeteries founded in other places. The re-emergence of barrow-grave burials does not, however, by any means signify a return to the original Tumulus Culture of the Bronze Age, but is only the expression of the symbiosis of the bearers of the Tumulus Culture with those of Urnfield Cultures, which in a new environment created a new situation. The return to barrow-grave burial was then successively influenced by the peripheral regions of the Celtic sphere — Etrusco-Italian, Carpathian or still more easterly regions, where, in connection with the burial of members of the upper social strata, a complicated burial ritual had evolved. Such a ritual also came into use, at least in the case of the burials of the most prominent persons, in the fertile Central Bohemian plain, where they are an accompanying feature of the mature Bylany Culture (named after the burial-place in Bylany, near Český Brod). The South Bohemian barrow-grave region had close contacts with the corresponding Bavarian (especially Oberpfalz) Culture, which again had much in common with the related Central Bohemian Bylany Culture.

A similar situation existed at this time throughout the whole Danubian Basin, from Austria to France. The Württemberg-Baden barrow-graves are related in their furnishings to the barrow-graves in Alsace (Hagenau). In addition, extensive barrow-grave cemeteries are to be found later in Burgundy, in Franche-Comté and to the west of Switzerland, in the direction of Dijon and the range of the Côte d'Or. It would seem that in the Hallstatt period there was a rapid increase in population, for, in some areas, for instance in the Forêt des Moidons (Jura Dep.), many thousands of burial-places are known; some investigators actually incline to the view that the population then reached a higher density than the present-day average.

II

The environment of the Hallstatt Iron Age Chieftains

The forts of the overlords and their contacts with the Mediterranean

The Hallstatt period saw the culmination and completion of the whole process of the coming into existence of the historical Celts and is of singular importance for the Celtic past. The name comes from the small town of Hallstatt in Upper Austria, in the Salzkammergut, situated in the mountains, beside a lake. In the middle of last century over a thousand graves were discovered there, in addition to many others that had previously been destroyed. The majority of the grave-finds belonged to the older Iron Age, which, in the seventies of last century, was generally designated the Hallstatt period, after this find-place. A later division of the period was carried out by the Munich archaeologist P. Reinecke, who divided it into four phases (A—D), the first two phases (A and B) being really Late Bronze, in which iron was a rare and not easily procurable luxury metal in the territories north of the Alps. Here we understand the term Hallstatt to cover the oldest Iron Age period, Reinecke's C and D phases, dating from the 7th century and extending to past the middle of the first millennium B. C.; from this period date most of the finds in the Hallstatt burial-grounds,

The importance of the Hallstatt period for the culmination of the process of Celtic ethnogenesis

The Hallstatt Culture, in art production of a mainly geometrical character, evolved gradually from antecedent cultures already in the time of the Urnfielders, and, at its height, embraced especially the Central European zone of the Danubian Basin. More marked individuality is possessed by two regions; the East Hallstatt (from the eastern half of the Alps to the Carpathian Basin and south-east to the shores of the Adriatic), which had a greater feeling for figural motifs, and the West

Hallstatt (in the main, South Germany and Eastern France), which inclined more to geometrical forms. Roughly on the border-line between these two regions is situated Hallstatt. The Hallstatt period in Central Europe corresponds chronologically to the Villanova Culture in Italy, in the district of Bologna, to the Etruscan culture in present-day Tuscany, and, in the older phase of the Reinecke chronology (A-B), to the geometrical style (Dipylon Culture) in Greece and in the island region of the south-east.

Fig. 4. Fortification technique remounting to the Hallstatt period (Heuneburg) and still in use in the La Tène period. The front wall of the rampart is articulated by wooden posts let into the ground; these form part of the timber construction of the stronghold. Kimming's reconstruction.

Hallstatt was at that time an important trading centre, which is reflected in the high level of culture. An important factor in its prosperity was the local quarrying of salt and a widely branching and especially long-distance trade in salt. From here there was a close connexion with Italy in the south, and also with the territories to the north, as far as Bohemia. An important transit-station for salt from Hallstatt and Hallein-Dürrnberg was present-day Linz on the Danube, which also shared in the trade in lead (graphite) from the České Budějovice Basin, goods being transported from there to the west, by way of the Danube. An unwonted traffic arose on the routes over the Alpine passes, formerly used only in a limited way. The routes from Italy started from Lake Maggiore on the Italian side of the Alps (Sesto Calende, Bellinzona) over the St Gotthard and the Splügen Pass, and wound their way down into Switzerland and the Rhine Valley. Similar use was made of the route over the Taurus Mountains down to the river Salzach, or across the Glockner down to the river Drava. All this opening up of trade routes was not stimulated artificially, but took place in response to the economic development and requirements of Hallstatt society, especially of its leading groups. Increasing demands were made on transport facilities and the waggon underwent considerable structural modification to enable it to carry heavier loads. Four-wheeled waggons mounted on a wooden axle, with wheels usually of equal height, now came into general use. The wheels had narrow iron tyres (2.5—4 cm) nailed to the wooden felloes with iron nails, but they still sank deep into the soft ground. In time further improvements appear, the back wheels are higher than the front wheels (Bruck a. d. Alz), and the steering capacity of the waggon is better; the construction of the wheel-hub is altered and great care is devoted to the metal-work, iron and bronze being combined. From these purely transport waggons there soon developed the four-wheeled cult chariots of similar construction, but with more metal-work and more richly decorated; they were used on festive occasions and often accompanied notable persons into their graves, for the funerary rite, too, grew in pomp and complexity. All these waggons, of which scores from the Hallstatt period have come to light in the region north of the Alps, were not yet fast war chariots; the light, two-wheeled chariots of this type did not appear in the Celtic world till later — in the Early La Tène period.

From the 7th century onwards, hand in hand with the development of the waggon, there is an increasing wealth and variety of harness fittings. Instead of the one-link snaffle-bits of an earlier time, two-link bits now come into use, the length of which (10—11 cm) would seem to point to a new and evidently heavier breed of horses, with a broader mouth, the bits they replaced being on an average 2—3 cm shorter. Instead of the semi-circular cheek-pieces, a 'bar' type comes into prominence, bent at the upper end, and with three box-shaped openings (*fig. 2*); this points to a better and more flexible command of the horse. Accompanying these, from the 7th century (Phase C), are numerous small ornaments on harness bands, button-hole and loop-shaped openings, terrets, leather straps and belly bands, with disc-shaped, mostly square-section and pierced horse-brooches, along with a horse-yoke for a pair of horses, consisting of a wooden core covered with leather and decorated on the surface with innumerable bronze studs and discs, grouped in geometrical patterns; besides the simpler forms, there are luxurious yokes with wings at either tip, decorated with special bronze rosettes. Well preserved and finely executed examples of complete sets of harness fittings and some particularly splendid specimens of horse-yokes from the Central Bohemian region have come to light in numerous find-places (Plates I, II).

Social differentiation
Chamber-graves and chieftains' burials

At the end of the 7th and on the threshold of the 6th century, throughout the large region with mature Hallstatt cultures, where iron was already in common use, a notable feature is the reappearance on a considerable scale of spacious chamber graves, beneath a mound or barrow, often with an inner wooden kerb and sometimes surrounded by a circular ditch at the circumference of the mound. Of special significance in this area are rich burials with four-wheeled waggons, splendidly decorative yokes and small harness fittings, the number of which, in some graves (Hradenín near Kolín, in Central Bohemia), reaches several hundred. As a rule they are male burials, the grave furnishings including a bronze or iron sword in a scabbard terminating in wings, and a large quantity of pottery vessels, sometimes richly painted with geometrical patterns. Most of these graves are practically without personal ornaments, notably without brooches; only in Bohemia do there appear exceptionally in such graves, especially in the older phases, lyre-shaped brooches, or brooches of spectacle type, with a figure of eight loop, which are otherwise more typical of the south-east. In the greater number, however, we often find a whole quarter of boar, with an iron knife beside it, and, in the corner, large amphorae as proof of a complex burial rite, or occasionally half-moon symbols of baked clay. The grave chambers of these Hallstatt leaders were not very high — just sufficient to accommodate a four-wheel waggon, with the body laid out on it, and other grave goods. The burial was then covered with a wooden construction, and a barrow built up over the whole.

The region of these rich chamber graves under a barrow begins in Bohemia, and the Central Bohemian Bylany Culture has produced some unique examples. Thanks to the Kolín investigator, the physician Dr F. Dvořák, there has been preserved from them, in Hradenín near Kolín, besides waggons and rich harness fittings, a very fine horse yoke (*Plate I*); but similar finds also come from the Prague region, from Straškov near Roudnice, from Lhotka near Litoměřice, and, more recently, from Lovosice (*Plate II*, excavated in 1956). Wood-built burial chambers also appear in the South Bohemian tumulus region and, in general, completely analagous counterparts (except for the pottery, which everywhere is locally differentiated) in the basin of the Main (Grosseibstadt, southwest of Römhild), almost to the borders of present-day Thuringia, then in the Oberpfalz and in the whole region of South Bavaria and of South Germany generally. Further west, we find them in Eastern France and in North-west Switzerland, at that time a region with a fairly unified culture, from which various finds from the 7th and the beginning of the 6th centuries and from places mutually remote are practically identical and easily mistaken one for the other. The burials are mainly of men, especially chieftains, and, in the broader sense, are burials of the leading social group. The majority of corpses are unburnt, but there is also an example of a main burial of a man, with sword and yoke, and beside it a heap of broken bones from a cremation (Plaňany near Kolín, in Bohemia). This does not mean, however, that the whole region indicated above was under unified rule or merged in a single large confederation. It would seem rather that it comprised numerous independent groups of patriarchal character, sharing the same kind of social order.

Many European investigators (Kossack, Krämer, Powell and others) consider that the oldest such chieftains' burials occur in Bohemia, in Upper Austria and in Bavaria, and that from these regions the complex rite connected with the burial of members of the leading group penetrated further west, so that they date the majority of such burials in Württemberg, Switzerland and the Upper Rhine, with outliers in Burgundy, as later, mainly from the 6th century and the turn of the following century. The situation in the different burying grounds, insofar as these have been systematically excavated, indicates, however, that more is involved than a mere taking over of the pomp and show of a burial rite. It is evidently rather the outcome of gradual economic and social changes throughout the whole region, in which the gulf has widened between the leading group, headed by the chieftain or prince, on the one hand, and the commonalty, on the other, the latter not sharing in the subsequent rising social and cultural standards of the first group.

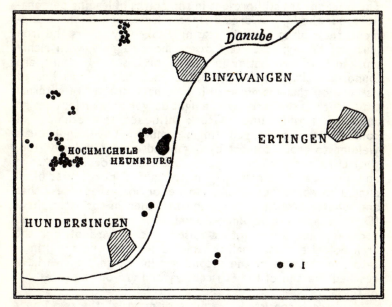

Fig. 5. Stronghold Heuneburg on the Upper Danube, from the Early Hallstatt period, surrounded by groups of larger and smaller barrows.

At this time burial honours are still paid mainly to men, usually equipped with at least a sword, but without showy personal ornaments and rare imports from other lands. In the different burial-grounds, we find spacious wood-built chamber graves, with the grave furnishings noted above, including a waggon and yoke, but also simpler chamber graves or quite simple interments. Later on, however, the rich burials are not confined to men, but include those of women, and, indeed, of all the members of a certain clan (or branch of it), which has won for itself the power over a larger population group, probably a tribe. We cannot help feeling that here a kind of family nobility, an aristocratic class, has slowly formed, sufficiently powerful, wealthy and securely established to be able to raise their social and living standards very rapidly. The contrasts between them and the rest of the population quickly become accentuated, as we shall endeavour to show on the basis of the archaeological excavations from the last decades.

In the 6th century, in the period which archaeologists designate Phase D (sub-divided into an older Phase D 1 and a younger D 2), the situation had changed very substantially. The waggons are still present in the graves of leading personalities, but the long swords disappear from the personal equipment, their place being increasingly taken by spears and iron (cutting) knives; in certain cases, short daggers, with richly worked hilt, terminating in a hoof- or U-shaped mount, are found. It looks as if the aristocratic class had so consolidated its position that members of it now have distinctive external traits, such as the carrying of a light dagger of luxurious design and workmanship; under Greek influence, the technique of combat had also changed, single combat between individuals yielding to group combat by organized units. Gradually, too, the rich harness fittings disappear. Dress undergoes some change and personal ornament begins to have a place; first of all simple bow brooches *(fibulae)*, snake- or boat- shaped brooches and lunette brooches with pendants, then in the later phase (D 2), characteristic knee-shaped and mainly drum-shaped brooches, and forms with a raised, decorative foot. For the archaeologist, these small ornaments are a chronological indicator, in the case of the second group, a sign that we have reached the end of the 6th century and are on the threshold of the 5th.

Men's garb consisted of a piece of material, the two upper ends of which were clasped by a brooch or pin, belted to form a kind of kirtle or tunic. Women's dress, after the manner of the Dorian *chiton*, was held in place by a clasp or brooch on either shoulder. A specific trait of this period is the increase in the quantity of women's personal ornaments, most marked in the leading social groups. Woman takes her place by the side of man as an equal representative of the aristocracy, and in death is furnished with grave goods of great richness and splendour, contrasting sharply with the poor ornaments of the ordinary folk. The court society thus taking shape lived in remarkable luxury, bordering often on ostentation, at the expense of the commonalty.

The highest aristocratic group, undoubtedly dynastic in character, as we shall see from further indices, the class of the leaders of single tribes, with almost unlimited resources, consciously separated themselves more and more from the rest of the population, both during their lifetime and after death.

They founded isolated residences on hill-top sites, real fortified halls, where their life was centred. Native workshops at first satisfied the growing demands; later, however, valuable imports from the Mediterranean appear in this environment, so that, by the end of the 6th century, long-distance trade had already developed and overstepped the boundaries of the Celtic world. The graves of these princes, immense barrows, are set up either on the edge of larger barrow cemeteries, or separated from the other mounds by a larger intervening space (Aislingen, Wellenburg in Bavaria, and others); sometimes they are sited quite independently. This is a phenomenon which was earlier non-existent, or only very rare. The barrows of these chieftains are noticeably grouped round fortified hill-residences. In the large barrows, there are often a number of grave chambers of considerable dimensions, some occupying an area of over 20 m².

All this would indicate that the upper social stratum had grown stronger and more flourishing and was anxious to raise its living standards evidently in the attempt to imitate and vie with some splendid extra-Celtic environment. In this respect, the 6th century and the turn of the 5th century was a time of special importance for the Celtic territories, and so we shall try to build up a picture of the general situation on the information obtainable from the archaeological record.

In Bohemia, too, the old Bylany "aristocracy" and leading families of the barrow-building culture lived on into this period, but many circumstances point to its no longer being in the centre of development, but rather on its periphery. Even in Hradenín near Kolín, famous in the preceding period for several prince's graves, with yokes and harness fittings, we may date provisionally to this time Grave No XXVIII: it contains the burial of a man of about fifty, on a four-wheeled chariot, with rich metal *décor*, along with harness fittings, including three iron bridle-bits and bronze frontlets, further, a bronze dish, whereas only a small quantity of pottery was among the grave goods (10 vessels), of a divergent and evidently later type. There was no sword in the grave, the waggon was, in construction and decoration, more for ceremonial use than for travelling or combat. It should be noted, too, that in several other graves in Hradenín, instead of a sword there were only spears.

Centres of development in the 6th century. Chieftains' strongholds

In the 6th century, the centres of development, however, shifted further west, partly into Southern Bavaria, mainly into the basins of the Upper Danube and the Upper Rhine, into Southern Germany and the north-west part of Switzerland, as well as into Eastern France. There a specific culture arose in the north-western foothills of the Alps, the true focal centre of the Celtic world *(fig. 10)*. There, too, greater contrasts developed in the social structure, and from there the liveliest contacts were initiated with the southern cultural and literary world, at whose sources the upper Celtic class drank deep and eagerly.

In the younger Hallstatt period, side by side with fortified tribal strongholds, serving as a place of refuge in times of danger and uncertainty, we come across for the first time in the history of the western part of Central Europe chieftains' residences, in whose immediate neighbourhood are usually barrows covering the graves of the lords of these first fortified castles. These seats were not necessarily sited in inaccessible places, but, on the contrary, often in quite open country, for it seems as if the ruling caste felt itself for a time perfectly safe. The surprising results of excavations carried out in recent years revealed the secrets of Heuneburg on the Upper Danube, and another such chieftain's hall, in the vicinity of exceptionally rich chieftains' graves, was discovered on Mont Lassois, near Châtillon-sur-Seine. Indications of others are in Württemberg, in the neighbourhood of Stuttgart, Hohenasperg near Ludwigsburg, with the chieftains' or princely burial grounds, Römerhügel and Klein Aspergle. Rich burials in the Zürich area (Altstetten), with gold ornaments, point to the existence of a similar residence somewhere in Ütliberg, south-west of Zürich, unfortunately, hitherto not systematically investigated. A pointer to the existence of more such centres on Swiss territory are the rare imports in the barrow-grave burials. In the district north-east of Dijon, too, a strong concentration of rich graves presumes a not distant princely residence of a similar kind, perhaps on Castle Gray, on the Saône.

Heuneburg near Hundersingen, on the left bank of the Upper Danube, not far from Sigmaringen *(figs. 4—6* and *Plates IIIA to IV)*, is a fortified princely hill-residence, surrounded by a group of barrow-graves. It is called Little Heuneburg, to distinguish it from Great Heuneburg, about 11 km further north in the wooded range of hills known as the Rauhe Alb. Castle Heuneburg was built on an elevated plateau overlooking the Danube, on a ground plan area of 300 × 150 m, with an outer ward facing the river. Access to the main gateway on the north-west was such that any assailant would be a direct target for the defendants on the castle ramparts. In the Earlier Hallstatt period the castle was rebuilt at least four times, as a rule

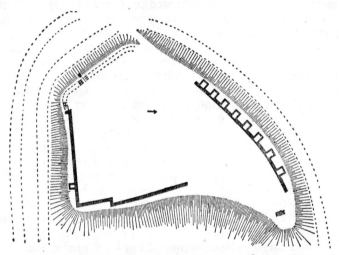

Fig.6. Heuneburg on the Upper Danube. The excavated part of the stronghold of a Later Hallstatt prince (Heuneburg IV), with lower stone courses and bastions of brick, after a south-eastern pattern. Contemporary excavations by W. Dehn and W. Kimmig.

after damage or destruction by fire. The oldest fortifications were of timber, stone and earth. One building phase, however, testifies to a mature building technique — Heuneburg IV. On a stone foundation wall, about 3 m broad and 60 cm high, a wall was raised of sun-baked bricks about 4 m in height (in places still standing to a height of 2 m); it is the first use of bricks of which we know in the Danubian territories. Jutting out from the masonry, at regular intervals, are four-sided bastions (so far 8 have been uncovered); in parts more easily accessible and so more exposed to attack, this technique was not employed, but the old native manner of fortification, with timber-laced and stone-faced earthworks (*fig. 4*) was retained. The stone for the building was transported from a distance of about 5 km, from quarries in Dollhof.

The brick structure in Heuneburg is a completely alien element in the North Alpine region and was carried out after south-east (Mediterranean) patterns. Such patterns may easily be found, for instance, in Sicily (Gela), or in the Macedonian region, near Ochrida and in Castle Larissa. A builder-architect was evidently called in from the south to carry out this work in the Danube Basin. In the new environment, however, it had a rather different function. The dimensions of the paving-type bricks of clay, sand and chopped straw, and the breadth of the wall-work followed southern patterns, but the close succession of forward projecting bastions, at ten-metre intervals, is not conceivable as being part of a system of fortification; the tower-like bastions were used as domestic dwellings. Here the motive was evidently a kind of ostentation, the endeavour to emulate the Mediterranean cultures, a tendency observable in other domains. From the Greek colony of Massilia (Marseilles), wine for festive banquets was imported into the Celtic territories in amphorae (fragments of which were found at Heuneburg only recently), along with Greek Black-Figure ware, goods from Provence and other typical southern imports. The last fortifications at Heuneburg, from the beginning of the La Tène period, were not constructed according to the above southern technique, but again in the manner of the old native fortifications. Excavations at Heuneburg are not yet completed. In the surroundings of Heuneburg are nine chieftains' barrows, some of them rich in gold, of which one barrow, Hochmichele, 13 m high, probably covered the burial of the ruling prince, as we shall have opportunity to show.

The Celtic centre, *Latisco*, a fortified hill site on Mont Lassois, is about 6 km north-west of Châtillon-sur-Seine; the upper area on the height is 500 × 120—150 m. In 1949 massive earthworks for defence were uncovered on the western slope and, beyond them, a rich cultural stratum, 40—60 cm deep; on the Late Hallstatt stratum are later deposits from the La Tène period. A preparatory probe revealed the presence of immense quantities of pottery sherds, running into hundreds of thousands, among them some painted with geometrical patterns (rarely with zoomorphic motifs), numerous fragments of imported Greek Black-Figure pottery made in the second half of the 6th century, about 200 brooches from the end of the 6th century and the beginning of the 5th century (double-reel brooches and others with a richly decorated foot, sometimes carrying a setting of coral), as well as numerous ear-rings, finger-rings and bracelets. Weapons, on the other hand, are rare — an occasional dagger or the head of a spear and a flesh-knife. In many respects, this settlement can be compared with other hill strongholds on the Marne, in Camp du Château at Salins, in the Jura region, or with the cemetery in Jogasses.

Mont Lassois is situated at the junction of long-distance trade routes, in a region rich in iron. In 1953, however, a rich and surprising find was made in Vix (beside Châtillon-sur-Seine, in the region of the range of the Côte d'Or). Here, the French archaeologist, René Joffroy, discovered the burial of a princess of about 35 years of age, which provided conclusive proof that among the ruling class, women, too, enjoyed all respect and honour and lived in a state of luxury. Beneath a barrow, once a striking landmark in the countryside (diameter 42 m, height at least 6 m), was a grave (area 9 m²), in which was laid out on

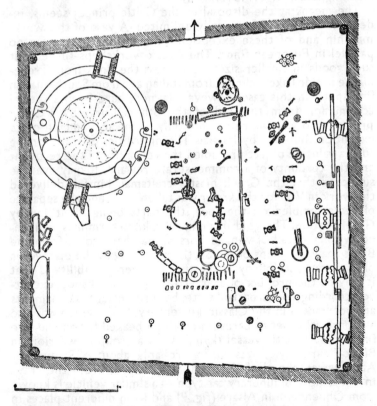

Fig. 7. Vix (Côte d'Or), France. The French archaeologist, René Joffroy, discovered in 1953 a barrow 'chamber' grave of a princess, about 35 years of age, with a gold diadem on her head and rich grave furnishings. Lay-out of the grave; in the corner a large bronze vessel.

a waggon, the body of a youngish woman, with a golden diadem on her head (wgt. 480 g, *fig. 7* and *Plates XI—XIII*), containing a great quantity of other personal adornments, bracelets, circlets of amber beads and brooches. The four-wheeled waggon, with rich metal-work, was propped up against the eastern wall of the grave chamber. In the north-west corner was a large bronze vessel (krater) 164 cm high and weighing 208.6 kg. It is rare work of Greek provenance, with a low-relief frieze on the neck, in which warriors on foot alternate with charioteers on two-wheeled chariots, driven by a team of four horses. The heavy lugs of the vessel have a tail-piece in the form of a gorgon, the face twisted into a grimace (*fig. 8* and *Pl. XII*). The detachable lid of the vessel is decorated in the middle with a free-standing female figurine (*Pl. XIII*).

The means at the disposal of the Celtic princes seems, indeed, to have been practically unlimited. A vase of this workmanship and of these exceptional dimensions has so far no parallel in European finds. The Greek workshops turned out such goods in smaller sizes, as witness the finds from Trebenichte beside Lake Ochrida, from Italian and from South Russian find-spots. In this case, however, it must have been a special commission from the end of the 6th century, by a Celtic prince, who was impressed not only by the art and craft of its execution, but also by its size. The difficulties of transporting such a valuable object presumed the reliability of the recipient and the certainty of a commensurate reward. It may even be supposed that the Greek master-craftsman himself delivered the work in Vix, for the *krater* was taken apart and the separate pieces assembled on the spot, the parts being identified by Greek letters. The gold diadem, with knob terminals, enlivened with a detail of winged horses, may have come from the Black Sea workshops of the Scythian culture, as the discoverer of the grave, R. Joffroy, suggested; another possibility is that it may be the product of a Graeco-Etruscan workshop, executed according to 'barbarian' taste, because analagous ornaments are not known in the Classical inventory. In the grave was also a bronze table set of Etruscan origin; a beaked flagon and two flat pans. An Attic vessel (kylix), with a group of warriors in Black-Figure style, was made probably about 525; another Attic vessel, shortly before 500. The waggon from the grave in Vix is more of funerary car type — a similar vehicle is known from Ohnenheim in Alsace (*fig. 9*) and from different places in France, in the Franche-Comté, in the valley of the Saône, or in the not far distant neighbourhood of Latisco, only about

3 km from Sainte Colombe. There, in the barrow at La Garenne (Mousselots), was found, among other things, a bronze cauldron with iron tripod, also a product of Greek workshops. If we take into consideration a certain time-lag for circulation of the above imports and types of brooches, then we can date the burial of the princess at Vix to the beginning of the 5th century.

The above examples throw a clear light on the status of the ruling class. A glimpse into the grave chambers of several other barrow burials serves to fill in the details of the picture. It is sufficient to cite a few examples of the younger phase of the Hallstatt princely graves covered with barrows from the 6th and the beginning of the 5th century. They have many features in common, though they are not by any means uniform. Above all, the lay-out of the burial-place is monumental. The heaping-up of a barrow of large dimensions presumes the pooling of labour by a large collective, for it was often necessary to transport the material from a considerable distance. The interior construction of the barrow, especially those consisting of several grave chambers, points to it being a permanent burial-place, in which successive burials were inhumated of a certain family, men and women, sometimes young persons of either sex. One common feature is the richness of the grave furnishings, the elaborately decorated waggons with ornamental metal-work, still four-wheeled, harness fittings, gold-thread materials, tooled gold *objets d'art*, gold diadems and head-rings, bronze vessels and other objects, in the earlier period still mainly products of native workshops; in the course of time, however, the number of imports from the south increases, as the court environment enters into closer relations with the more mature cultures of the Mediterranean.

In the 6th century Scythian influence penetrated from the east into the Carpathian Basin (burial-ground in Chotín, near Komárno in Slovakia, and others), forming a Scythian barrier in the valley of the Tisza and along the present-day Slovako-Hungarian frontier. In the Scythian cemeteries, burial with horses was customary, and we come across them also in the Tisza Basin (the Szentes-Vekerzug cemetery in Hungary). In the Celtic territories where, at this stage of development, splendidly caparisoned horses were needed to crown social prestige, horses were not as a rule placed in princes' graves. Only exceptionally do we learn of such cases (Simmringen), or of the find of a horse's head in a grave chamber (Hundersin-gen), and where they do occur it is evidently for special personal reasons, as the burial of horses was not part of the Celtic burial rite in use at that time.

A surprisingly large quantity of artistically worked gold has been found, especially in the South German region, in Burgundy and in part of Switzerland. It seems to have come from local workshops, for gold had been won in those parts, from the Late Bronze Age (Hallstatt A-B), mainly from alluvial deposits in the Upper Rhine lowlands, carried down by the river Aara from the area between Bern and Luzern. In the later phase of the Hallstatt period, as O. Paret showed earlier, it was the raw material for personal ornaments, especially for women. A girl in a wood-built burial chamber in Sirnau (Würt-

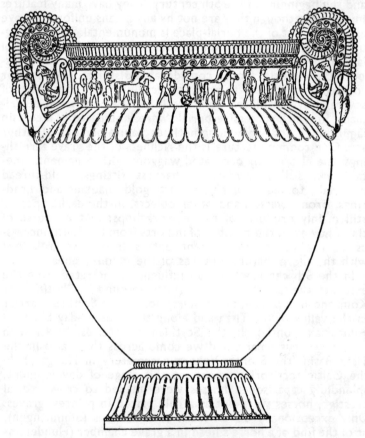

Fig. 8. Bronze vessel from the princess's grave in Vix, 164 cm high. See also Pl. XI—XIII.

temberg) had her arms adorned with gold bands, and under her head lay 18 small gold rings, possibly for hair adornment. A barrow-grave in Kappel, in the Rhine Basin, contained a necklace of gold plate, weighing 160 gr., a gold bracelet and other jewels; in another, in Ins near Bern, there were gold beads, and in Gunzwil-Adiswil, 4 tubular and ring necklaces were among the treasured personal belongings buried with the departed. In this part of the Celtic world, the concentration of gold at this time is particulrarly striking: in an easterly direction, as far as Bohemia, gold objects appear here and there, but they are the exception rather than the rule.

Let us return for a moment to the burial-places of the princes of the Celtic world in order to get a clear survey of the archaeologically ascertained facts.

The Hochmichele barrow-grave near Hundersingen, in the close vicinity of the Heuneburg stronghold, is impressive for its size and height. It was last investigated in the years 1937—39. The main chamber, lined with wood and occupying an area of almost 20 m² (563 × 348 × 581 × 350 cm), had its wall hung with a material draped in folds. Although the grave-chamber had earlier suffered considerable depredation, fragments of the waggon were still preserved in it, originally also draped with some textile, as well as gold belts with inset discs, as ornaments for the waist. A woman was laid to rest here, adorned with a necklace of amber and glass beads, and a braid of her hair, plaited from three strands, is still preserved. The remains of materials in the grave are covered with a diagonal pattern and, even according to present-day standards, are of fine quality. In the adjacent chamber (242 × 306 × 250 × 296 cm), which is undisturbed, is the skeleton of a man, on a bull's hide, with an iron arrow and a headband, and beside it that of a woman, adorned with a snake-coil brooch and a three-metre-long necklace of amber and pearl beads. Near the adjacent chamber is the burial of a man, with a spear and a bronze belt.

Similarly, in Apremont (Haute-Saône, France), a barrow-grave of an average diameter of 70 m and at least 4 m high contained a four-wheeled waggon, draped with material; from the grave-chamber come a gold circlet (232 g), gold brooches and small gold vessels. Textiles are, in general, a usual feature in these Late Hallstatt graves of high-ranking presonages. In Gieshübel-Hundersingen I, there were three burials in the wood-built chamber — two women and, between them, an older man. One of the women was dressed in a mantle, with a gold-thread border. In Tannheim, in Upper Swabia (Barrow VI), the waggon was covered with a textile of cruciform design forming a stepped pattern.

The dimensions of some barrows are truly imposing. The barrow in Buchheim had originally a diameter of 120 m, that in Kappel on the Rhine, 74 m, the barrow in Hügelsheim near Rastatt, 70 m, and a present height of 3 m. At Villingen, in

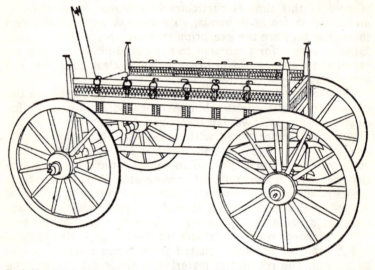

Fig. 9. Ohnenheim in Alsace. Reconstruction of a four-wheeled cart or hearse from the Later Hallstatt culture.

Schwarzwald, a barrow was heaped up, at an altitude of 771 m above sea-level, 118 m in diameter and 8 m high; the grave-chamber, occupying an area of over 36 m², is constructed of oak timbers, 20—35 cm thick, and has also a wooden floor. The barrow had already been robbed at the time of excavation (1890), only some fragments of the chariot still remaining. In Winterlingen, too, the barrow is at a considerable altitude (820 m). Not infrequently in these barrows, some of the grave furnishings are laid out on strips of birch bark, and are sometimes covered with them (e.g. St Andrä bei Etting, Pullach).

One other burial monument deserves special mention —the princely barrow-grave in Pflugfelden, 6 m high (Römerhügel), which was already investigated in the 19th century. In the wood-built chamber (3.5 × 3.5 m) was the burial of a man in a splendid robe, with a gold diadem and an iron dagger in a bronze scabbard, the hilt inlaid with amber. The grave-goods included bronze vessels, a four-wheeled waggon, on which the departed had evidently been brought from his hall (the hubs of the wheels were covered with bronze plate), and magnificent harness fittings. About 3m further north was a second burial, also with gold and amber objects. Over all this a barrow had been raised of heavy stone blocks, brought from the surrounding countryside. The somewhat later barrow-grave in Klein Aspergle, in the same neighbourhood, of which we shall hear more later, contained in a wood-built chamber the burial of a woman in a robe ornamented with gold, with a silver chain, bronze vessels, an Etruscan beaked flagon and other imports. Barbarian taste clothed with an openwork mantle even the Antique beauty of pottery (a bowl). This was actually the adjacent grave of a woman, the principal grave-chamber in the centre of the barrow (5 × 4 m) having been robbed long since — perhaps some thousand years ago.

The reader has doubtless realized that the Celtic history of the 6th and 5th centuries B. C. is almost exclusively the history of a single class — a ruling class, with almost unlimited means and opportunity. The results of archaeological research give a perfectly unambiguous and convincing picture of its privileged character and make it plain that the commonalty, while providing the basis for its power, did not profit from or share in its rise. The isolation of the leading social group became ever clearer. Whereas in the Hallstatt period proper (phase C) burials of leading personages are furnished with large quantities of pottery, which is also a common item in the inventory of ordinary folk, in the graves from the latest (D) phase of the Hallstatt period, pottery in the graves of the upper class and of the chieftains and princes is rapidly ousted by the characteristic products of native workshops and then by expensive imports from other regions, whose purpose was to add to the show and prestige of the leading class. In the halls of the princes gold spoons and sieves make their appearance (Heuneburg), bronze table services and more and more objects of personal adornment. In the settlements of the common folk, native pottery continued to play its role, with an occasional bronze brooch of the "drum" type, a simple bronze neckring and, of imported wares, only a few glass or amber beads making up their prized possessions.

Among the dynasties burying their members on waggons, a tradition of heroic glorification grew up, motivated first by triumphs on the field of battle, and, later, ever more by the splendour of the banqueting hall, for which the south supplied the furnishings and a sufficiency of wine. We shall see how this trend went still further in the 5th century, and how, after several generations, it led to a continual refinement of taste, at first still accompanied by markedly barbarian traits, which laid the main stress on outward effect; later, artistic values came to be increasingly appreciated, especially with the rise of the Early La Tène art style. Was it possible then for the contrasts between the two groups to widen indefinitely? At a certain juncture, the inevitable breaking-point was reached.

A source of subsistence for the leading class was not only the fertile soil of the plains, but the hill uplands which, to this day are mainly cattle-raising country. The noticeable concentration of later Hallstatt phase princely graves in the Upper Danube, on the Rhine, from Basel to the Neckar, in Burgundy or in the region of the Côte d'Or range, continues only down to the beginning of the 5th century. Though for a certain space of time it would seem that the ruling class lived in relative security, yet it was not spared passing shocks. However, all that took place throughout the 5th century in this territory north-west of the Alps is still for us only a matter of surmise. From the archaeological record, however, it is clear that, in the 5th century, when the Celtic power was preparing to make incursions into other parts of Europe and when at least a part of these expansive thrusts had already been realized, the centres of Celtic rule, as represented by the princely courts and richly furnished graves, clearly shifted to the north-west, to the territories of the Middle Rhine and to the rivers Mosel and Saar. The earlier centres in the Upper Danube were evidently passing into decline. The most southernly point in which continuity is preserved is in the Stuttgart region, namely, the above-mentioned princely burial in the barrow-grave in Klein Aspergle. Farther south, as far as Switzerland, princely graves, which we designate Early La Tène. have not so far been discovered, and the former power centres in the uppermost parts of the Danubian waterway were losing their importance. In the old environment of rich graves, the trend of development takes another course; slowly the number of barrow-graves declines, and later there appear cemeteries with flat graves, in which men are buried with their fighting gear. Formerly this transition to a different burial rite was usually explained as being due to movements of population. P. Reinecke still considered that Celts irrupted into South Germany from the west. Today, however, it is becoming increasingly clear that the causes of change were of an internal character and that we are here dealing with the same people in the same environment. The new burial rite becomes more generally widespread from the 4th century onwards and represents a well-armed class and no longer only individuals. Horse gear disappears and iron sword and spear gain predominance. As these cemeteries appear later in the more fertile regions, some investigators have taken into consideration the possibility of the emancipation of the farming people, Kahrstedt even going the length of premising a revolt of the farming people against their overlords, in a liberating process.

It seems to us, however, that in interpreting this phenomenon it is necessary to evaluate certain other factors. The whole region of the later phase of the Hallstatt period princely graves, as above delimited, became in the 5th century the assembly area for the already historical expansion of the Celts; from here armed groups, comprising a leader and his followers, irrupted not only into contiguous areas, but also into distant regions, and even into contemporary southern centres, which hitherto had supplied the Celtic courts with luxury wares. There had earlier already been indications of a striking increase in the density of population in this trans-Alpine territory. Nor can it be doubted that, considering the social structure as it then existed, it must have led to considerable strains and tensions. Besides, Heuneburg itself, with its frequent rebuildings, mostly following destruction by fire, may be the testimony to such unrest, in the course of which the people of one tribe rose in arms against the people of another. In times of expansion and colonization, it is usually the discontented who leave in the hope of being able to better their economic and social position in a new country. These dissatisfied elements may have belonged not only to the commonalty, but might number among them members of the ruling families or dynasties. And so the explanation suggests itself that in the growing crisis there was no other alternative than to arm and equip the greater part of the male population fit for military service and send them on plundering raids into other parts of Europe, and so satisfy the demands of larger groups of population. As we know from the archaeological material that at the head of these groups and bands ("Gefolgschaften") of armed warriors were leaders, whose equipment links them up with the *milieu* of the princely courts, and from the tradition, preserved in Livy, which also speaks of the sending out of the nephews of King Ambigatus of the Bituriges, Belloves and

Sigoves, at the head of a band of armed followers from the over-populated land in order to seek new settlements (the oracle named the region of the Hercynian Forest as the new home for Sigoves and Italy for Belloves), it is quite reasonable to assume that members of the ruling families, who were not fully satisfied with their opportunities, placed themselves at the head of such warrior bands. Thus it would seem that the land formerly supporting the princely courts was substantially depopulated and the rulers who remained with the rest of the population moved the centres of their power further north-west, in the direction of the Middle Rhine, the Mosel and the foothills of the Hunsrück range, that is, into the region commonly known as the Hunsrück-Eiffel region. There the princely courts continued to flourish in all their splendour throughout the whole of the 5th and a part of the 4th century.

Internally the situation on the Middle Rhine had not changed very much. The burial rite continued to be observed in the traditional way, only the four-wheeled waggon yielding place to the lighter two-wheeled war chariot. Instead of Black-Figure pottery, the more fashionable new Red-Figure ware appears, from the second half of the 5th century.

The concentration of these princely graves of the Early La Tène period increases with continual new finds. In the Saar alone, at least 8 rich burials were known earlier — from Besseringen, Remmsweiler, Weisskirchen (2 burials), Schwarzenbach (2 burials), Theley, Remmsweiler and Freisen. All are situated in the northern half of the region, on the southern edge of the Hunsrück range and in the hilly country beside the rivers Saar and Moselle. They were monumental barrows, most of which had been explored already in the 19th century, and not always expertly. Nevertheless some finds from here have been preserved, especially gold personal ornaments. From two barrow-graves in Schwarzenbach, south-east of the massive fortifications in Otzenhausen, opened as early as 1849, come two bronze beaked flagons, with figurally designed handles, a bronze amphora, the handle of which is decorated with figures of Silenuses, a dish-shaped vessel covered with a gold openwork mantle, and a quantity of other gold ornaments, also with mask-like motifs (*fig. 22*). In the princely grave in Dürkheim (Rhenish Pfalz), a woman was buried with a gold neck-ring, two gold bracelets, with mask-*décor*, fragments of gold plate from a belt and a bronze table set (a beaked flagon, a tripod cauldron and a bucket-stamnos). In Rodenbach near Kaiserlautern, a large barrow contained the rich burial of

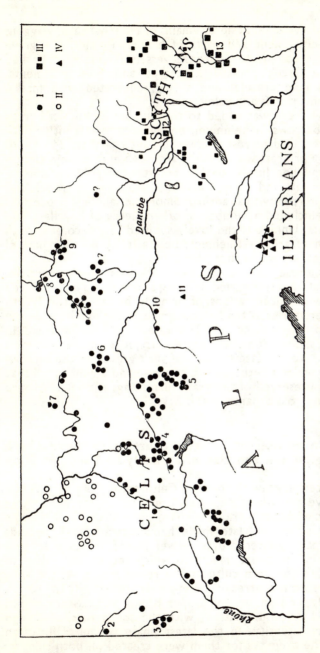

Fig. 10. *Central Europe in the Hallstatt period and in the period of Early La Tène*: I. Burials with chariot or with yoke and horse trappings (7th — beg. of 5th cent.); II. younger chieftain's graves from Early La Tène; III. Scythian burial-places and single graves or finds (smaller symbols); IV. region with finds of bronze helmets and fighting-gear. — 1. Ohnenheim, Alsace; 2. Jogasses, France; 3. Vix (Côte d'Or), France; 4. Hundersingen-Heuneburg; 5. Uffing; 6. Oberwiesenacker-Parlsberg; 7. Grosseibstadt (south-west of Römhild); 8. Lhotka and Lovosice, Bohemia; 9. Hradenín near Kolín; 10. Uttendorf in Upper Austria; 11. Hallstatt; 12. Chotín, Slovakia; 13. Szentes Vekerzug, Hungary. — Map drawn up by J. Filip, on the basis of finds as at 1959.

a man and a woman; besides remains of a four-wheeled waggon, fighting equipment and parts of harness fittings, the grave furnishings comprised 5 bronze vessels (including a beaked flagon), a Greek painted kantharos and gold ornaments, mainly a gold bracelet and a ring, decorated with masks, zoomorphic motifs and palmettes.

In 1954 there was added to the number of known burials 2 more barrows in Reinheim, on the southern frontier with Lothringen. Laid to rest in a wood-built chamber (346 × 270 cm) was a princess with a gold torc, both ends terminating in human and lion heads; on her breast were gold ornaments, gold bracelets and a ring, a bronze mask-motif brooch and a bronze mirror, with an anthropomorphic handle. The personal treasure included a number of other pieces of jewellery and ornaments. Unique is the lovely spouted jug, decorated with a pattern of great refinement; beside it lay another part of a table set — two bronze plates.

As has already been pointed out, the most southernly princely burial from this period, forming a connecting link between the former concentrations of princely burials in the North Alpine territories, is the barrow-grave, in the middle of fertile fields, in Klein Aspergle. The celebrated double-grave in Waldalgesheim (Hunsrück) belongs, to judge from a part of its inventory, to the latest group of such graves. In the barrow-grave, in which are the burials of a man and a woman, all that has been preserved of the grave furnishings is a set of bronze vessels and gold ornaments *(Pl. XIV)*.

Contacts of the princely courts with the southern region and the rise of an Early La Tène art style

The 5th century saw the birth in Celtic society of a remarkable decorative art, whose patrons were first and foremost those chieftains whose rich graves we have come across in the Middle Rhinelands and which later made their appearance in the uplands of Champagne, watered by the river Marne. The new art germinated in the court *milieu*, to which the artistic values of the mature southern cultures had ready access. At the time when the main centres of Celtic power were still in the region of the Upper Danube, the Upper Rhine and Eastern France trade and cultural relations with the south reached a high degree of intensity. In the latest phase of the Hallstattian period, the premises for them were created on both sides by the growth in power and the correspondingly increasing demands of the chieftains and princes in the relative luxury of their strongholds, on the one hand, and in the new organization that had taken place in the Mediterranean on the other. About 600 B. C. the Greek colony of Massilia was founded on the site of present-day Marseilles and soon it became an important trading centre. It flooded the surrounding regions and then even more distant lands, as far as the waters of the Danube, especially with Greek wares, thus bringing the mature Greek environment into contact with the barbarian *hinterlands*. Today it is certain that the trade connection, Massilia — the Rhone valley — the Burgundian Gate, became a principal purveyor of the products of Asia Minor, Rhodes, Greek and local Provençal products, which found their way as far as Heuneburg. True, already in the 6th century the routes over the Alpine passes had seen a considerable increase in the volume of traffic, and, on the south-east side of the Alps, there arose a production centre, as a link with North Italy, based on the wealth of the surrounding region, especially rich in deposits of iron ore. We find the rulers of this region in graves, along with bronze fighting gear, helmets, leg-armour and tooled bronze gauntlets (Klein Klein). The importance of the Ateste-Adriatic region, in North Italy, also grew and, later, Greek trading colonies were founded there in the basin of the Po (Spina, Adria). Here the warehouses of Greek merchants, stocked also with pottery, were still flourishing in the 5th century. Caput Adriae became a new influential factor, and not least for a part of Central Europe. On the Italian side of the Alps, beside the lakes in the neighbourhood of Bellinzona, a series of trading posts arose marking the routes over the Alps into Switzerland and the Rhinelands.

Thus undreamed-of possibilities were opened, especially to the West Hallstatt Culture of the Central European zone, and these it fully exploited as early as the 6th century. From the Greek workshops of the Miletus-Rhodes type wares of all kinds were imported, and, later, their Italian imitations. They appear only rarely in the burials with waggons in the Late Hallstatt environment of the Upper Danubian-Eastern French Culture (Vilsingen in the Sigmaringen region, Kappel-am-Rhein, Agnel-Pertuis, in the valley of the Durance, in the Vaucluse area, in the Southern French *hinterland* of Massilia, Vienne). The imports represented here are mainly bronze flagons of Rhodian type, from the middle of the 6th century or, from a slightly later period, with a trefoil spout which, unlike later Etruscan

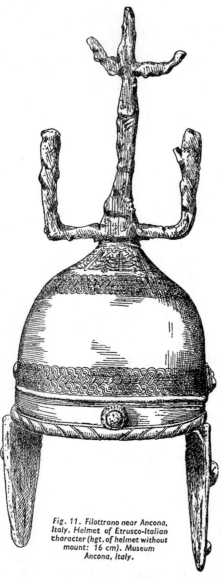

Fig. 11. *Filottrano near Ancona, Italy. Helmet of Etrusco-Italian character (hgt. of helmet without mount: 16 cm). Museum Ancona, Italy.*

flagons, had squatter, more bellied bodies, and the attache of the handle was decorated with vegetal elements combined with vestiges of geometrical motifs. Such wares appeared elsewhere, too, in the Mediterranean, and the European finds allow the conclusion to be drawn that they reached the Upper Danube and the Rhinelands mainly by way of Massilia.

It was not, however, only occasional examples of Rhodian metalwork that reached the north-Alpine territories from the middle of the 6th century. In 1851 there was found in a barrow-grave in Grächwil-Meilkirch, in the Bern canton, besides fragments of a waggon, brooches and pottery, a large bronze jar (hydria), also of Greek manufacture, from the first half of the 6th century. The neck is particularly richly decorated. The lug is in the form of a winged ruler of animals (the so-called Persian Artemis), surrounded by four lions and crowned with an eagle and snakes; in either hand she holds a hare, one by the hind legs, the other by the forelegs, possibly as the symbol of fertility (*Pl. V, VI*). It is a rare piece of metal embossing.

It would seem that other rare pieces were conveyed north

by way of Massilia, such as the bronze *krater* already mentioned, from the princess's grave in Vix. Among them must be counted the cauldron with griffon *décor* from La Garenne (*fig. 3*).

Very much in favour in the latest phase of the Hallstatt cultural area was Attic Black-Figure pottery, most of it imported through Massilia. It is widespread in the whole of Provence, as far as Languedoc, and recently it was found in the Malpas stronghold near Soyons, south of Valence. As, however, it occurs in the Bologna district and near Adria, it is not to be ruled out that at least a part of the import was by way of the Alpine passes. The majority of Black-Figure pottery belongs to the period designated as Hallstatt, Phase D 2, that is, the latter end of the 6th century and about 500. It must also be mentioned, however, that it seems likely that wares were made to order, so that, for instance, when Red-Figure pottery had become the fashion in the country of origin, Black-Figure pottery was still made for export, in order to satisfy the taste of customers abroad; the fragment of the Black-Figure jar in Heuneburg is one of the largest type of this kind known. The dish in the same style from the grave in Klein Aspergle was provided with a gold mantle by a native goldsmith. Similar imports probably continued for long in circulation.

From south of Massilia came other kinds of pottery as well — simpler, grey, decorated with wavy lines, usually described as from Asia Minor; it was common, everyday ware, which turns up in settlements, not in graves, as, for instance, in Camp-de-Château near Salins, in the strata with double-drum brooches and with brooches having a decorated foot, that is, evidently from the very beginning of the 5th century. From Massilia were exported as far as Heuneburg earthenware wine amphorae (they are present in the latest, that is, the Early La Tène strata), which here and there also appear in rich graves (Mercey, Mantoche). It seems likely that several such kinds of wares were of Magna Graecian origin, others came direct from Massiliote workshops (termed "amphores micassés" by F. Benoit, to which group the Heuneburg find belongs). Transport was by mule caravan: at Heuneburg, a donkey's tooth was found among other things, the first such find in the Hallstatt cultural area north of the Alps.

Massiliote trade was still in full swing when, in the Transalpine area, Etruscan trade began at the beginning of the 5th century to develop more intensively. The balance of power and the economico-commercial situation in the Mediterranean underwent radical change in the course of the 6th century.

Etruscan power was based on the city centres on the shores of present-day Tuscany and a rich goldsmith's art industry (fine granulated work), as well as metal-working, in connection with which several towns became specially famed for their bronze vessels (e. g. Vulci). The wealth of the whole Etruscan world lay in its widely-branching trade relations. In the 6th century the Etruscans had a clear supremacy at sea and exported their wares to the whole for them accessible world, from the Pontic Steppes to the shores of Spain. Their products reached Central Europe only rarely and by chance, mostly by way of the cultural regions of North Italy (a small bronze bowl and a pyxis from the grave in Kastenwald near Colmar, a gold bead from Ins and a gold granulated pendant from Jegenstorf in the Bern canton, here and there an Etruscan tripod cauldron which, in Italy, was usually associated with Black-Figure pottery). The main Etruscan market, in the latter part of the 6th century, was still the Mediterranean. At the turn of the century, however, Etruria lost her markets in South Russia, Greece, Asia Minor and on the North African coast. A dangerous trade rival arose to threaten the Etruscan monopoly, first in Carthage and then in the young Roman Republic. At the beginning of the 5th century the tyrant Anaxillas closed the Straits of Messina (between Sicily and South Italy) to the Etruscans and, after annihilating defeats at Himera and Cumae (474), Etruria was completely cut off. As at the same time Massilia initiated colonizing activities along the coast of Southern France and of Western Iberia, Etruscan trade sought new markets — the only ones then still accessible — north of the Alps. Prior to 500 B. C. the Etruscans had actually seized power in the region of Bologna (the Certosa period, lasting to the time of the Celtic invasion) and, almost simultaneously, they opened up trade with the north and north-west, by way of the Alpine passes. This led to a marked increase in the importance of the North Italian lake districts, as trading posts and entrepôts (the Tessin region of the Ticino valley, the surroundings of Bellinzona). There, bronze beaked flagons have been found, among other things, and later their imitations, also made in earthenware.

The production of Etruscan beaked flagons had begun in Italy before the end of the 6th century and continued for some considerable time, possibly for a whole century. Exports included not only the usual production runs, but also commissioned pieces, as R. Frey showed, often of unusually large dimensions. The main source of supply were the workshops at Vulci. It is true that the beaked flagon and other associated pieces of bronze table sets soon became, probably after the Etruscan manner, a part of the grave furnishings, but this does not mean that every such flagon was deposited in a grave shortly after its acquisition. Some of them were for long in circulation and Celtic goldsmiths had embellished them with chased patterns after their arrival north of the Alps, as is the case with the beaked flagon from Besançon. The Czech flagon, too, from Chlum near Zbiroh (*Pl. X*), evidently of later date and not of the best quality, has unskilled decoration of the throat.

Fig. 12. *Artistically executed torcs, with mask and seal terminals wrought in high relief, were the mark of the high rank of their wearers: 1. Filottrano, Italy (gold); 2. Frasnes-les-Buissenal, Belgium (gold); 3 Courtisols (Marne), France (bronze); 4. Oploty near Podbořany, Bohemia (gold); 5. Waldalgesheim (Kr. Kreuznach), Germany (gold).*

The first deliveries of Etruscan beaked flagons still reached the territories north and north-west of the Alps in the later phase of the Hallstatt period, that is, at the turn of the 6th and 5th centuries and at the beginning of the 5th century. They appear in graves where at least part of the furnishings possess Hallstatt character, for instance, in the princess's grave in Vix, or in the graves in Mercey and in Hatten. Fragments of imitation beaked flagons of pottery found at Heuneberg testify to their exemplars being familiar and popular also in the Upper Danube Basin. The main stream of these imports, however, was directed somewhat later farther north, to the princely courts of the Middle Rhine; the most northernly finds are in Belgium.

The beaked flagons, which are so common an item among the grave goods of the rich graves of the Middle Rhine, did not come alone. They were imported along with whole sets of bronze vessels for banquets, with tripod cauldrons, buckets and other vessels for mixing wine. And with all these came the wine itself — and seemingly in large quantities. This is confirmed, for instance, by the chemical analysis of the deposits on the walls of the vessels; one of the best authorities on these flagons, P. Jacobsthal, thinks that the bronze services were only an accessory item accompanying the regular large transports of wine, and not an independent import.

These Etruscan products also reached Bohemia and, it would seem, by a more direct route across the Alps and *via* the Salzburg-Hallstatt region. An Etruscan import of first-class workmanship is the beaked flagon from the barrow-grave in Hradiště (near Písek in South Bohemia), found along with two bronze dishes and a pair of gold, boat-shaped ear-rings; other finds, among them, gold bracelets, have not been preserved. In Hradiště there is little doubt that the barrow covered a princely-type grave. The find belongs to the group of beaked flagons with figural ornament. The attache of the lug is in the form of a four-winged Siren, with human arms and bird talons (*Pl. IX, X*). The upper part of the handle clasps the rim of the flagon by means of two recumbent lions, and in the corners of the spout are two more animal figures, perhaps also intended to be lions. The edge of the spout is decorated with a triple row of pearl-like *décor*. On the throat is a finely engraved design incorporating flower and palmette motifs. The flagon is an Etruscan product of the 5th century.

The other beaked flagon, of which the handle has not been preserved, is from Chlum near Zbiroh (*Pl. IX*). It is a second-

Fig. 13. Ornamental motifs in the La Tène style: 1. Klein Aspergle near Ludwigsburg; 2.—3. Waldalgesheim (Kr. Kreuznach); 4. Mannheim, Germany (décor of a sword scabbard); B. Kiskőszeg, Hungary (scabbard in Sword Style); 6. Colchester, England (mirror with incised ornament, after Fox); 7. Talián Dörögd, Hungary; 8. Bussy-le Château (Marne), France (sword scabbard, breadth c. 4 cm); 9. Aylesford (Kent), England; 10. Hunsbury (Northants), England; 11. Marlborough, England; 12. La Tène, Switzerland (sword scabbard).

rate piece, with throat *décor* of inferior workmanship. From the Písek district comes the handle of another beaked flagon, with a palmette attache, and yet other handles from Čínov near Žatec and from Modřany near Prague. As a bronze vessel (situla) has been recovered from the Hostouň barrow-grave in the Domažlice district, the handle of which is already decorated with the "fish bladder" motif, which appears as the border of masks on the bronze horse phalera from Hořovičky near Podbořany (*Pl. VII*), it seems extremely probable that in parts of Bohemia, too, there was a similar environment to that in the Middle Rhinelands. It did not, it is true, reach such a high material and cultural level, but it was still capable of acquiring valuable imports from the south. Finds of beaked flagons on Austrian soil document the route by which these vessels reached the north, and their earthenware imitations from the Hallstatt-Salzburg region indicate that they long served as a type-pattern.

Thus in the 5th century two main regions come into relief, where rich graves with foreign imports are most concentrated; the main region in the lands of the Middle Rhine and later in Champagne, as the principal region, and the Bohemian or Bohemian-Austrian peripheral region, as the most easternly outpost of the contemporary Celtic world, exposed in part to other cultural trends.

The western region imported, in addition to products of the bronze industry, many other goods, especially (from the second quarter of the 5th century) Greek Red-Figure pottery, then various South Italian products, Late Corinthian wares, and so on. These products did not reach Bohemia.

Surveying the situation as a whole, the important question arises as to what the North Alpine consumers offered or could offer in exchange for these goods. It is possible that, in the west, it may have been gold, of which there must have been a sufficiency, as it was quite commonly worked up in local art and craft workshops. In the view of the majority of investigators the main article of exchange was people, slaves, then agricultural products, especially cattle and hides. The transport of goods over the Alpine passes was presumably provided by the native Alpine inhabitants, under the supervision of the merchants.

From the above-described state of development, reconstructed mainly on the basis of the archaeological record, the earliest references to the Celts, which date from the 5th century, become perfectly comprehensible. Hecataeus of Miletus places the land of the Celts near that of the Ligurians, and the Greek historian, Herodotus of Halicarnassus, is informed that the river Danube has its source in the land of the Celts. The contacts of the leading Celtic society with the cultured south provided ample opportunity for merchants and traders to spread information about the Celts and their territories to the most remote parts of the then known world.

The environment of high living standards and growing requirements of the leading social class of the Celts provided, in the second half of the 5th and the first half of the 4th century B. C., the suitable context for the rise of a proper Celtic art, which was the first contribution of the "barbarians" to an all-European culture. Its development, from its initial phase to its full flowering, will be the subject of another chapter. The Celtic artist-craftsmen created and brought to maturity an individual artistic style just at the time when armed bands of Celts streamed into Italy and other parts of Europe.

III

Armed expeditions of the Celts into the rest of Europe

Period of Celtic expansion and later Central European concentration

The former Upper Danube-Eastern France homelands of the Late Hallstatt chieftains, which in the 6th century were still flourishing, gradually became depopulated about the middle of the 5th century. The glory of the princely strongholds faded and with it the testimony of the wealthy graves. Perhaps inner tensions caused by a too great density of population and the flagrant social contrasts between the mass of the people and their rulers were finally resolved by the latter taking part of the people and setting out to found new settlements, first in neighbouring regions populated by related peoples and then, by way of armed excursions, into more distant lands. These former movements of population took place at a time when the barrow-grave burial rite was still predominant. One part of the people, with their leaders, advanced in a northerly and north-westerly direction into the lands extending from the Lower Neckar to the Middle Rhine and the Moselle, and, somewhat later, into Champagne and other parts of France. Other groups shifted their settlements further towards the north-east, through Bavaria and into south and a part of Central Bohemia, where they reinforced the related tumulus-builders already settled there, and also perhaps entered Austrian territory in the direction of Hallein-Dürrnberg. A similar deconcentration was demanded, too, by the situation in Burgundy, in Franche-Comté, in the neighbourhood of Salins (les Moidons, Alaise), between the Upper Seine and the Upper Saône, where huge barrow-grave cemeteries point to a rapidly increasing density of population. It is thus to be presumed that pressure was also exerted in a southerly direction. All this however, did not as yet mean a forcible irruption of the Celts on the Greek and Roman spheres of the Mediterranean world. In the Rhine Basin, it was the timely occupation of the lands mainly on the left river bank, for from the north there was already growing pressure by the Germanic tribes;

for the future the area between the Rhine and the Elbe was, with small exceptions, already lost for the Celts.

All that we have noted above builds up to a picture reconstructed on the basis of archaeological indices, because the changed situation must have had its causes and consequences. In the specialist literature, the daring suggestion is occasionally made that the Celts may have pushed forward at this time as far as Noricum, and that Nyrax, a Celtic power centre, mentioned by Hecataeus (c. 540—475 B. C.), may be identified with Noreia, mentioned at the end of the pre-Christian era as being in Styria and the centre of the Norican kingdom. Archaeological evidence for such a view is not yet sufficiently convincing. It is, however, very likely that already at the end of the 5th century the first Celtic bands penetrated into Northern Italy.

The Celts in Italy

For long the southern world had no foreboding that it might one day be the victim of sharp attacks by armed bands from the still little-known trans-Alpine Celts. Round about 400 B. C., however, it had become an unpleasant reality. Over the Alpine passes, through which a steady stream of southern products had flowed northwards to the Celtic courts, armed bands of Celts now penetrated, thirsty for plunder and enrichment, making the rich valley of the Po their chief goal — those flourishing centres of the North Italian sphere of Etruscan influence, which, especially in the Bologna area was, in the 5th century, predomin ant (so-called Certosa period, after the place-name Certosa, near Bologna). The majority of these invaders were no doubt from Eastern France, Southern Germany and a part of Switzerland. It is unlikely that whole tribes moved in; presumably only parts, comprising the youthful and more dissatisfied elements, and so all the more daring and enterprising. Classical sources assert that the first were the Insubres, who penetrated to the neighbourhood of present-day Milan, and these were followed by the Boii, Lingones and Senones, who settled in Lombardy. Rich centres, with accessible plunder, tempted these warrior bands further south, to as far as Rome, to Apulia on the south-east seaboard and to the shores of Sicily. A later tradition describes this migration as the military adventures of the nephews of King Ambigatus of the Bituriges, of whom the one, Belloves, made for the Italian regions.

The Insubres sacked the great Etruscan city of Melpum and

occupied the neighbourhood of Milan. The main stream of Celtic people, however, settled in the valley of the Po, the Cenomani in the north-east, the Boii in the Bologna district and the Lingones, south of the lower stretches of the Po, as far as the Appenines. The Senones penetrated still deeper and reached the Adriatic coast in Umbria, between Rimini and the mouth of the river Aesis, north of Ancona; there they settled permanently and the region actually bore their name for a time, being known as Ager Gallicus. This was, however, only the first phase of expansive Celtic impacts on the peninsula, for only a part of the intruders settled in the newly conquered land; the others went on, plundering, laying waste and spreading terror and destruction wherever they went. Above the little stream called the Allia, about the year 387, they defeated the Roman legions and made a direct attack on Rome. The Gauls, led by Brennus, sacked and burned the city and seized enormous booty; only one part of the city resisted their onslaught, namely, the Capitol. For Rome this catastrophe had far-reaching consequences. It was evidently after this Gallic raid that a reorganization of the Roman forces was carried out and effective stone ramparts built for the city's defence.

The attack on Rome caused widespread uneasiness in the Greek towns of Southern Italy, for the Gauls continued their southward thrust, down into Apulia, and everywhere they behaved like victorious conquerors. In South Italian Canusium they buried their chieftain in a grave reserved for the native ruling family.

After the defeat of the Latini in 338 Rome became the strongest military power in Italy, gaining predominance over the disintegrating federation of Etruscan towns and over the Samnite tribes. In the anti-Roman confederacy, Gauls were regularly represented. In 299, when the Celts advanced into Etruria, they succeeded in destroying a Roman force beside Clusium and joined with other tribes to oppose Rome. In 295, however, beside Sentinum in Umbria, they suffered a devastating defeat. After a series of further bloody clashes the Celts were pushed farther and farther back; the Romans subjugated the land of the Senones and founded there, in 280, the civilian colony of Sena Gallica.

Under these circumstances, the Insubres and the Boii were obliged to call to their aid their kinsmen on the other side of the Alps; they are said not to have been able to reach agreement with them on the matter of the division of the arable land. Gallic resistance was not as yet completely broken, and new revolts and raids followed. Finally, after the famous battle of Telamon (225 B. C.), Roman forces entered the North Italian territories occupied by the Boii and successively occupied the whole region annexed by the Boii and Insubres.

Thus slowly the end drew near of Cisalpine Gaul. Between 225 and 190 the struggle continued unabated. When, however, in 192, the Romans destroyed the power of the Boii and their strong-point, Bononia (present-day Bologna), a large part of North Italy passed (191—190) under Roman suzerainty. A part of the Celts (among them probably also the Boii) moved out of their territories in a north-easterly direction, a part remained and the remnants were, according to Polybius, forced back by the middle of the 2nd century to the foothills of the Alps. Gallia Cisalpina then became a Roman province under Sulla in 82 and, in the same century, acquired full rights of Roman citizenship. Several cemeteries in the Alpine foothills document the last phase of Celtic culture at the end of the pre-Christian era.

Celtic incursions into the Carpathians and into the Balkans

Tradition has it that it was the Celtic tribe of the Sigoves that first undertook armed raids into the Danubian lands, Illyria and Pannonia. We do not know exactly where these bands settled, for the writers of antiquity have not left us sufficiently detailed information about the Carpathian region. According to the archaeological record, it would seem that, at the turn of the 5th and 4th centuries, the Celts aimed first at the then richest centres in the wide Danubian region, at Salzburg in the north, at Hallein-Dürrnberg and at Hallstatt, then in the direction of Lower Austria. In the course of the 4th century the Celts then extended their raids to the Carpathian lands. There, however, the situation was rather different, for the Celts came up against the Scythian barrier along the river Tisza and they had no alternative but to turn their main thrust more to the south-east, to the lands of the Balkan Peninsula. All these armed expeditions into the Carpathian region, however, brought the Celts into direct contact with local cultures, not only Scythian, but also the native cultures of Thraco-Dacia and, of course, with the contemporary Greek world.

The presence of Celts in the Carpathian region is confirmed about 358 B. C. by Pompeius Trogus, when he speaks of their clashes with the Illyrians. Alexander the Great, in 335, received

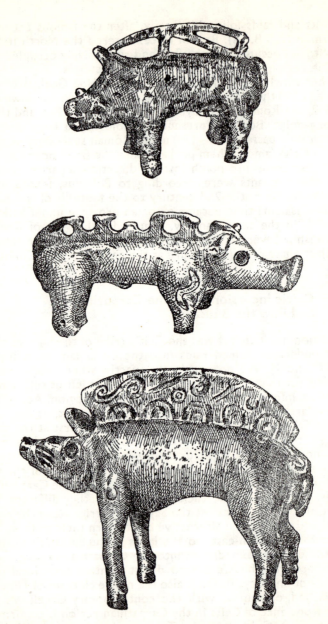

Fig 14. Bronze figurines of boars from Late La Tène; Salzburg-Rainberg, Austria; Tábor, Bohemia (centre); Báta, Hungary (below).

envoys from the Danubian tribes, among them being representatives of Celts, perhaps from regions near the Adriatic.
However, the Celtic assaults became ever sharper and more
destructive, so that, for instance, in the year 310, panic broke
out among certain Illyrian tribes when they learned of lands
being laid waste by Gaulish raids. In 298 B. C. one Celtic group
penetrated into present-day Bulgaria, but was repulsed; a second stream reached Thrace. After the death of the Macedonian
ruler, Lysimachos (281), new opportunities were open to the
Celts. In Illyria, a strong group under Bolgios appeared and the
bands of Kerethrios attacked Bulgarian territories. In 279 Celts
laid waste Macedonia, King Ptolemaios Keraunos was killed at
the time, and the Macedonians withdrew into the mountains.
Bands led by Brennus and Akichori̇us invaded Thrace and
reached Greece by way of Thessaly. At Thermopylae, Brennus
met with the opposition of Athenian forces. The main stream
of Celts, havings kirted Parnassos, made the Temple of Delphi
their goal and, it is said, plundered it. Strabo relates that the
Tectosages also participated in the raid on Delphi and that
they carried off immense booty, part of which is said to have
turned up in Tolosa (Toulouse) in Southern France. Thanks
to the Phocaeans and the Aetolians, the Celtic assault was
warded off. The invading forces withdrew to Thessaly (Brennus
committed suicide in Herakleia) and a part, originally under
Brennus's command, aimed for the Chersonese.

Celtic mercenaries in foreign service. Celtic armed bands
hired out their military services without any scruples. It was
thus not only the expansion of a people seeking new homes,
but expeditions of armed adventurers for whom military
service had become a profession and source of livelihood.
Celtic soldiers were quite a common feature of Hellenistic
armies. Antigonus Gonatas had such a Celtic unit under his
command when he was defeated by Pyrrhus in 277. At
Megara, a Gallic division revolted in 265 because of inadequate
or irregular pay. Pyrrhus, too, the most famous King of Epirus,
employed Celtic mercenaries and allowed them to desecrate
the graves of the ancient Macedonian kings in Aigai (Edessa).
King Nikomedes of Bythinia (a region on the coast of Asia
Minor bordering the Sea of Marmora [Propontis]) invited a large
number of Galatae (Celts) into Asia Minor estimated at about
20,000 of whom about half were in arms. These then held in
terror the towns of Asia Minor and actually threatened Syria.
In 270 Antiochus Soter settled them beside the river Halys
(present-day Kizilirmak) and in the neighbouring territory,

roughly in the region of the Turkish capital of Ankara. Since then the region has retained its name of Galatia; here the Celts created some kind of State, but remained a foreign minority among the indigenous native and Greek populations. Among the Celtic tribes in Galatia, mention is made again of the Tectosages, who turn up in different places in the contemporary Celtic world. Finally, in 244, the Celts were defeated in Europe by Antigonus Gonatas, 'the second founder of Macedonia', and in Asia Minor by Attalus I. of Pergamum and his ally Seleucus.

We come across Celtic mercenaries, too, as far afield as Egypt. Antigonus Gonatas ceded a Gallic troop to Ptolemy II, called Philadelphus, (277—276), and Ptolemy III also acquired Celtic soldiers who were later settled in Egypt. Celtic mercenaries are mentioned again, in 187—186, in connection with the suppression of a revolt in Upper Egypt.

The figures cited by ancient writers as to the number of Celtic armed bands in the Balkans and in Greece are high: they speak of as many as 70,000 men, though we must make allowance for some exaggeration due to the sharpness of the assault, in which mounted units took part. The Celts did not, however, get a permanent footing in Greece, and so they later retired northwards to more thinly populated regions. Thus there arose, at the junction of the Sava and the Morava with the Danube, the domain of the Scordistae (a Celtic or, more likely, a Celtiberian tribe), with its centre at Singidunum, in the present-day region of Belgrade. Other groups penetrated into Bosnia or intermingled with the Thracians and even founded a Celtic kingdom, which stretched as far as Dobrudja, in the Danube Delta, and contained a number of power centres (Ratiaria and Durostorum-Silistria on the Danube, Noviodunum above the Delta). Its influence extended as far as Byzantium, and not till the beginning of the 2nd century was this dominion overthrown by a revolt of the Thracians.

Thus the situation in this part of the world, just as in Italy, steadily deteriorated from the latter end of the 3rd century, so that it is probable that the Celtic bands withdrew more and more into the Central European regions, into the Carpathian area and also, evidently, into the Czech Lands, as we shall see below. In the Carpathian lands and on the Danube, it is difficult if not impossible to delimit the area of setlement of Celtic tribes, nor can we always determine with certainty their ethnical character. The environment was too thoroughly saturated with non-Celtic, especially Illyrian, groups of population. Somewhere near the frontiers of Slovakia, in the earlier

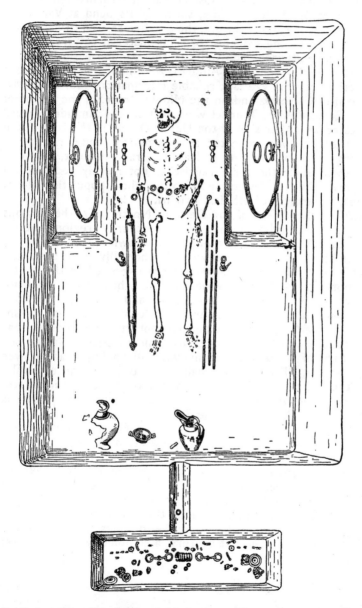

Fig. 15. Somme-Bionne (Marne), France. Burial of a Celtic warrior, with a two-wheeled chariot.

period, was a tribe named Osi, perhaps Illyrian in origin. On the right bank of the Danube, south of its bend at Vác, were settled, at the end of the era, the Eravisci, related to them, but, according to the evidence of their material culture, already strongly celticized. The Celts in the Danube basin had even earlier held in check the Autariti, who, in 310, had fled before them in terror. We lack reliable information, too, about the Carni in Carinthia and on the Middle Drave. In the region of the Eastern Alps, Taurisci were settled and Ambidravi were located on either side of the Upper Drave. In the land of the Taurisci gold was extracted as well as iron and here the Romans tried to penetrate at least for trade. It is not, however, clear whether the term Taurisci is not merely geographical and whether it does not apply to the whole population of this area, regardless of ethnical origins.

After the defeat of the Celts in North Italy, the Romans organized an advance into more northernly regions. About 182 or 181 Latin colonists founded the town of Aquileia, which soon handled the trade between Northern Illyria and the Celtic lands. From here Italian goods were exported to the north, important items being wine and oil, while in the opposite direction was a flow of slaves, cattle and wool. The territory known in the time of Ceasar as Noricum had become organized at the turn of the 2nd and 1st centuries as an independent State, the kingdom of Noricum (*regnum Noricum*). In the last century of the era Noricum was still an important power factor; not till the second half of the century, and especially in the 'thirties' did it come under stronger Roman influence, to be incorporated then, in the year 16, under Augustus, as the *regnum Noricum*, in the Roman Empire, and later, under Claudius, to become a Roman province. From the 2nd century Roman power systematically penetrated directly into the Carpathians. In 146 Roman forces reached the river Drave and beyond to Siscia on the Save, and again in 119 B. C. Within the Carpathian area, the possibilities for the Celtic tribes were also shrinking rapidly, and, finally, only Pannonia and the surrounding territory still provided the opportunity for a more peaceful development for some few decades. But there, too, in the middle of the last century, a completely new situation arose.

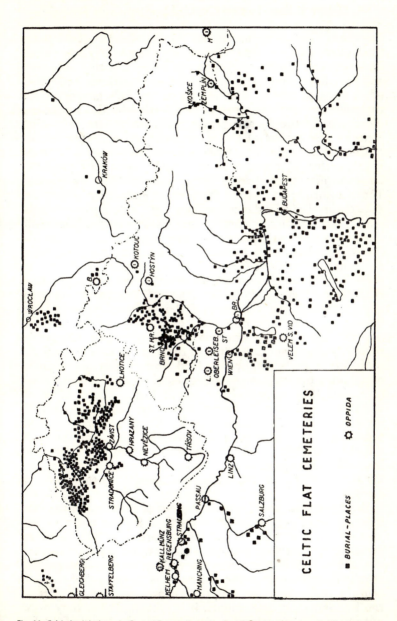

Fig. 16. Celtic burial-places in Central Europe, from the time of Celtic occupation: distribution map.

Celtic tribes in the Czech Lands and in Slovakia

The most frequently mentioned of the Celtic tribes in the Czech Lands are the Boii, after whom the country was named Boiohaemum, Bohemia. We do not know exactly when they entered these territories or how far their settlements extended. It must be borne in mind that part of Bohemia, especially the southern half, had been earlier settled by Celts from the older area of the barrow-graves and that, as late as the 5th century, the results of that settlement are apparent in part of Central Bohemia. The influx of Celts, confirmed by literary sources, that is, the arrival of armed groups that gradually became differentiated from the tumulus-builders by their La Tène Culture in its classical form, dates undoubtedly from the 4th century B. C. Evidence for them are Celtic burial-grounds, with a strong warrior component, whose concentration is in the ensuing period especially striking (apart from the Central Bohemian area) in the foothills of the Krušné hory and along the banks of the Ohře (Fig. 16). It is not possible, however, to date the beginnings of these cemeteries, on the basis of archaeological findings, to earlier than well into the 4th century and, preferably, to the turn of the 4th and 3rd centuries. Burials then continued on these sites, without a break, throughout the third and second centuries B. C. These streams of militarily organized Celts limited their land-taking to only the most fertile parts of Bohemia (and Moravia) and did not penetrate into the old barrow-grave region: it would seem, therefore, that they respected the earlier Celtic region of South Bohemia. In Central Bohemia, however, there was also an indigenous population, for which we have, today, reliable archaeological evidence, and there the Celts formed only a higher social group, relatively small, which was later reinforced by further accessions not unconnected with the changing fortunes of armed Celtic expeditions into other parts of Europe.

We have seen above that a number of branches of the Boii federacy were settled in other parts of Europe and that, especially in North Italy, in the 4th and 3rd centuries, they had highly effective fighting units, which caused the Romans and the peoples in the Etruscan zone of influence considerable trouble. At the end of the 3rd and the beginning of the 2nd century their dominion was overthrown and a large part of the Boii left their settlements. It is presumed that they drew out in a north-easterly direction towards the Middle Danube, and possibly also into Bohemia. These conclusions are based on a comparison between the culture of the Italian Boii and that of the Central Bohemian and Moravian Celts, between which there are not such essential differences; certainly these differences are much smaller than, for instance, between the Central Bohemian La Tène Culture and the South Bohemian Barrow-grave Culture. The latter culture continued more or less on the older Hallstatt basis and did not undergo the same process of development as the culture of the Celtic warrior groups which occupied the various parts of Central Europe.

About the same time as the movement of Celts out of the North Italian area, roughly in the 2nd century B. C., we can observe attempts by the Central Bohemian Celts to penetrate at least in places into the South Bohemian barrow-grave region, where they sought new sources of raw materials, iron ore, alluvial gold from the South Bohemian rivers (Otava) and, possibly, also lead.

Military defeats and setbacks in various parts of Europe from the 3rd century onwards had deprived the Celts of a number of territories. Inevitably a large part of these displaced peoples had either to withdraw into their lands of origin, into Gaul and its neighbouring territories, or concentrate as much as possible in their own Central European environment, where the danger of a similar fate to that of the Celts in Italy and in the Balkans did not so far threaten. These changes had also economic reflexes, for, under the altered situation, it was no longer booty that could satisfy armed bands, but what they needed was a well organized economic base of their own, with fully developed production and growing trade, as the premises for their further survival.

The name of the Boii, in connection with the Czech Lands, appears clearly for the first time in the sources of the Mediterranean world just before the end of the 2nd century, when, prior to 113 B. C., they had repulsed an irruption of the Germanic Cimbri. It cannot be safely affirmed that the power of the Celtic Boii was necessarily confined to Bohemia. A survey, however, of the archaeological situation in Central Europe in the 2nd century points to the basis of their power having been Central and North-west Bohemia. In this century the Celtic Central Bohemian area is in full flower and also sufficiently strong to resist alien intrusions: the same cannot be said of South Bohemia at this time. It is important to recollect, too, that in the neighbouring Oberpfalz and North-east Bavaria there are no burial-places of the character of these in Central Bohemia: the nearest appear further south, in the basin of the Bavarian Danube, and extend in an easterly direction to about Passau. Insofar as certain groups of Boii were contemporarily settled in a part of Bavaria, then the only possible area of settlement must have been roughly between Regensburg and Passau (near Passau there is a place called Boiodurum), but they could not have had direct contact with the Central Bohemian area. And then, on the right bank of the Danube, to as far east as about the river Inn, were the Rhaetians, and further west, opposite the Danubian waterway, was the land of the Vindelici, whose important stronghold was the oppidum Manching, near Ingolstadt.

From the beginning of the last century B. C. the number of burials in Celtic cemeteries shows a marked falling-off, so that a part of the Celts may possibly have moved out of Bohemia after the clash with the Cimbri, as the Germanic threat continued to grow throughout the century. On the other hand, from the 2nd century and into the early part of the 1st century, there are indications that Celtic settlement became denser in the Pannonian-Slovak region, and, according to the most recent archaeological investigations, there are numerous Celtic cemeteries in Southern Slovakia, on the left bank of the Danube and in the Nitra district. Thus it is not impossible that a part of the Boii left Bohemia for this region, where, as we know, the Boii had an important power-centre.

Another view seeks to identify the Boii with the barrow-grave culture in South and South-west Bohemia and in North-east Bavaria (E. Šimek), basing it on Strabo's statement that the settlements of the Boii adjoined those of the Vindelici, so that the southern frontier of the Boii territory would be the Danube. In this case, the archaeological evidence of the Boii is taken to be the barrow-grave culture which, in the La Tène period, was not on a comparable level, in economic and cultural importance, with that of the Central Bohemian Celts. Here, too, the problem of the Boii is taken in isolation and not seen in the context of its relation to the other groups of Boii in Europe, whose culture would show deviations from that of the tumulus-builders. The Central Bohemian cemeteries, with a preponderance of unburnt burials, is attributed by E. Šimek to another Celtic tribe, the Volcae-Tectosages, to whom he would also attribute all the finds in Moravia and Slovakia. According to this conception, there would have existed an extensive tribal territory of the Volcae-Tectosages from

Thuringia, across Bohemia and Moravia, and reaching to Slo-vakia. In the environment of the Celtic tribes and the frequent shiftings among them, this would be a very unusual pheno-menon. We come across the Volcae-Tectosages, in the La Tène period, also in France and in the Balkans, and later in Asia Minor. They are said to have survived in Moravia far into Roman times (to the 4th century A. D.), and their name is

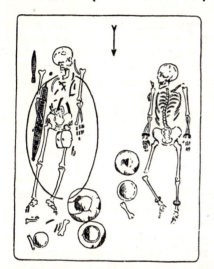 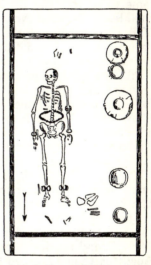

Fig. 17. Velká Maňa (Nitra District), Slovakia. Celtic cemetery, double grave No 28 (warrior with shield, pig bones at his feet) and grave No 14 (burial of a woman, in a wooden-built grave). Excavated by B. Benadík.

thought to be identical with that of the Wallachians (Valacho-vé), which has entered the Slavonic vocabulary. Remnants of the Volcae are held by some scholars to be the Cotini, another Celtic tribe which, in Roman times, engaged in the extraction of iron ore. Others, again, would locate the Cotini in Slovakia, in the hilly Středohoří (Central Massif). The name of the Cotini first appears in the time of Augustus, about 10 B. C., on the so-called Tusculan elogium, an inscription on a stone found in Tusculum, south of Rome.

The Volcae-Tectosages were, according to Caesar, a brave and by no means insignificant people. The possibility of their having settlements in Moravia is worth considering, and ar-chaeologically it cannot be ruled out that at least a smaller part of them remained in Moravia longer than a compact Celtic settlement of Central Bohemia continued. Further conclusions, which would entitle us to infer the existence of these settlements into the 4th century of our era, are not sufficiently supported by the evidence of archaeological finds.

We have already mentioned that, in the first half of the last pre-Christian era, there existed a powerful Boii dominion in Pannonia, a territory extending from Lake Neusiedl in the east to the Southern Slovak plain north of the Danube. At the same time, too, the Dacians had gained greatly in strength, their leader Burebista venturing to attack the Boii region. About 60 B. C. (according to the latest results of Rumanian and Hungarian research) he defeated the forces of the Boii and plundered Pannonia, which was then called "the desert of the Boii", the greater part of whom left this territory — men, women, old people and children, according to Greek lists found in a camp of the Helvetii, to the number of 32,000. They headed for Noricum, where they vainly besieged Noreia, and then joined the Helvetii in present-day Switzerland. They aimed to go farther into Gaul together with the Helvetii, but Caesar forced the latter to remain in their own territory and allotted the Boii, well known for their exceptional bravery, settlements in the territory of the Aedui in Eastern France. The Boii settled permanently there as a farming people.

The kingdom of Dacia, which had brought about the fall of the Boii in Pannonia, did not survive long. Burebista died in 44 B. C. and his dominion was divided. The Roman Emperor Augustus then advanced the frontiers of the Empire to the Danube.

The invasions of the Cimbri and of the Teutones

An important dividing line in the history of the Celts on the continent of Europe was the incursion of the Cimbri. Before the end of the 2nd century these Germans started moving south from their homelands in Northern Jutland, in order to find new land for settlement. Their assault was repulsed by the Boii before 113 B. C., perhaps somewhere to the west or south-west of Bohemia. The stream of Cimbri first turned against the Scordistae, a Celtic tribe on the Danube, and then westwards against the Raurisci, where they were defeated by the Romans at Noreia in 113. The pressure of the Cimbri also forced the Helvetii to leave their earlier settlements between the Rhine and the Danube and move into present-day Switzerland. The Cimbri then joined with the Teutones, perhaps a Celtic tribe from the area south of the Main, and became the scourge not only of the Celtic world, but a threat even to Rome. The Celtic territories in the 2nd century had their fortified centres or oppida, and it would seem that in this time of heightened danger increased care was devoted to their construction. In 109 the Cimbri were victorious in the land of the Sequani and advanced, in association with other tribes, as far as Aquitania. Twice, in 107 and in 105, they suffered defeat at the hands of the Romans, and Italy was in great fear of a direct invasion of the peninsula. Finally the Roman commander Marius inflicted on them a decisive defeat at Aquae Sextiae, in 102, and the Cimbri, groups of whom had crossed into the valley of the Po by way of the Brenner, were routed in 101 at Vercellae, not far from Milan, by the combined forces of Marius and Catullus.

Gaul in the La Tène period and in Caesar's time

The most detailed information about the Gauls in present-day France and in Cisalpine Gaul is contained in G. J. Caesar's De Bello Gallico, a diary of his campaign in Gaul, which he waged from 58—51 B. C. He divides Gaul into three large regions: south of the Garonne, the Aquitanians; from Garonne to Seine, the Celts; and from Seine to Rhine, the Belgae. This, however, represents the situation at the end of the pre-Christian era. The original homelands of the Celts did not, as we have seen, embrace the whole of France, but settlement spread gradually from the area of the barrow-grave culture in a westerly and south-westerly direction. In later times we know of many larger and smaller tribes in Gaul, as well as of some of their centres, the majority being of the oppidum type.

West of the Helvetii (settled in present-day Switzerland), and on the other side of the Juras, were the Sequani (Franche-Comté), and still further west the Lingones and especially the Aedui, between the Saône and the Loire, in whose territory on Mount Beuvray was situated the well-known oppidum of Bibracte. Their western neighbours, in the Loire Basin, were the Bituriges, with the oppidum Avaricum, and, in the same area, mention is also made of Boii. In Auvergne and on the Allier were settlements of Arverni, a numerous tribe, with well-equipped forces, which for a time held a leading position; in their territory was situated Gergovia, known from Caesar's campaign in 52 B. C. On the lands watered by the Iser, from present-day Lyon (Lugdunum) to Lake Leman, was the territory of the Allobroges, also at one time famed for its warrior bands. Of other important tribes mention must be made of the Senones in the basin of the Seine, south-east of present-day Paris. On the Moselle were the Treveri.

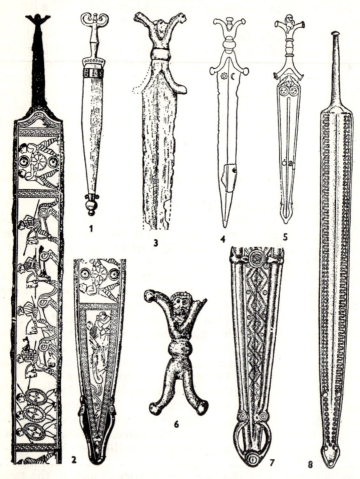

Fig. 18. *Chieftain's swords and swords of high-ranking persons from the Early Hallstatt and the La Tène periods: 1. Hundersingen, Württemberg (Early Hallstatt dagger, H D, about ¹/₇ actual size). 2. Hallstatt, Upper Austria. Sword with scabbard decorated with figural motifs (lgth. 81 cm). Museum Oxford. — Anthropoid and pseudo-anthropoid Celtic swords: 3. Křenovice, Moravia (from a Celtic grave). — 4. Mainz-Kastell, Germany (gold and silver decorated sword, lgth. 45 cm). — 5. River Witham, Lincolnshire, England (lgth. 45 cm). — 6. Dinnyés Puszta, Hungary (bronze hilt of an anthropomorphic sword). — 7. Sword with "lipped" (pierced) chape, from Vert-la-Gravelle (Marne), France. — 8. Jenišův Újezd near Bílina, Bohemia. Chased bronze scabbard from a Celtic grave (about 1/6 actual size).*

Aquitania, at the beginning of Roman administration, was only a small province, extending from the Pyrenees to the uplands in the basin of the Garonne. Several tribes were settled there, all of them of smaller size; although the peoples of Aquitania had a fair admixture of Celtic elements, they differed from the Gauls proper and were closer to the Iberians who were settled in present-day Spain.

The Belgae occupied settlements in the territory north of the Seine, south and west of the Ardennes. They were described as being closest in appearance to the Germans. Their lands of origin were still farther north, but under pressure from German tribes moved south, penetrating in places deep into present-day France. They had a simpler mode of life and so preserved the virtues of courage and daring. They had not so many towns or fortified strongholds as the other Gauls, considering thickets and swamps to be a sufficient defence. Of the fifteen or so tribes, recorded as living on their territories, mention must be made in the first place of the Bellovaci, in the region north of present-day Paris. Beyond them to the north were the settlements of the Ambiani and Atrebates; their neighbours were the Nervii, and still further east, on the river Maas, were the Eburones. Of the Menapii, on the coast of the German Ocean, Caesar merely notes that he never had any dealings with them. A part of the Belgae later crossed over into the British Isles.

The situation in the south of France. The region in the south of France, at the mouth of the Rhône, showed a very different development. From the time of its foundation, about 600 B. C., Massilia had occupied a key position there, surrounded by olive groves and vineyards, but without grain, which it had to import. As a trading centre, it long acted as middleman between the Greek world and its own *hinterland*. Later it founded colonies along the coast: to the east, at Nicaea (Nice), to the west, on the Spanish coast, near the Pyrenees, Emporion and Rhode. The *hinterland* of Massilia was long cut off from the Celtic world by the barrier of the Ligurians. The Celts did, however, finally penetrate there, and, in the 3rd century, we find them settled in the region. The Carthagenian commander Hannibal made contact with them in 218 B. C., when he led his forces from Spain, over the Alps, into Italy, and the Gauls then helped him to make good the losses he had suffered in the difficult crossing of the Alps. Rome had a special interest in the southern coast of France and Massilia was in permanent trade relations with Rome. It was the time when Rome, having rid herself of the rivalry of Carthage in North Africa after the Punic Wars, and gained complete control of the western Mediterranean, had penetrated deep into the Iberian Peninsula, where, in 133 B. C., her forces destroyed the Celt-iberian stronghold of Numantia. This brought with it a tightening of the ring round the coast of Southern France, where the Romans sought further markets for their goods. In 154 and again in 124 B. C., when the Salyes made assaults on Massilia, Roman forces came to its aid and, having defeated the insurgents, proceeded to subjugate the neighbouring tribes. North of Massilia, the Romans built the stronghold of Aquae Sextiae and cut a canal enabling Roman boats to penetrate deep into the interior. In 118 B. C. another Roman fort arose at Narbo, and the Romans, at a time when Gaul was as yet unconquered, founded the first Roman province outside Italy — Gallia Nar-bonensis, Braccata, present-day Provence — as the starting-point for the exertion of economic and cultural pressure on the Gauls. From then on Gaul was overrun by profit-seeking traders, whose activities were reflected in rising imports into the territory of Italian goods, especially wine. And more than one governor of Gaul got into difficulties for unlawful personai enrichment by the extortion of high duties on imported wine.

Under these circumstances, Massilia was the last outpost not tributary to the Roman power. In 49 B. C. the Romans at last laid siege to the town and took it. Under Roman administration, it then became an educational and cultural centre, for hither Roman notables sent their sons for Greek studies.

Gaius Julius Caesar in Gaul. The last century of the era witnessed the outbreak of political crises in Central and Northern Gaul. The old kingdoms were in decay and regroupings were taking place among the Arverni, as well as the Sequani and the Aedui. Of this situation the Roman commander, G. J. Caesar, took full advantage. He profited by his friendship with several Gallic tribes in the war of subjugation lasting 8 years (58—51 B. C.) and not only subdued the Helvetii, but also pressed back the Germans, led by Ariovistus, behind the Rhine; twice he made expeditions to Britain and suppressed a large-scale popular revolt of Gallic tribes under Vercingetorix. After Caesar's victory at Avaricum, followed by a severe check at Gergovia, where he was forced to raise the siege, Vercin-getorix declared himself the supreme leader of the Gallic tribes at a great assembly of Gauls in Bibracte, but at Alesia, north of Bibracte, Caesar brought the war to a successful close. The whole of Gaul thereupon lay subject to Rome and was thus completely opened to Romanization. At the end of the era, under Augustus, the systematic pacification of the whole Gallic territory was accomplished, it being divided into 4 provinces: Gallia Narbonensis, Aquitania, Gallia Lugdunensis and Belgica; Roman influence then made itself ever more strongly felt in all fields — in the way of life, in the country's economy, in art and in coinage. The old oppida were abandoned, new towns were founded and organized according to the Roman pattern. Gaul was soon full of Roman traders and citizens, a knowledge of Latin became widespread and Roman influence penetrated through Gaul still further north.

In Caesar's time there still existed a broad arc of Late Celtic civilization, stretching from France to Slovakia and best represented by a series of oppida. It is, however, already subjected to pressure from two sides: from the Germans on the north, who, like the Celts before them, aimed their thrusts at the most flourishing centres, this time Celtic centres, and, from the south, where the rising Roman Empire was endeavouring to reach the Danube with as little delay as possible. In Gaul the pace of Romanization was very rapid and for many of the other centres of Celtic power it was better policy to look for support to the more civilized south than to the still rude German north. Thus, in the second half of the last pre-Christian century, Roman traders and Roman goods appeared at some of the Celtic oppida north of the Alps, as well as in Bohemia, at Hradiště by Stradonice, not far from Beroun.

Historical Celts in the British Isles

The settlement of the islands by British people is usually dated to the end of the 4th century, and the area from which colonists were received is taken to be Brittany in France. In South England the names of a number of tribes are historically established: the Dumnonii in the tin-quarrying region of Cornwall, the Dobuni on the Upper Thames, the Ordovices in Wales, and other groups of Britains (Pretani or Preteni) in Scotland and Ireland. Mediaeval Irish sources speak especially of the immigration of Dumnonii, whose advance was made at the cost of the Goidel inhabitants settled there. About the middle of the 3rd century, a new wave of Celtic immigrants reached Britain from France, evidently from the territory roughly corresponding to the modern department of the Marne (hence their name 'Marnians'), their goal being the south coast and Sussex in particular. From then a La Tène Culture in Britain is recognizable and becomes the starting-point for an independent British La Tène art. Another route taken by La Tène immigrants was into the south-west and Bristol Channel region, a percolation which continued to the time of Caesar, when the movement became a stream of refugees.

In the last century B. C., Belgic tribes represented the last phase of colonization in Britain before the arrival of the Roman legions. Cantii settled in Kent, the area south-east of Londinium (London), to which they gave their name. North-west of them, in the present shires of Cambridge and Bedford, were the Catuvellauni. Round about 50 B. C. Atrebates and Durobriges came across the Channel (out of fear of Roman subjugation) and landed on the Isle of Wight and on the southern coasts of Dorset and Hampshire.

IV

Celtic languages and the oldest surviving literature

Gaelic-Goidel and Gaulish dialects

The family of Celtic languages can be divided into two main branches: Q-Celtic and P-Celtic. The first comprises the group of Gaelic dialects (Irish and Scottish), in which Indo-European kw changed to qu (k, c): they are also designated Goidel languages and are the more ancient branch, it being presumed that it was a form of Q-Celtic that was spoken by the Celts who early entered the Iberian Peninsula. The second group comprises the Gaulish dialects, to which belong, in addition to the Continental dialects, the language of the inhabitants of Wales and Brittany. This second group changed kw to p. All the above languages have a certain common lexical stock and certain features of declension and conjugation in common: originally, they were dialects mutually more or less closely related.

The words Gael and Gaelic are anglicized forms of names long in use by the Irish people to designate themselves and their language. The name Goidel would seem to have first appeared towards the end of the 7th century and probably owes its origin to the word Gwyddel, the Welsh name for the Irish. In North Wales, the cognate Gwynedd is a re-

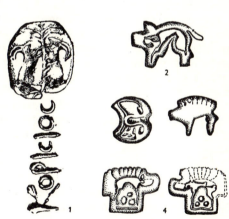

Fig. 19. Punch-marks on the blades of Celtic swords from Switzerland; 1. Port, punch-mark with the Greek name of the maker, Korisios. — 2. Basadingen (Kt. Thurgau), mark with a boar-motif. — 3. Mandach (Kt. Aargau), warrior's grave. Double punch-mark, with stylized human mask placed sideways and boar with raised bristles. — 4. Brütisellen (Kt. Zürich). Double punch-mark, on the inside is outlined a second figure of a boar and three bosses. Drawing: Provincial Museum (Bern) R. Wyss.

gional name deriving from Irish settlers there, known in their own land, before the coming of Christianity, as Feni.

Gaulish is the name given to the group of Celtic dialects spoken in Gaul, in a part of Britain and in the Central European area in the period of Celtic expansion. Not even in Gaul, in the wider sense of the term, was there complete linguistic unity. Caesar notes that in the three main parts of Gaul (to which we made reference above), the corresponding groups of tribes (Belgae, Aquitanians and Gauls) differed in language and customs.

A certain minority among these Gaulish speaking tribes, especially the chieftain class and also the trading class, undoubtedly had some knowledge of Greek, for the numerical data on the tablets found in a camp of the Helvetii in the time of Caesar, regarding the number of Boii and other Celtic tribes, were written in Greek characters. Also the blade of the La Tène sword from Port, in Switzerland, has an inscription — Korisios — in Greek letters. The priestly class of druids, a very influential group in Celtic society, had no wish for written records, and none have been handed down from them. In the last century B. C., especially in Gaul, and, to a lesser extent, also in certain Celtic domains in Central Europe, a knowledge of Latin began to spread. After Caesar's subjugation of Gaul, Latin quickly became the language of the upper classes, the common folk, however, still speaking Gaulish, especially in the country districts. In Central Europe, too, remnants of Celtic peoples survived even under the altered circumstances, and proofs of their existence are preserved, for instance, in Pannonia, in literary sources and epigraphical material. With the progressive Romanization of present-day France and part of Switzerland, the Gaulish languages died out, only some few elements being preserved in the Romance languages that took their place.

Our present-day knowledge of Gaulish language
Interpretation of place-names

Literature, in the sense of connected writing, has thus not survived in the Gaulish dialects. Our present knowledge of the language is based mainly on incriptions from the 4th-lst centuries, written in Greek, Etruscan or Latin scripts. These inscriptions contain mainly personal and place-names. In addition, there are certain words in the works of Greek and

Latin authors taken over from the Celtic world, then a number of inscriptions on Celtic coins, as well as Gaulish names from grave monuments from Roman times, in Pannonia, and also in the west, in the region of the French-Rhine Basin: there the names of the Gallic makers are inscribed on metal and even ceramic wares.

The interpretation of personal and especially of place-names is particularly difficult, not even the specialists being unanimous in their views. Nor is it even certain whether some place-names which have survived up to the present and which were originally considered to be Celtic are not of still older, pre-Celtic origin.

Surprisingly enough, France itself is not particularly rich in Celtic place-names. The greatest concentration is in the area between the Rhine and the Danube and the surrounding region, which fully conforms to the archaeological evidence. Adjudged to be Celtic are the names of several rivers: the Rhine, the Danube and some of its tributaries, the Neckar, the Main and the Ruhr-Raura, from which it is deduced that the Raurici, whom Caesar mentions as being in the Basel area, originated in the Ruhr basin.

As regards the older period, place-names ending in -briga are considered to belong to an early stratum. The suffix indicates a fortified place and, according to H. Rix, dates from the time when the Celts in Gaul had not yet reached the western seaboard, but when they had already penetrated into Spain. Later, it is said, names ending in -dunum, -dunon, having similar meaning, became widespread, namely in the time of the historical expansion of the Celts, roughly in the 4th and 3rd centuries. In the same period the designation of open settlements with names ending in -magus (magos) became common. As examples of the above, we may mention Boudo-briga (Boppard) or Tarodunum (Zarten), both in the Rhine-lands. However, the mapping of the distribution of these place-names gives only an incomplete and possibly even a misleading picture, as the survival of place-names contains a large element of chance. Names ending in -briga, insofar as we take into account only those for which we have evidence in antiquity (and not first in mediaeval times), are most widely spread in the north-western part of the Iberian Peninsula and occur only sporadically in North-eastern France and in the Rhine-lands. On the other hand, names in -dunum are fairly widely distributed throughout France (with the exception of Aquitania) and crop up also in the Rhine Basin and in the Upper

Danube (their frequency decreasing towards the east) in Britain, and only sporadically in the Iberian Peninsula. Bosch-Gimpera makes use of names ending in -dunum to support his theory, according to which he establishes connections between the Catalanian urnfields and the Celts.

A very different situation arose in the British Isles and, especially, in Ireland. The Roman occupation of Britain embraced only a part of the territories and almost a century later than that of Gaul. Ireland itself was never brought under Roman rule and so an old Celtic language, the ancestor of modern Gaelic, survived undisturbed and, in time, gave birth to an independent native literature. In Roman times it was mainly the folk tradition that kept alive a picture of the past and this was later committed to writing. The monks of the Irish monasteries were thoroughly familiar with this tradition and, in the course of time, recorded it in the native vernacular, thus giving rise to a literature which is the oldest in the 'barbarian' part of Europe, ranking immediately after the literatures of Greece and Rome.

The oldest survivals of Irish literature

The oldest Irish literary monuments are held to be the inscriptions executed in Ogam script, from the 5th—6th centuries A. D. This curious kind of writing is composed of dots and strokes, the latter in various positions relative to a central horizontal straight line, and presumes at least a partial knowledge of Latin. It was made use of mainly in inscriptions on gravestones and similar monuments (just as were Runic characters in Northern Europe), of which the greater part is to be met with in Southern Ireland and on the opposite British seaboard.

The 5th and 6th centuries saw the spread of Christianity in Ireland and the Irish monasteries took over some of the functions of the traditional druidic schools. Monks, well versed in native learning, for the first time committed the ancient vernacular literature to writing. The oldest examples of Irish are Church books of the 8th and 9th centuries, in which the Latin text is accompanied by glosses in the native language of the monks of that age. As these books are easily dateable, they provide an important chronological criterium for the age of the language of manuscripts dating from as late as the 15th and 16th centuries.

From later times epic poems and sagas have survived of an

Heroic Age, in which it is hard to differentiate between fantasy and reality, and often, running like a ground bass through the bardic songs of ancient exploits and heroic glorification, is the thought of death and that other world, inhabited by the souls of those whose mortal days are ended. We shall have opportunity to mention these monuments below and in our final chapter. As they provide a key to the essential fabric of Celtic society in its earliest phases, we shall nevertheless list here the most important.

The principal monuments of Irish literature may be divided into three cycles. The first of them, the Book of Invasions (Lebhar na Gabala), is usually regarded as a scholastic compilation of the 8th—11th centuries. It speaks of waves of immigrants, of which the Goidels were said to be the fifth; they forced the defeated native population to seek refuge, so it is maintained, in great megalithic monuments (on the borders of the Late Stone Age and the Early Bronze Age). Some experts, however, consider the whole work to be a genealogical fiction, designed to explain the origin of all free Irishmen. The second cycle describes the changing fortunes in the struggle of Ulster against Ireland; and the third gives an account of the exploits of Finn and his son Ossian, along with some references to cults and the old social structure.

Celtic literature also includes the stories about Arthur, a Celtic king of Britain, who with his followers opposed the invading Germanic Angles and Saxons. Along with these may be grouped the histories of various small kingdoms. The centuries passed, court verse and the compositions of country poets revived the old traditions, but they themselves came under new influences as the social structure underwent gradual change. In their late garb, it is thus very difficult to isolate the original historical core which they contain. Celtic-speaking peoples were, however, a vehicle for the continuity of language, customs and usages, so that many ancient elements have been preserved which throw light on the character of the Celtic past.

V

Celtic society and its structure

Appearance and character of the Celts

Some ancient writers describe the Celts as tall, with blue eyes, fair hair and fine skin. This may have been a characteristic description of a certain group of population (the chieftains and warrior freemen), without being applicable to the population as a whole. The burials of Celtic warriors, also in Central European territories, show considerable differences in the height of men. Thus, in the Celtic cemetery in Brno-Malo-měřice, are the skeletal remains of men who are relatively small (c. 150 cm), side by side with men of medium height and very tall men (Grave No 42 contained an occupant about 195 cm in height). The evidence of the Slovak graves confirms this. In Horní Jatov-Trnovec nad Váhem, skeletal remains indicating a height of 150—160 cm, of both males and females, are quite common, of 180 cm, rarer, while in the burial-grounds in Dvory nad Žitavou, the average height runs between 160 and 170 cm.

Other anatomical evidence shows the same mixture of types. Where anthropological measurements have been carried out, as, for instance, in the Swiss burial-grounds, the indications are that both long- and round-headed subjects are present. Earlier and more recent analysis of the skeletal material in Czechoslovakia and in other Central European areas confirms the heterogeneous character of the Celtic people, as regards racial composition. Only in Bohemia, it would seem, dolichocephaly is more frequent, in which case the Central Bohemian Celts would then differ somewhat from those in Moravia and Austria, where brachycrania is more the rule. It is significant that the long-headed type ascertained in Bohemia is also to be found in relatively later burial-places in Slovakia, especially in Horní Jatov-Trnovec and in both cemeteries in Hurbanovo. We have still insufficient material to enable us to draw definitive conclusions, so that these must be considered to be merely tentative.

In general, there was no great difference in the physical appearance of Celts and Germans. This is stressed by Strabo in his Geography, written under the Emperors Augustus and Tiberius, the Germans being only, according to him, taller and of a wilder disposition. The fact that it was difficult to distinguish between Celts and Germans is confirmed by the report that when Caligula required extras for his 'triumph', in 37 A.D. to represent captive Germans, he procured Celts from Gaul for the purpose.

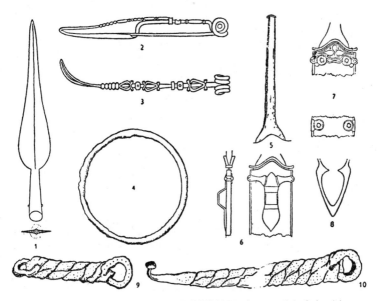

Fig. 20. Kobylnice, Moravia. Cremation grave No IX (Celtic warrior, turn of the 2nd and 1st cents. B. C. (4 = 16 cm, 9 = 12 cm, 10 = 56 cm).

Fair hair cannot be considered a generally recognizable trait either, for, from various allusions in the sources, we know that the Celts often dyed their hair, making use of different solutions, soaps and dyes. They also used cosmetics, and, in Rome, the poet Propertius bitterly reproaches his mistress for making up like the Celts. Men, too, treated their hair with a wash of lime to stiffen it and then brushed it straight back from the forehead to look like a horse's mane. Thus we find references in the Classical writers to the long stiff hair of the Celts. According to Diodorus, the men shaved their cheeks, but grew long moustaches covering their mouths.

Disposition of the Celts. In Antiquity, the Celts were generally described as a fighting, courageous and high-spirited people, but sometimes of an almost childish naivety. Strabo writes of them that as a nation they were war-mad, loved feats of arms and adventures, and also feasting and entertainment. Their eloquence often bordered on loquacity. They would stop travellers and traders and inquire all about the countries they had passed through. The information thus acquired was often exaggerated in the re-telling. According to Caesar, they were an unstable people, always running after something new, but very apt to imitate all they saw and quick to learn. Archaeological finds testify to the ability of the Celts not only to imitate foreign patterns, but to adapt them creatively and give them an individual content. They had a weakness, however, for glorification and show.

Celtic dress

In their dress, according to Diodorus, the Celts were fond of bright colours and favoured striped and checked materials. As early as the Hallstatt period they produced high-quality woollen materials, with gay patterns. In the La Tène Age, women adorned their dress with flowers and the women of rank gave it lustre by the running in of gold thread, as in ancient times. Prior to the Roman Occupation, fringes were said to be a common adornment of dress and mantle.

The costume worn consisted of a coloured tunic or shirt and trousers (*braccae*, whence breeches). Over this was worn a cloak or mantle, of wool in winter and of a thinner, smooth material in summer. Trousers were an innovation in the European environment. They had so far been known only in the east, for instance, among the Persians and Scythians, but not at all in the Mediterranean world. Literary sources confirm the use of trousers among the Celts, but it is not clear whether it was widespread or confined only to certain tribes. The Insubres and Boii in Italy also wore trousers and a light-coloured cloak. The Gaesatae called in from beyond the Alps to help their kinsmen fought naked, in the front ranks, as was the ancient custom. In Caesar's time the Gauls wore wider and longer trousers, reaching to the knee; the German type was closer fitting.

The body garment among the Celts was held in place by shoulder brooches, fibulae, warriors most commonly having brooches of iron, women of rank, bronze or sometimes silver brooches, often very artistically wrought, set with coral and decorated with enamel. In some women's burials there is a strikingly large number of brooches, on the shoulders and the breast. The woman buried in Grave No 184, in Münsingen in Switzerland, had 16 brooches; a girl of twenty or so, in Dietikon near Zürich, had 14, while in another grave as many as 21 were counted. In a woman's grave, in Jenišův Újezd near Bílina in Bohemia, 6 bronze and 4 iron brooches were among the personal possessions buried with her. Rich women's burials show best the passion for adornment: women wore gold, silver or bronze finger-rings, neck-rings and necklaces, bracelets and ankle-rings, sapropelite rings and glass bracelets, splendid belts and belt chains and other ornaments of which we shall speak later. In men's graves, ornaments are rarer, but all the greater attention is paid to combat equipment.

The Celts wore the body garment gathered in at the waist by a belt. In the Late Bronze and Early La Tène times, belts and girdles were decorated with gold or bronze ornaments and discs sewn on in *appliqué* style. Ordinary folk had simple belts of material or leather. In the 3rd century B. C., when the general situation of the Celts underwent considerable change and led to a reorganization of the economico-social structure, the belt became an important part of the equipment of the freeman-warrior and the woman of free grade. From that time dates a clear differentiation between belts as worn by men and by women. Women of the highest rank wore splendid bronze chain belts, admirable products of the casting and enamel-working workshops: they are composed of cast disk-like members, linked by rings *(Fig. 24)*, and the effect of the gold-gleaming bronze is heightened by numerous inlays of red enamel. A more common variant of these chain belts composed of tubular members is decorated with red or white enamel, as were also belts of double chains, linked by rings. Later forms, which we find in cemeteries and in oppida, are chains with figure-of-eight members. When fastened, the end part of the chain formed a hanging loop, to which was attached a special pendant piece *(fig. 25)*. The 'hook-and-eye' clasps are usually artistically wrought.

Men's belts served also for hanging on the sword (or dagger) sheathed in a scabbard. They were either of leather or of bronze (figure-of-eight design) and consisted of two parts. From the turn of the 2nd and 1st centuries come iron chain-belts of flat plaited members (reminiscent of plaited leather thongs), on the surface of which was hammered out a dense 'punctuated' pattern (the hammered 'panzer' belts in use practically throughout the Celtic world, *fig. 20*).

Celtic footwear was well known as far as Rome, whether it was their small wooden sandals, linen shoes with a leather sole or shoes of leather.

Torcs and their socio-ritual significance in Celtic society

A special place among articles of personal adornment is occupied by the neck-ring for which antiquity used the word torc (Latin = *torquis*), as referring to the type twisted from a number of strands, although few examples of these have been preserved. More frequent are those consisting of a curved rod or hollow tube, with more or less enlarged seal-like terminals. Torcs appear in the middle of the 5th century B. C., the idea being a borrowing from the east where, in Persia, for example, we find splendid exemplars. In the period of the rise of an Early La Tène art, at the end of the 5th and in the 4th century, Celtic workshops turned out neck-rings of this kind, of gold, as objects of high artistic value; especially the terminals of these rings are richly decorated, mostly in relief, with vegetal or mask motifs. These exquisite torcs are widely distributed wherever the armed Celtic bands penetrated: in France, in the Rhinelands, in Italy, the Alps, Bulgaria, as well as in Bohemia (Oploty) and Slovakia (Myjava, Hrkovce, *fig. 12*). They were worn by persons of high rank and were the mark of their social status and wealth.

Later bronze neck-rings were made of simpler design, with seal or rounded buffer terminals (*Pl. XXVIII*). Not even these, however, appear frequently enough for us to speak of popular ornaments; it seems that these, too, had social significance, for they are most often found in the graves of warriors and of wealthy women.

About the 2nd century, a change came about. At the time of the height of Celtic power torcs appear on coins in a severely schematized form, but disappear from grave furnishings. The torc, originally of gold, ceased to be the mark of an individual's social standing in everyday life and entered the world of religious-mythological conceptions, in which it was closely associated with concepts of gods and heroes. This change took place in the 2nd century at the latest, for the torc then figures

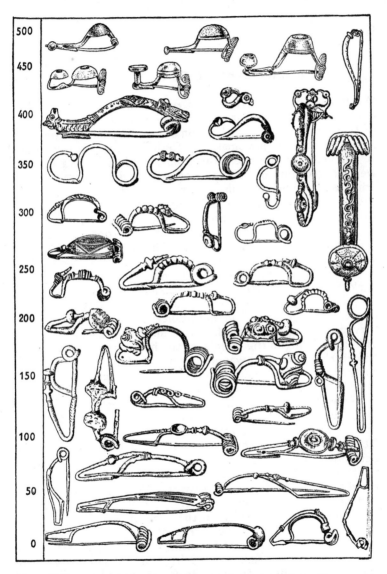

Fig. 21. Evolution of the fibula in the La Tène period. The brooch, as a fashionable ornament, is a reliable period pointer, and so of value in helping to date associated objects in archaeological finds.

in sculptural representations of Celtic gods and heroes by southern artists as well as in native representations (head from Mšecké Žehrovice in Bohemia, *Pl. XX*). The same motif is present on the richly decorated cult cauldrons from Rynkeby and Gundestrup *(Pl. XXIV, XXV)*.

Food and feasts of the Celts

We have it on the authority of Poseidonius that the food of the Celts consisted of bread and plenty of meat, either boiled or roasted on glowing coals or on a spit. The men cut the meat from the bone with a small iron flesh-knife, which they wore at the waist beside their sheathed sword. Beef and mutton were served, but also salt-pickled pork and baked salted fish. Pork was a favourite dish, either roasted or boiled in a cauldron. The bones of boar and pig are a common feature of Celtic graves and were probably the remains of the burial feast. In Ireland, tradition has it that the proper portion for a champion was a whole porker. Fish were broiled in salt water, with the addition of vinegar and carraway seeds.

A larger company sat down to a meal in a circle. The Celts took their food squatting on the ground or on skins, sometimes they had a low table in front of them. There was a fixed etiquette of precedence and hospitality, which was strictly observed. Seating was according to rank and prowess, the seat of honour being in the middle, at the head. Strangers were fed before their business was inquired. The food was served on earthenware, bronze and wooden platters; sometimes a cauldron with glowing coals was brought in, on which were pans with the cooked joints of meat. At some feasts, a wrestling match was part of the entertainment. Occasionally the sham contest turned into the real thing, so that injuries, sometimes fatal, were inflicted. The victor was awarded the thigh, as the best portion.

The drink of the wealthy in Gaul was wine, drunk undiluted or with a small admixture of water. Wine-drinking became widely indulged in among the leading Celtic class as early as the 6th century, and later, in the time of armed raids, it increased inordinately. Polybius reproaches the Celtic warrior for his love of drinking and feasting. The greater part of the wine in the western half of the Celtic world was imported from the south in amphorae made in Provence and in Rome, and these are not seldom found in the graves of Celtic notables.

But the drinking of wine spread, though to a smaller extent, also among the leading grades in the lands of the Upper Danube and particularly in Bohemia. Already in the 5th century a wine drinking service reached Bohemia (beaked flagon and vessels from Hradiště, near Písek), and in the last century B. C., when Roman influence had greatly increased in the Celtic lands, wine amphorae also turn up in the oppida, alike in Bavarian Manching and in Bohemian Hradiště near Stradonice. For long Greek and Southern French wine had been imported through Massilia, and Italian wine, in smaller quantity. From the 2nd century, however, Italian wine comprised the bulk of the export. The wine trade in the south of France passed completely into the hands of Italian merchants. The occupation of Gaul by the Romans corresponds in time to the development of viniculture in Southern Italy: Gaul then became an important wine import market up to the beginning of the 2nd century A. D.

The common folk drank home-brewed beer made from barley, sometimes improved with the addition of hops. Carraway seeds were also an ingredient in the brewing of beer. This home-made beer was called 'korma'. Oil was little used among the Celts, butter, which was plentiful, being preferred.

It was the custom, at drinking bouts and feasts, for bards to sing the praises of those present, especially of the host. They sang to the accompaniment of an instrument similar to the lyre. The kings, especially, had their court bards, who glorified the heroic deeds of their patrons. The tradition of court eulogistic verse struck deep roots and continued far into mediaeval times.

In the course of time a fixed ceremonial became established for official banquets, which allotted to each rank the appropriate joint of meat. In Ireland, a leg of pork went to the king, the haunch to the queen, and a boar's head to the charioteer. According to Poseidonius, the thigh always went to the best man present. On warring expeditions, a feast was part of the reward of fighting services. In general, the sources praise the cleanly eating habits of the Celts, while disparaging their voracity.

The structure of Celtic society

Family and kin. The basic unit of Celtic society was the family and kin (Irish *fine*). The father had, according to Caesar, in a legal sense, unlimited power over the members of his family — the power of life and death *(potestas vitae necisque)*, devolving apparently from his patriarchal authority. If the death of a man awoke suspicion, his wife was interrogated and brought to judgement. This did not mean that a woman did not enjoy respect, especially in the higher social grades. We have seen that in the later Hallstatt period there were women who lived in the lap of luxury and were shown the highest honours in burial. According to Classical sources, the Celtic woman was the equal of her men-folk in bravery. In Ireland and in Gaul, a man could have more than one wife, but Irish sources show that only one could be the principal wife, the others occupying various grades down to what amounted almost to slavery. At the end of the La Tène period polygamy was still permitted by law, but in practice society enjoined monogamy. Insofar as the paternity of a child was not in dispute, the mother had no particular rights in this connection. Traces of matriarchal rights are observable in illegitimate offspring, who took the name of their mother. Irish law actually bound illegitimate children to their mother and accorded them civil rights. In later times the wife brought her husband a dowry, in the west, in silver. Husband and wife were joint owners of this property, which was heritable on the death of one partner by the other.

Members of a family and of a kin were bound by collective responsibilities and obligations. It was possible, in the form of sanctions, to exclude a member from certain rights and privileges, while his obligations remained. The organization of the family also determined the manner of conveying property and of heritage. Sometimes it caused serious complications in the leading classes, and in the royal family itself. If a king had no son to succeed to him, his successor was chosen from the male line of descent (father, uncle, cousin) reckoned from a common great-grandfather. In the upbringing of children there were, too, certain rules and usages. In Gaul, sons might not appear in the company of their fathers before they had reached an age when they could bear arms.

The development of the kin society had advanced very far in the Celtic environment and was accompanied by various features which created the pre-conditions for the rise of a class society; it was, however, interrupted by the fall of Celtic power. An aristocracy of birth points to an advanced stage in the break-up of primitive communism, but does not yet imply the rise of a class society. There are notable differences between the course of development in Central Europe, in Gaul and in the British Isles. These cannot be dealt with here in detail, but a special study will be devoted to the subject; the divergency of the situation in the British Isles was already pointed out by F. Engels in the last century.

Tribes. The largest social unit was the tribe (Irish *túath*, in Gaul, civitas-pagus), whose members claimed a common

Fig. 22. La Tène art: 1. Waldalgesheim, Germany. — 2. Schwarzenbach, Germany, mask motif. 3. Pfalzfeld (Kr. St. Goar). — 4. Holzgerlingen (Odenwald), reconstruction of a double-faced head (limestone, columniform figure, see also fig. 41).

ancestry. Traces of kin organization and an earlier totemistic conception long continued (the taboo on certain foods, animal cults, the Celtic love of symbolism, and so on).

The Celtic tribes were very numerous. The name of sixty tribes were, according to Strabo, inscribed on an altar dedicated to Caesar Augustus at Lugdunum (Lyon). Some tribes were small, others large and powerful, with large armed forces, and these contended among one another for the hegemony over the whole of Gaul. These were especially the Arverni and Aedui, the Salyes in the south, evidently at least partly of Celtic origin. The latter were defeated, as we saw above, by the Romans, in 124 B. C., on their beginning hostilities against Massilia.

During the period of Celtic expansion parts of individual tribes reached many different European regions. It cannot be presumed that in their further development the ethnic composition of the group or tribe was maintained. Historical sources show that the Celts frequently moved their settlements and that often parts of one tribe split off and joined up with another tribe. Besides, the archaeological record shows that in the Carpathians and in Moravia, by the 2nd century B. C., at the latest, a closer amalgamation of the Celtic groups with the older indigenous population had taken place and that elements of the native culture percolated into the La Tène culture of the leading class. Several groups, including those of mercenaries who had entered foreign service, were gradually absorbed into the new environment. It must be borne in mind that the La Tène Culture, in its stricter connotation, was, in Central Europe, the culture of only a single ethnic group and of an upper social stratum.

Kingship and aristocracy

We have evidence that as late as the La Tène period kingship was still common among the Celtic tribes, as an ancient institution whose beginnings we can trace to the later phase of the Hallstatt environment of the stronghold chieftains. In some tribes, however, the king was elected. On his ceremonial inauguration, he entered into all the powers and rights of kingship; he was also bound to observe lavish hospitality. In the last century B. C. we still come across kingship among the Senones and the Nitiobroges. It is known, too, that in the triumph of Fabius Maximus a captive Celtic king was in the procession. Florus relates that his chariot was inlaid with silver and his weapons flashed in different colours — being probably richly decorated with gold, silver and coloured enamels. Famous for his prodigality was Luerna, the King of the Arverni, later defeated and captured by the Romans. This king is said to have driven in his chariot through the countryside and thrown gold and silver coins among the people. Once, it is also reported, he had a square piece of ground fenced in where he installed barrels of drink and immense quantities of food, so that whoever wanted could help himself.

Social differentiation, however, continued to progress and the noble families tried to seize as much public power as possible. Economic conflicts and acts of revenge among the aristocracy were not unusual. The decline of kingly power among the individual tribes is ascribed by Caesar to the growth of the system of clientship, whereby the aristocracy greatly strengthened their power and influence. Nor can it be doubted that another operative factor was emulation of Roman institutions, for the tribes who gave up kingship (Arveni, Aedui, Helvetii) were all within direct reach of influences from the Provincia Narbonensis, which had been under Roman administration since the latter part of the 2nd century. In Aquitania and in the region of the Belgic tribes, kingship was maintained into much later times.

Fig. 23. *Stupava, Slovakia. Bronzé belt décor, with mask relief.*

In Caesar's time the form of rule by the aristocracy already predominated, which, however, sometimes led to an unstable situation, caused by internal strife between factions, and even to anarchy. The governing class sought a prop for their power in the system of clients, not altogether dissimilar from feudal customs. Personal clientship is fully confirmed among the continental Celts by Polybius, who also describes its advantages for the patron class. According to Strabo, the Gauls chose their king every year and, in time of war, every band of warriors had its captain. In the last century B. C. the Adui and the Sequanes were the main contestants for power in Gaul, so that the country was divided into two camps. For a time, too, the Arverni played an important role. The Arvernian Celtill, having gained the leadership over a large part of Gaul, was then killed by his countrymen for aspiring to kingship. In 52 B. C. his son, Vercingetorix, organized a rising against Caesar.

He called on his clients to fulfil their obligations and, out of necessity, forced poor people and worthless rogues into service; having established his power and gained the support of the Senones and other tribes, he became chief commander, taking action, with the cruelty of a military dictator, against offenders, in order to maintain discipline and subordination among his armed troops.

In Ireland, according to customary law, society was divided into three grades within the *túath*, a word originally meaning 'the people', but later acquiring a territorial connotation — the king, the nobles and the commonalty or body of freemen. The king was chosen from the kin of his predecessor, but was not necessarily his son. The royal power embraced a number of public functions, such as action in connection with warfare, the conclusion of pacts of friendship with other *túath*, and so on. The body of freemen included farmers and certain categories of craftsmen; the unfree population consisted of subjugated groups and mixed families. Small kingdoms, based on individual *túath*, did not form states in the proper sense of the word, for in them there was no organized public administration. A freemen had an honour-price, depending on his dignity or social status and on his wealth. In Ireland, too, in addition to ties of kinship, the institution of clientship was widespread. The client was under obligation of certain services, especially armed attendance, to his lord, in return for which he enjoyed protection and material support, without, however, losing any of his rights as a freeman, not excluding the owning of property. The rights of individuals had validity only within the *túath* to which they belonged.

The condition of the commonalty was never enviable, and sometimes, indeed, was not far removed from slavery. Many were deep in debt and were oppressed by the more powerful, who extorted from them onerous services and heavy dues. For this reason, many placed themselves under the protection of noble lords. The wealthier and more noble a free Gaul was, the more numerous were his client-dependents.

Caesar reports that in Celtic Gaul there were three main groups of population: druids, equites (horsemen, 'knights', i. e. the free governing grades) and the people. To these must be added a type of clientship as noted above, which was not altogether identical with the Roman institution of the same name.

The druids

Originally the priestly caste of druids was fitted into the social hierarchy in which they occupied a high place. They formed an aristocratic society, which not only fulfilled religious functions, but also exercised great political influence, greater than that of the 'equites'. It was an all-Celtic institution, established both in the British Isles and in Gaul, and may have played a role for a certain time also in Central Europe; only in Spain and in North Italy no mention is made of it, nor are there archaeological indications of its existence. Caesar's view that the institution arose in the British Isles is only his own presumption. Classical sources (Caesar, Pliny) attribute to the druids a wide range of functions, which it is difficult at present to verify.

Our knowledge of the substance of their teaching, philosophical and religious conceptions is still very fragmentary. They believed in the immortality of the soul; death for them did not mean the end, but only an intermediate stage. Under their priestly protection were the sacred groves of oak and their name is said to be derived from the word *drys*, meaning an oak. Sacrifices (for instance, of white bulls) were never offered without branches from this tree, for what grew on it was looked upon as a divine gift and the rites performed with it as the fulfilment of a divine commandment. The lunar symbols were also held in high reverence. The Celts measured time not in days, but in nights, and sacrifices were made to the gods at night, by the light of the moon. In addition to offering sacrifices (sometimes human), the druids forecast the future; they also influenced unfavourable forecasts and fixed auspicious times for important actions and enterprises. The druids were entrusted with the education of the young nobility. They did not, however, use writing and have, therefore, not left any written monuments to posterity; learning was by rote.

The druids and 'vates' (seers, the word being derived from a root meaning 'inspired' or 'ecstatic') were a group whose ranks were supplemented by novices from the sons of the freemen nobility. An account has come down to us of an instance of druidic trance, in connection with the choice of a new king at Tara. The druid ate of the flesh of the sacrificed bull, fell into a deep sleep, on coming out of which he was able to influence the decision. This rite was known as a 'bull dream'.

In later times the druids did not form such an exclusive caste, nor even a purely religious order. We know of druids who were sons of laymen. At the beginning of the Roman occupation of Gaul, druidism was still flourishing. The druids strongly resisted Romanization and took part in various risings and plots, so that the Roman power had a special interest in the suppression of this institution. Druidism survived long-est in Ireland. The successors of the druids in Early Christian times were the *filid*, the founders of permanent mediaeval schools

VI

The warrior organization of the Celts and their mode of warfare

The leading warrior group and their equipment

Besides the druids, a leading group in Celtic society were the mounted freemen-warriors, a kind of military aristocracy. The Celts in the west had no permanent armed forces, these meeting only in times of war and danger. When such danger threatened, it was the custom in Gaul to convoke an assembly of all the armed men. Such an assembly marked the beginning of warfare; by the rattling of arms and a shout the assembly expressed agreement with the proposals put forward. For the duration of hostilities the warrior bands remained organized according to tribes.

A different situation obtained in Central Europe, in the territories occupied by the Celts in the 4th—1st centuries B. C., where it was necessary for certain groups of freemen to be in constant preparedness, as they lived in an environment where there was a larger and older established population. This is clearly testified to in the graves of the warrior class in the cemeteries in Bohemia, Moravia and Slovakia. Burials of men, usually with their fighting-gear of sword in scabbard, spear and sometimes shield, comprise an important part of the total of more exactly recordable graves (Letky near Prague, Holubice in Moravia), elsewhere about a fifth or somewhat less. The general situation shows that it is not a matter of a burial rite which prescribed the inclusion of arms in the grave furnishings of freemen, but of the burial of active professional warriors. Some male burials are without arms and some even without equipment, so that not all men were buried in full fighting gear. On the other hand, the skeletal remains of the burials with arms show traces of armed encounters and warlike activities. Healed scars on the skulls of males have been verified in the Celtic cemeteries in Zábrdovice near Křinec, in Dolní Dobrá Voda near Hořice, in Nová Ves near Velvary, and elsewhere; in Křenovice, in Moravia, a warrior had had his skull fractured twice in his lifetime; in Trnovec nad Váhem another had healed injuries on his crown, and a third, in Hurbanovo, a bone scar on the forehead. Sometimes part of a limb is missing: in Červené Pečky near Kolín, a forearm, in Brno-Maloměřice, the right hand, as also in Hurbanovo in Slovakia. There is thus sufficiently convincing evidence of the character of this warrior group of population.

Undoubtedly belonging to this social group are the burials of richly furnished women's graves. They are usually located in the cemeteries in the immediate proximity of warrior graves — in some cases man and woman are buried in a single grave (Velká Maňa in Slovakia). The richness of these women's graves is in marked contrast to the average and sub-average furnishing of the other graves. Sometimes these women are buried in expensively furnished grave chambers, lined with wood. Above, mention has already been made of burials of women with a large number of brooches; along with these are bracelets, ankle-rings, finger-rings (some of silver and of gold) torcs, beautifully wrought belt-chains, decorated with enamels, sapropelite and glass rings; finally, there are usually pig bones from the burial feast. In the graves so far investigated in this context, the number of richly furnished women's graves is about 10 per cent or even more (Jenišův Újezd near Bílina, in Bohemia, Brno-Maloměřice and Bučovice, in Moravia).

Archaeological observations of recent years permit of our distinguishing, within the relevant Central European stratum, called by Caesar 'equites', the graves of leading personages, chieftains or overlords, according to a number of criteria. First of all there are the special burial arrangements for certain men buried with their armour and of rich women. In Horní Jatov-Trnovec nad Váhem lay the skeleton of a tall, older man, with fighting equipment, wrapped in an animal skin, in a spacious burial pit (Grave No 362), in which were the bones of almost a whole pig; round the grave was a square ditch, with sides measuring 10 m. A similar arrangement is observed in the burial of a rich woman (Grave No 233), also with a square enclosing ditch. Both burials, which would appear to date from before the end of the 2nd century, are somewhat isolated from the other inhumations. A similar situation is observable in the Celtic cemetery in Holiare. The cremation burial of a warrior (Grave No 29) and of a richly equipped woman (Grave No 185), from which comes the very fine bronze belt-chain (fig. 25), both from the turn of the 2nd and 1st centuries B. C., are in close propinquity and, unlike the other cremation-burials, are both surrounded by a circular ditch having a diameter of 10 m. In this case, too, the graves are somewhat apart from the others, in order to stress their importance.

Outward marks of social prestige

The principal weapon in the La Tène period was the sword, then the casting spear or lance, and later also a shield. Certain kinds of sword and scabbards were the outward symbol of power and rank and enable us to distinguish the leading personages in the warrior group. They are, in the first place, ceremonial swords, usually shorter than the fighting weapon, with anthropomorphic or pseudo-anthropomorphic hilt. They are apparently a development of the Late Hallstatt dagger of similar character, particularly associated with the culture in the north-west foothills of the Alps, from where the armed bands set out on their raiding activities. They turn up from about the end of the 5th century and continue in use for long, to the beginning of the last century, first in the environment of the barrow-graves and later in flat cemeteries throughout the whole region within the sphere of Celtic expansion, from the British Isles in the west to the Carpathians in the east, and, indeed, as far as the Mukačevo area. Five such finds have been made in Bohemia and the same number in Moravia. The shaft of the hilt of these swords runs up and down in a frame generally reminiscent of the letter X, or a stylization of the human limbs. Between the upper arms, sometimes on a special thorn, is set the representation of a bronze human head (anthropomorphic swords) or some other decorative motif (pseudo-anthropomorphic swords). Some of these swords are very skilfully wrought, the ends of the hilt arms being decorated with coloured inlays and the blade inlaid with gold. The sword from Nemilany, Moravia, decorated with gold, lay on the breast of the warrior and included in the grave goods were two more iron swords. The iron sword with bronze hilt from Klučov near Český Brod has hollows and a groove in the middle shaft for inlays.

The leading warrior class laid great emphasis on the artistic tooling of the swords, and especially of the scabbards. Associated with the ceremonial swords are bonze scabbards, with medallion-decorated chape (a group of 3—5 circular medallions, sometimes with enamelling or other decoration). These forms, too, appear from the 5th century and continue throughout the whole period of Celtic expansion. Well-known are the

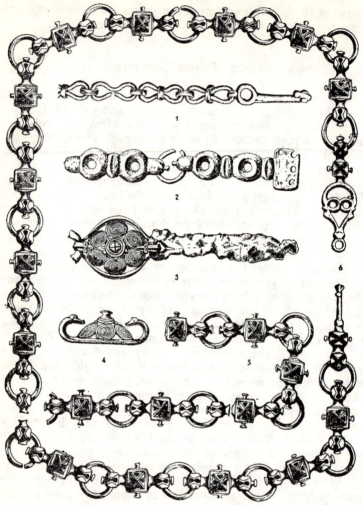

Fig. 24. Among the personal ornaments of women of the leading class were bronze chains, often decorated with red enamel-work (nos. 5—6). They were in particular favour also in Central Europe, in the 2nd and at the beginning of the 1st cent. B. C.: 1. Lednice, Moravia; 2. Nejdek, Moravia; 3.—4. Kozlany, Moravia; 5. Želeč, Moravia; 6. Stradonice near Louny, Bohemia.

Celtic scabbards in the 'beautiful sword' style, with arabesque or other design chased on the outer face, executed symmetrically or diagonally asymmetrically; the *décor* is usually embossed or chased, animal motifs are relatively rare (*fig. 18*). We still come across them at the end of the 2nd century and they often bear a punch-mark. The greater number of such finds have been made in Switzerland. Evidently for their magico-religious significance punch-marked swords favour boar and mask motifs, in one case, the name of the maker is inscribed in Greek characters in *repoussé* technique (Korisios, *fig. 19*). In the younger period, the insular sphere of the British Isles was outstanding for its production of richly decorated scabbards.

The actual fighting bands were equipped with effective iron swords, some of which were over 80 cm long, sheathed in a scabbard and hung on a leather, iron or bronze belt. These heavy swords were common already in the 3rd century (Polybius, for instance, mentions them in his description of the battle at Telamon, 225 B. C.), and, in Central European cemeteries of the 3rd and 2nd ceturies, they are part of the regular inventory in male burials; the majority are in graves of foot warriors either from the group of freemen or from the freemen who had entered into a client relation. Spears, too, were part of the equipment, sometimes with a shaft and head over 2 m long; spearmen were an important body in the Celtic armed forces and antique sources make express mention of them. The Celtic shield becomes a commoner feature in the archaeological display from the middle of the 3rd century; it was long, usually oval or rectangular in shape, with rounded corners. Originally the shields were of wood, without complicated metal-work, later they had a pronounced metal umbo (serving to protect the hand holding the shield) and midrib, the surround being strengthened with a band of bronze or iron sheet. Reconstruction of Celtic shields is not difficult, as in several places finds have been made of almost complete examples (La Tène in Switzerland, or the mass find of wooden shields, with wooden umbo, in the peat-bog in Hjortspring, Jutland) and also sculptural representations of Celtic warriors are accurately observed *(Pl. XIX)*. The shield motif occurs also on Celtic coins. Some shields were over 1 m high, among them one measuring 170 cm, so that they often cover the whole body (Velká Maňa): they were, however, not very strong, about 11 mm in thickness round the centre and only 3—4 mm at the edge. These archaeological data are in agreement with Caesar's account, where he comments that it was possible to impale a number of Gallic shields on one sword, so that they became a hindrance and the Gauls then threw them away.

Coats of mail and helmets were rare in the Celtic warrior environment and confined to the leading personages; insofar as any have been preserved, they are of artistic workmanship (fig. 11).

Mention has already been made of belt-chains. In Britain and Brittany, there is evidence for the use of slings for hurling flat pebbles or stones. The Celtic foot warrior had few ornaments, most commonly an iron brooch to fasten his cloak.

In the period of Celtic expansion, besides foot warriors, war chariots and mounted warriors took part in armed action. The two-wheeled chariot is in evidence from the end of the

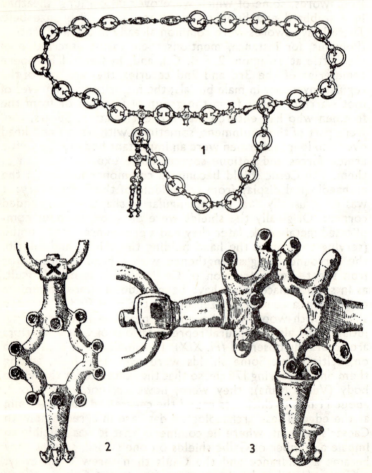

Fig. 25. Bronze belt-chains as worn by Celtic women: 1. Manching, Bavaria. General view of fastened chain. — 2.—3. Holiare, Slovakia. Enamelled clasp-hooks from chain-belts found in women's graves.

5th century. The warriors in these chariots drove furiously towards and in front of the enemy's front ranks, delivered missiles and kept up a terrific din of horn-blowing, shouting and beating on the sides of the waggons, this and the neighing of the horses all intended to intimidate the enemy and fill them with dismay. At an opportune moment, the warriors leapt from the chariots and delivered a challenge to an opposing champion, the ensuing encounter being fought out on foot. The charioteers retired with the chariots to the rear. As the result of daily training, the Celts were splendid horsemen and could stop and turn their horses on the instant, in the middle of the fastest gallop. Charioteers are said to have proved their agility by running along the chariot pole to the yoke, when driving at full speed. Burials with two-wheeled chariots are best investigated so far in the Rhenish-French region. In Britain this type of warfare was long kept up.

Mounted warriors (equites) among the continental Celts, especially in the west, formed the highest social group. They played a particularly important role in the armed excursions into the Balkans and Greece. The Greek writer, Pausanias, has preserved from the 3rd century the Celtic term, *trimarcisia*, denoting three riders, one of noble rank and two followers, who were able to provide the first with a fresh horse or go to his assistance. The number of mounted warriors undoubtedly increased during the struggle with the Romans. The main body of warriors fought on foot in tribal units and often had on their standard the figure of a boar (*fig. 14*). The boar had a special symbolic significance throughout the Celtic world, as we shall see in the chapter on Celtic art and religious concepts.

Methods of warfare

Celtic warriors had a wide reputation for daring and courage; women, it was said, fighting as bravely as their men-folk. Enemy fortifications were scaled by Celtic warriors with the help of wooden ladders, and earthworks were submitted to a hail of stones from warriors forming a circle round them, so that the enemy were unable to keep a footing on them. On mounting an attack, they formed a roof with their shields, under cover of which they undermined the earthworks and set fire to the gateways. Sometimes, too, they used waggons to form a defence. From higher positions some hurled missiles others attacked the enemy with casting spears and lances. Boiling tar and tallow brands, passed from hand to hand, were hurled at the enemy defences to start conflagrations.

Fighting methods were often of great cruelty. In certain areas of the Celtic world, we come across the cult of decapitation. According to primitive notions, the head represented the whole man, and it is likely that it was this idea that gave rise to the custom of warriors hanging the heads of foes on their horses' bridles, to be taken home and nailed to their dwellings. The heads of notables were sometimes embalmed and displayed to guests as the visible proof of the victor's prowess. References to this custom are made by Classical writers (Diodorus, Strabo) and it is documented in artistic representations in the south of France, in special sanctuaries (Entremont, Roquepertuse), of which mention will be made below. According to Orosius, the Scordistae on the Lower Danube used the skulls of their enemies as drinking cups. On Celtic coins, too, we often find the motif of a warrior holding a decapitated head by the hair. Here it may be recalled that in Central European graves we sometimes come across bodies buried without heads, as, for instance, in Letky near Prague.

In early times Celts surpassed even Germans in courage and Caesar can still praise this quality in the last century B. C. But then Celtic valour was already quickly deteriorating, especially where contact with the highly civilized south accustomed the Celts to a high level of material comfort. Roman influence then accelerated the trend to physical decadence. Finally there came a time when the Celts avoided conflicts and struggle and retreated before the vigorous thrusts of Germanic tribes.

VII

The economic basis and civilized achievement of Celtic society

House and village

The majority of Celtic people lived in villages in the middle of their fields. Their houses were built of wood and covered with thatch roofs which were easily inflammable, so that the setting of fire to a large number of villages in times of war was a simple matter. The accounts of Caesar, Tacitus, Strabo and Pliny are, in general, in agreement with the results of archaeological investigation; there is no evidence of any grand dwellings, but rather of huts, whose erection was neither arduous nor costly.

Most of the ascertained ground plans of houses in Central Europe are partially let into the ground, sometimes half a metre down, elsewhere even more. Most frequently they were rectangular structures. On the central axis, at either end of the hut, were usually two wooden posts about 4 m apart, which evidently carried the main truss of the roof. Along one wall, usually the longer one, there is often a kind of bench carved in the dried mud. We have already a sufficient number of such structures on which to base conclusions (the La Tène settlement near Tuchlovice in the Nové Strašecí district, in Soběsuky and Třískolupy in the Žatec district, in Hostomice near Bílina in Bohemia, and others). Most of the excavated examples are small dwellings, whose excavated ground plans are usually about 5—7 m long. Only it is very difficult in Bohemia to distinguish between the dwellings of the Celtic immigrants and those of the indigenous population.

In the younger La Tène period buildings become more frequent with a stone understructure (in the dry-stone technique used up to the end of the last century B. C., under Roman influence), and this especially in South Bohemia (Kbelnice near Strakonice, hut 6 × 3 m, with a stone understructure). Sometimes the huts were let into a soft rock foundation (Kuřímeny in the Strakonice district). Some Late La Tène structures are relatively long (as much as 13 × 3.5 m), with stamped earth floor, partly paved with stones; the walls of round timber are joined by means of iron nails and clamps, and are sometimes whitewashed; the doors are fitted with a good lock and iron keys (Karlstein near Reichenhall, Upper Bavaria). The hearth is usually inside, in a small alcove. A similar lay-out is also found in a number of oppida. The houses and huts of the Aedui in Bibracte were erected on a dry-stone substructure, sometimes partly let into the ground, so that stone steps led down into the dwelling. There is evidence, too, however, of post-built houses and of a circular ground plan in farm buildings, where other building techniques are employed, including wattle and mud.

In some regions, rectangular structures, with stone foundation walls, are joined up by a wall to form a kind of courtyard, several such courtyards forming a village (Wasserwald near Zabern in the Vosges). The interiors have various lay-outs: most frequently they consist of a single room, but some have more, the maximum being four. The courtyard arrangement is also present in places inside the oppida, an example occurring in Hrazany, Bohemia.

In Scotland and Ireland, the Celts built dwellings with dry-stone double walls, the space in between being filled with rubble. In the boggy flat lands of Ireland, they built large round farm-houses on an artificial island, with tie-beams and stone facing (crannogs). In Ireland, we must add to the list of dwellings many thousands of raths, fortified Celtic farm-steadings, mostly on elevated ground (hilltops), protected by earthworks and a ditch; in districts with a sufficiency of stone, their counterparts are 'cashels'.

Farming and land ownership

The economic basis of Celtic society was cultivation of the soil and cattle-rearing, which, in the west, was carried on by the Celtic peoples themselves. In the east, especially in Central Europe, where the Celts formed only an upper stratum of population, they depended at least in part on the farming production of the indigenous population.

Farming was profitable in Gaul and the country was accounted rich in the last century B. C. Caesar was able in the course of an almost eight-years' war to provision his numerous forces, mainly with grain, in the country itself. All kinds of grain were cultivated there: wheat, barley, rye and oats. Among the Irish Celts the principal grain for long was barley, and it would seem that it had priority elsewhere, too, for barley porridge, bread and the brewing of beer. They also grew white and yellow turnips, flax, hemp, onions, garlic, several kinds of vegetables and plants to provide vegetable dyes. The grain was stored in special pits or silos sunk deep into the ground, within the house or farmstead enclosure; we come across large numbers of such storage pits in the later oppida (see below), for instance, in Manching, Bavaria. In the south of France (oppida in Ensérune; Coyla de Mailhac), the silos were sunk into the limestone, in Languedoc these went later out of use when large earthenware jars, *dolia*, took their place. In the La Tène period grain was ground into flour in a rotary quern of the type still in use in some parts of Europe up to modern times.

An important aspect of farming was the rearing of cattle, which in some parts, where circumstances favoured it, as, for instance, in the uplands of the Rhine Basin or in Ireland, took first place. The herds were pastured for the most part of the year in meadows and grasslands, in summer also at higher altitudes. Pigs, cattle, sheep and horses were the principal animals reared. Herds of swine fed mainly on acorns in the oak woods. But also the hunting of boar, as well as of deer and other game, was a favourite sport and source of food; boar's fangs, mounted and made into pendants were the pride and adornment of men of rank, being placed in the grave with them among their other treasured possessions. From the Hallstatt period we find the remains of parts of a pig, in the case of the graves of leading personages, sometimes of a whole pig: in the woman's grave in Horní Jatov-Trnovec nad Váhem in Slovakia, bounded by a square ditch, were the remains of the greater part of a year-old porker, as also in the grave of the warrior (No 362), to both of which reference was made above. A pig (*Sus scrofa dom. L*) was a common funerary gift in La Tène graves, or at least a leg of pork, but the head is never found. Less frequently cattle bones are present (*Bos taurus L.*) and still more rarely a goat or a goose (in four graves in Hurbanovo, Slovakia).

Sheep-rearing in Gaul was on a relatively large scale. The wool from Celtic lands was well-known in Rome. Horses, too, were widely reared and, according to Tacitus, the skill and effectiveness of Celtic horsemen was still greatly admired even in Roman times. Gaul supplied the Roman armies on the Rhine both with draught horses and cavalry mounts. Epona, the Gaulish goddess-protectress of horses, was worshipped in the west and also in the eastern territories, as, for instance, in Pannonia.

There are still traces, in certain areas, of the old prehistoric division of the land into fields and strips. Often these field systems are held to be Celtic, but it is possible that they are of even older date, for they appear in those regions where Celts were not actually settled: not only in South Britain, but also in North-west Germany and in Denmark. In the Celtic environment, the field system was connected with the concept of land ownership. Some fields had well-defined boundaries, others were open, and all varied in size. Especially in Great Britain and in Ireland, it was quite common for fields to be bounded by ditches or fences of different kinds.

The Celtic concept of land ownership in the period of expansion came to be identified with the common occupation of newly taken land. Such land, acquired by conquest, was divided among the tribes and further subdivided within the tribe. The frontiers between tribes (especially in Gaul) were belts of uncultivated land, the idea of frontier merging with that of waste land or forest. Such border lands came to serve as tribal assembly places or as meeting-places for trading transactions.

For the west, H. Hubert, the notable French specialist in Celtic antiquities, presumes two types of ownership: arable land in the ownership of the family and arable land owned by the community as a whole. In Ireland, land for long belonged to the tribe, which allotted plots to the families. In Gaul, shortly before the Roman occupation, the greater part of the land belonged to noblemen-landowners; private property existed and was a fully developed concept. During the period of expansion the right to land derived from the right of conquest acceeding to individual warrior groups or parts of tribes, which then gave their name to the territory. However, an older population survived, and the thin stratum of Celtic overlords, as their cemeteries clearly testify, had to keep a considerable part of their male population under arms, even though they were not regular military units in the form of garrisons. The real content of the relation between the holding of land by the Celts, on the one hand, and the subjugated people on the other, is not known. One thing is certain, however, namely, that to judge from the archaeological evidence, the native people as a whole continued to farm their land as before, but they had to share to some extent the product of their labour with their conquerors. There are grounds to suppose that the Celts cultivated a part of the land themselves, one of the indices being the traces of shifting of settlements within the new areas of settlement.

Crafts and trades and the high level of Celtic technology
Iron bloomeries and forges

Already in the Late Bronze period the Celtic environment had overstepped the limits of simple domestic production. Increased washings of gold from the Rhine were the basis for the flourishing development of goldsmiths' workshops, which produced articles of fine metal-work, such as diadems, circlets, bracelets and other ornaments, most of them with chased designs. The complicated making of waggons and chariots, with well-wrought hubs and fellies, presumed the existence of a body of skilled artisan-craftsmen. And this is true in still greater measure of the metal-work on these vehicles, in which wrought iron-work, partly combined with bronze, provided the often elaborate *décor*. Fine metal-work also reached a high level in Central European territories at the turn of the 7th and 6th centuries, whether it was in the making of daggers and swords, or in the artistically wrought linch-pins of the Hallstatt chariots, or the complicated metal fittings. Of all these we have innumerable examples in archaeological finds. As they represent the output of local workshops, it is clear that there must already have been, in the 6th century at the latest, in the whole Celtic world, fully developed metal-founding, on a scale much greater than the finds of smelting furnaces and traces of iron-working would hitherto indicate.

The later La Tène metal-founding techniques became the basis of Central European civilization as such. During the Celtic expansion it was necessary to equip the warrior bands with first-class weapons. In the course of time the production of iron and iron-working techniques had no secrets for the specialists in these branches in the Celtic-dominated lands. Among the large inventory of tools made by them, many of which were of quite special-purpose character, were iron files, rasps, drills with spiral spindle, a variety of axes, hammers and tongs, hand-punches, pokers, riveting tools, special cooper's tools (adzes, rivers, draw-knives etc.), knives, hand-saws, scythes, harrows, plough-shares, and so on. Certainly these cannot all count as Celtic inventions. On their raiding and land-taking expeditions, the Celts became acquainted with methods of production in other more technically advanced lands, but it is to their credit that, in the endeavour to increase production, they not only introduced various working procedures, but also adapted them to their tools, all of which technical progress was to become part of the Central and North European pool of skills and knowledge on which later developments were founded. The Celts, too, systematically sought new lodes, especially where they occurred near the surface. Thus, large iron-working centres arose in Bohemia, in the district of Nové Strašecí and in the foothills of the Ore Mountains, and, later, in the southern half of the country and in the Prostějov —Brno region of Moravia.

A hutment in Mšecké Žehrovice (Nové Strašecí district), from where comes, too, the well-known softstone head of a Celt, had an iron-smelting hearth in front of the roofed-over part; the iron founder here also engaged in the making of sapropelite ring-ornaments. Indications of parallel production are to be found in many places in the Nové Strašecí locality. But from the end of the 3rd and, especially, throughout the 2nd century, production obviously assumed a large-scale character. The Kladno district has also a tradition for the working of iron ore and sapropelite which goes back to the last century B. C. Originally, it was a purely domestic production, but the quantity of sapropelite raw material, semi-products and almost finished products found in the course of excavations of sites in the neighbourhood of Slané (Královice, Mšecké Žehrovice, Honice and elsewhere) far exceeds the probable local consumption. Sapropelite (incorrectly called lignite) in the Kladno—Rakovník region, occurs in the upper deposits of coal seams often reaching to the surface; it is a sedimentary dark-brown carbon substance, similar to slate and easily workable into the black armlets frequently found in Celtic graves and smaller rings. The Celts systematically quarried it and worked it for the requirements of distant regions. The second smaller region of outcrop sapropelite, in North-east Bohemia, between Semily and Jičín, was only partially exploited. The most recent investigations carried out by M. Claus have discovered sapropelite products as far afield as Pipinsburg near Osterode (in the German Harz Mountains), and laboratory analysis of the finds there and those in Královice near Slaný have shown that the material is identical. This would presume the existence of organized long-distance trade in this raw material and in products from Bohemia of as early as the 2nd century B. C.

The Celts soon went over, too, to the mass production of iron and iron products. In Tuchlovice, west of Kladno, a whole foundry, with a battery of iron-smelting hearths and a large quantity of slag, was excavated; in Chýně, another foundry with hearths; in Podbořany, two hearths, and, in Vyklice near Ústí nad Labem, others of the same kind. In Kostomlaty near Nymburk, a hearth for the smelting of iron was found half let into the ground. In addition, there was the well developed production of iron in the Celtic oppida, in Bibracte in France, as well as in the oppida in Bohemia and in Moravia (Hradiště near Stradonice, Třísov near Český Krumlov, Staré Hradisko). Thanks to the Celts' well-organized production, iron became a metal for everyday use, within the means also of country settlements. The ore was refined in hearths with flues, by means of charcoal, the end-product sometimes being hammered into ingots with pinched-up ends, weighing 6—7 kg. We find them from the Late Hallstatt period onwards, in Switzerland, in South Germany, in France and in Britain, reference to them also being made by Caesar, who praises the skill of Aquitanian and Biturigesian miners. Bar iron was exported to non-Celtic, especially Germanic, regions and was sometimes used as a currency equivalent.

Equally well-developed was the mining of silver ore and washings for gold. Gaul was looked upon as an auriferous region. In the 3rd and 2nd centuries, however, the Celts gained alluvial gold in different parts of Europe, not only on the banks of the Rhine and the Danube, but also in South Bohemia, on the Otava where, in Modlešovice, B. Dubský found the hut of a Celtic goldwasher. F. Pošepný attributed to the Celtic about 75 km^2 (?) of heaps of alluvial washings in the Otava Basin, and it seems that washing for gold was carried on as far south as Sušice. A large quantity of the gold thus won was used for the minting of Celtic coins.

Domestic production and later mass production
Different branches of manufacture

It would be possible to list numerous other branches of production, ranging from skilled domestic to organized large-scale workshop production, which, as early as the 2nd century B. C., reckoned not only with local consumption, but with export of a surplus to more distant regions, or which Celtic producers also placed in non-Celtic lands, as, for instance, parts of

Poland and South Germany, from about the end of the 2nd and the beginning of the 1st century B. C. Nevertheless, production was, of course, very much dispersed, as in the Celtic world every tribe and locality aimed to have its own mines, foundries and workshops.

We have ample evidence of the high level of metal-casting and metal-working among the Celts already in the Hallstatt period. Mention was made above of the large numbers of harness fittings found in graves, many of which contained some hundreds of items, as well as horse-brooches, rosettes, harness mounts and plaques, terrets, bronze bosses, domed studs, bronze plates with shaped openings, bridle-bits, and other types of metal ornament for harness and chariot. Founding technique presumed a good knowledge of the different kinds of alloys and their properties and used more and more moulds of the *cire perdu* type, especially when the workshops went over, in the 5th century, to the making of mask-motif brooches and other objects designed in relief. The complicated model for serial production was carried out with masterly skill in wax and was then enclosed in an earthern form; after the drying and baking of the earthen form the wax was removed and the form filled with molten bronze. On completing the process, the earthern form had to be broken off, so that each casting was really a valuable individual piece. In the La Tène period these Celtic techniques were constantly being improved and culminated in the 2nd century B. C. in the greatest flowering of the style of metal relief ornament. At the same time, however, fine smith's work was important for its production of complicated personal ornaments, brooches, pins and various tendril- and- leaf design bracelets (*fig. 20*), which can bear comparison with the best of their kind (Ponětovice in Moravia). The literary sources show that Celtic artist-craftsmen were also sought after in the mature cultures of the south; as we learn, a Celtic smith, Helicon, lived and worked in Rome, where he was known by the name of Brennus.

In the younger phase of La Tène the art of enamelling became widespread. It took the place of the Hallstatt-La Tène *décor* with coral, supplies of which did not suffice for the growing demand, and enamel inlays decorated a wide variety of objects of daily use, as well as warrior's shields, wrought jewel caskets and horse trappings. The enamellers' workshops were scattered throughout the whole Celtic world and there is evidence for them also in Bohemia, for instance, in Hradiště near Stradonice. From the middle of the 2nd century glass arm-rings became increasingly popular, often decorated with knobby excrescences and tubular sections, with coloured glass-thread surface decoration (*Pl. XXIX*). Their production was widespread in the more westerly part of the Celtic world; in the Rhinelands, and in parts of France and Switzerland, where there is an exceptional concentration of finds. A glass-making tradition became established there which was to play an outstanding role in Roman times and in the period of the migration of peoples. The most easterly siting of this branch of production for which we have reliable evidence is in Bavaria, at the Manching oppidum, where unworked lumps of glass material were found, but it is not impossible that the technique also reached Bohemia, though so far we have no certain evidence for it; but in Bohemia, too, we find an unusually large quantity of glass bangles and variously coloured beads.

A technically fully developed tanning industry supplied saddlers and shoemakers with a sufficiency of raw material, and a great deal of leather was required for daily needs and for warriors' equipment. Leather jackets, too, were a prized possession; they appear as trophies on the altar in Pergamum, in Asia Minor, and the torso of the hero in Entremont is similarly garbed. A long iron sword, which was laid in the Gaulish manner in the grave on the warrior's right-hand side, usually hung from a leather belt, and his helmet or cap was, as a rule, also of leather. Certain regions of Gaul were famed, too, in Celtic times, for the making of fine materials (Franche-Comté, Artois, the region of the Lingones). The Allobroges supplied Hannibal's troops with warm materials when he crossed the Alps into Italy. Classical writers also wrote of the excellence of carpentry and cooperage among the Celts; this is fully borne out by the results of archaeological excavations, in the course of which have been found, in addition to remains of buildings and fortifications, special-purpose iron tools for the making of barrels and pitchers, with shrunk-on hoops, and of a variety of vats. On the Atlantic coast, the building of sea-going vessels grew to be an important industry.

A special place among the crafts was, of course, occupied by the pottery workshops, which turned out wares on the potters' wheel. This greatly improved technique had already made its appearance in certain localities in the 5th-4th centuries, but the greater part of pottery continued to be hand-made. In the 2nd century and at the beginning of the last century B. C. there is evidence of a very dense network of potter's workshops throughout Central Europe, where the new technique is applied with masterly skill, and this is true of Bohemia, Moravia and Slovakia inclusively. Sometimes there seem to have been whole colonies of potters, as, for instance, in Bratislava, below the Castle, or in Šárovce. There a series of pottery kilns have been excavated, complete with hearth, flues and

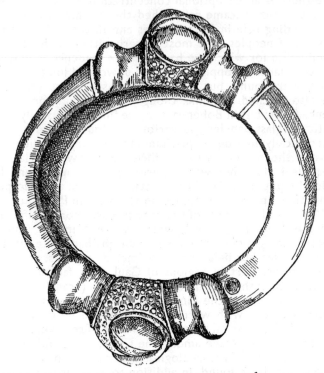

Fig. 26. Bronze bracelet with high-reliefwork, from a Celtic grave. Nový Bydžov, Bohemia. Diameter: 56 mm. Museum in Vienna.

earthenware grating, and with circular openings into the oven itself. Such centres, the number of which constantly kept growing, supplied the surrounding countryside with first-class ware and, in addition to purely Celtic types of pottery, sometimes met the demand for other types of ware traditional among the older indigenous population. The merging of the two groups of population now proceeded apace and the mature La Tène Culture powerfully influenced that of the older inhabitants, who till then had maintained to a considerable extent their characteristic way of life and material culture.

Graphite pottery, for which there was a good market, was also exported to distant regions. For the period of flourishing Celtic oppida painted pottery is particularly characteristic; in the Carpathians its production was centred, in the last century, on a number of non-Celtic or only partly Celticized centres.

The output of rotary querns for the grinding of grain was highly specialized, being based on selected kinds of stone, as, for instance, in the foothills of the Kunětická Hora, near Pardubice, in Slovakia, in the Štiavnica region and elsewhere. These querns, made of two discs of coarse-grained stone (sometimes weighing over 40 kg) came into general use in Central Europe in the La Tène period (*fig. 48)* and remained a permanent part of the domestic inventory till mediaeval and even well into modern times.

At the height of the La Tène period Celtic workshops had a mastery of almost all production skills and techniques, thus raising to a high-point the development of material civilization in Central and Northern Europe and creating the basic fund on which succeeding centuries were able to draw. We saw above that the increasing density of Celtic settlement in Central Europe called for this far-reaching economico-social revolution, making it necessary for the Celtic peoples to substitute their own economic activity for the former influx of wealth in the form of plunder, to seek new resources and new productive possibilities based directly on the Central European environment. Thus it was that this culminating period exercised a strong influence on the neighbouring regions, as far north as the Baltic and Southern Scandinavia, and reaching deep into Poland and far into the Ukraine. In place of the former military expansion, there was an equally many-sided economico-commercial expansion, and individual groups of Celtic craftsmen-producers apparently set up their workshops even outside the Celtic territories, as, for instance, in Poland, in the Cracow region. This merging of Celtic and non-Celtic in the middle of the last century B. C. had progressed so far that in some regions of Europe it is very difficult to distinguish what is purely Celtic from what is older native. Production techniques were taken over by the non-Celtic environment and developed in conformity with consumer requirements and all the other prevailing conditions.

This civilizing and economico-commercial campaign of the Celtic world towards the end of the pre-Christian era is best illustrated in two other specifically Celtic manifestations — the fortified Celtic oppida, power-centres with a high concentration of population, and Celtic coinage, the oldest in Central Europe.

Celtic oppida and their systems of fortification

Oppidum originally signified a fortified place defended by a rampart — a stockade (wall) and a ditch, usually on elevated ground or in less accessible situations. The word probably derives from the Latin *ob pedes*, it being necessary to walk round the site as an enclosed whole. In the special literature of different countries, this expression is used for fortified places of widely varying character, sometimes indicating a place of refuge for the whole population of a district in times of danger, sometimes a fortified place with a permanent population and a considerable amount of productive activity, identified not always quite accurately with the idea of the oldest towns. Nor are the Celtic oppida of unified character and it would be difficult, without systematic investigation of the different sites, to decide whether any given example was a place of refuge, or the stronghold of a chieftain or prince, or a centre similar in its basic features to later boroughs or towns.

In the earliest times the Celts had, in addition to their fortified strongholds, also fortified places of refuge, often in high and inaccessible positions (hill-forts), which come into special prominence during the great movements of population in the Late Hallstatt and Hallstatt-La Tène period, from the latter end of the 6th century to well into the 4th century B. C. Among them are many places in Central Europe, such as the South Bohemian barrow-grave region. The stronghold Věnec, on the Pržmo Height near Lčovice, in the basin of the Volyňka, is situated 763 m above sea level. The hill-top has still a wreath (whence Czech Věnec) of massive stone fortifications. The combination of steep slopes and rock wall with the stone rampart turned Věnec into a practically impregnable fortress, with an inner dominating bailey (90 × 70 m, rampart 1,529 m long), and with an outer bailey divided into two parts, of which the circumferences measure 668 m and 1,140 m respectively. The stronghold, as early as in the 5th century, had clearly the character of a temporary refuge, and retained this character throughout the La Tène period. It was thus not permanently inhabited, nor was the impressive stronghold of Sedlo, near Sušice (*Pl. XV*).

Sedlo is the highest situated stronghold in Bohemia, the altitude being about 900 m. There, too, advantage was taken of rocky slopes and sheer rock, which were topped by a stone-faced rampart. Thus arose a structure of elongated form, of which the axes are 403 × 114 × 32 m, which served as a place of refuge already in the 5th century when, in times of danger and uncertainty, the people retired to the forests and hills, taking their herds and flocks with them; here simple hutments were erected as temporary dwellings. The stronghold continued to serve as a refuge right through the La Tène period into Roman times. None of these, however, were oppida in the strict sense of the term. It must be remembered that in the Hallstatt-La Tène period a whole series of such refuges were erected, some larger, some smaller, in a belt extending from the present-day borders of Bohemia to Bayreuth in Bavaria and to the region north of the river Main, in Southern Thuringia.

From the middle of the 2nd century B. C. there arose Celtic oppida in the proper sense of the term, namely, fortified strategic and productive centres, many of which at the turn of the second and last centuries represented places with a considerable concentration of population. Besides urban influences from the Mediterranean world and the example of Southern France (see below), there was also outside pressure, mainly from German tribes, the incursions of the Cimbri being especially strong about 113 B. C. This pressure was felt in various parts of the Celtic world, in many places with catastrophic effect, so that in other regions, too, it was imperative to take safety measures. Considering the progressive changes which the economic structure was undergoing in Central Europe, it is understandable that population groups with movable property preferred, under such circumstances, to take refuge in fortified places.

A certain difference exists, however, between the Celtic oppida in present-day France and Switzerland, on the one hand, and in Central Europe, on the other. Small tribal strongholds and larger places of refuge had existed earlier in the west. Our best informant about the Gallic oppida of the last century B. C. is again Julius Caesar. Individual tribes had a number of such oppida, the Helvetii having, according to him, twelve such points, only a few of them being of large dimensions. In the whole of France there must have been at least 200 oppida. Central European oppida are larger, as a rule, and it would be incorrect to identify them all with urban-type settlements. Some of them were in fact important fortified centres, with workshops and their own mint, and were set up in the proximity of accessible mineral wealth — iron ore or graphite. Sometimes former settlements or strongholds were chosen as sites. Other oppida had strategic significance or, in the last century, when Germanic pressure became more intense, the hastily constructed and sometimes uncompleted

Fig. 27. Murus gallicus, a true Gaulish rampart from the end of the 2nd cent. and the first of the last century B. C. In the front of the wall are visible the ends of the horizontal timbers of the structure. Based on K. H. Wagner's excavation-work at the Manching oppidum, near Ingolstadt.

strongholds were intended to maintain at least a backguard action for the Celtic power now forced into the defensive by the intruders.

The surrounding walls of the Celtic oppida were of two kinds. The so-called "Gallic wall" (murus gallicus) described by Caesar is repeatedly documented today by the results of archaeological excavation. It became widespread above all in present-day France, where about 24 examples are known, and also in Switzerland, in Belgium and in parts of the British Isles, whereas in Central Europe it is relatively rare; the farthest east authenticated example is, so far, Manching near Ingolstadt in Bavaria. This Gallic wall was raised from ground level (figs. 27—28), the lengthwise and cross timbers being held together at their points of intersection by long iron nails (fortifications of the Avaricum type), forming a skeleton structure which was filled in with rubble and stones; the front was stone-faced, the technique employed being that of dry-walling (i. e. without mortar). Thus arose a wall about three metres wide, whose stability was ensured by its timber construction; it was not easy either to demolish it or set fire to it, for only the ends of the cross-timbers were visible in the stone face. On the inner side of the wall was a broad ramp designed to allow not only foot soldiers, but also mounted forces to reach the top of the wall, which rose to a height of several metres. This type of fortification did not first come into use in Caesar's time, as many investigators assume. It must have been employed already at the end of the 2nd century, as the *murus gallicus* at Manching is associated with older fortifications.

The other method of fortifying oppida is older and was in use in the Hallstatt period and more commonly still in the La Tène, sometimes being employed in the rebuilding of oppida or in the reconstruction of their fortifications, so that both types of fortification sometimes appear in a single oppidum (Manching). We come across it in the Heuneburg stronghold (*fig. 4*), and archaeological excavations have confirmed its use in Czech oppida as well. The rampart had also timber lacings and a facing of stone on the outer side, but here the timbers were vertical, let into the ground and projecting above the top level and thus visible from a distance; even today the empty space originally filled by these vertical posts is still distinguishable in the wall-face.

The entrances to the British and Germanic oppida are often in the form of a street; the rampart kinks inwards at an angle, forming a narrow entrance-way, sometimes 20—40 m long. This feature goes back to the Hallstatt period, an example being the stronghold, Plešivec, near Hořovice in Bohemia.

Many of these oppida represent a great investment of labour, it being necessary to accumulate for their construction huge quantities of stone and timber. Only the well-organized labour of a large collective could have constructed such ramparts, several metres high and broad, in a relatively short time.

Of the Gallic oppida, Caesar has left us a description of *Avaricum*, the centre of the Bituriges. It is the only Gallic oppidum the Roman general took by assault during the Gallic Rising of 52 B. C., led by Vercingetorix, and has not a few points of resemblance with Otzenhausen near Trier, presumed to be a stronghold of the Treveri. Many Gallic oppida arose in the course of the Roman advance and they bear in their semi-urban character the strong imprint of Roman influence.

Avaricum was reputed to be the best fortified and the best situated, being well protected by a river and by swamps.

Bibracte, the main centre of the Aedui on Mount Beuvray, about 27 km from the present-day town of Autun, is described by Caesar as the largest and wealthiest in the whole of Gaul, and he himself chose to set up his winter quarters there after his victory. It was situated on four heights, the highest of which was 822 m above sea level. The area of the fortified

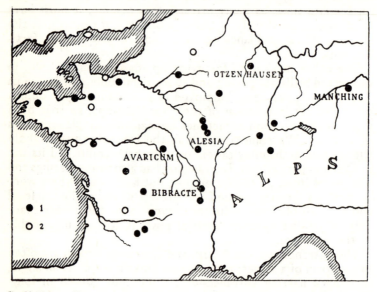

Fig. 28. Murus gallicus, main area of distribution (1. authenticated finds, 2. probable finds). M. A. Cotton's map, revised and extended.

enclosure is about 135 hectares, and on its slopes were numerous terraces with dwellings. It is the most thoroughly investigated of the oppida so far (excavations were carried out by Bulliot and Déchelette), and the finds from here have much in common with those from Hradiště near Stradonice in Bohemia. Excavations uncovered numerous house foundations, some still from Gallic and others from Roman times. Gallic houses, either built on stone foundations, with lower courses of masonry in dry-walling technique, or partially let into the ground, consisted mostly of a single room. Only after the country's subjection to Rome, in the second half of the last century B. C., were larger houses built containing a number of rooms (peristyle- or atrium-type houses). Under the Emperor Augustus, about the year 5 A. D., the population moved to the newly-founded town of Augustodunum (present-day Autun), and a temple was then the only reminder of the past in the once populous Bibracte.

Alesia, in the territory of the Mandubii (present-day Alise-Sainte-Reine) was situated on a steep- sided hill between two rivers, surrounded by ramparts and a ditch, and occupied an area of about 97 hectares. *Gergovia* (present-day Clermont) had a defended area of 75 hectares and *Noviodunum* covered about 45 hectares. The Belgic oppida (Fécamp type) were mostly of spur-formation, with a transverse rampart, the entrance forming a narrow street as described above. The Belgae, however, not seldom regarded forests and swamps as the best protection. The same is true of Britain. Some fortified places were erected in remarkably short time. The Nervii, in time of danger, are said to have raised a rampart round their winter camp of about 3,000 ft in circumference, with a ring-work 10 ft high and a ditch 15 ft wide, in something less than three hours. As they had not a sufficiency of iron implements, they cut out, so it is reported, turfs with their sword, scraped up the earth with their hands and carried it in their cloaks. It is possible that a large number of people were able to do this work very quickly, but it was not of course a proper defensive rampart such as enclosed the oppida, but a temporary earth-work to defend a camp.

The oppidum of the Vindelici, *Manching* near Ingolstadt, on the upper Danube, in Bavaria, at an important junction of trade routes, is situated 363 m above sea-level and is at present being systematically investigated. The fortifications, originally over 7 m long and about 12 m wide, enclosed an area of about 380 hectares, that is, an area about three times as large as that of Bibracte. Numerous finds of weapons, broken swords, spears, iron chain-belts and shield-bosses, as well as human skeletons in various chance attitudes, point to some catastrophe of war. This would also explain the two phases of fortification; the older, incorporating a true *murus gallicus*, and a later, reinforcing the former, with upright timber-lacings in the stone-faced wall, carried out in the old native technique. A broadish belt on the inner side of the fortifications contained no hutments, the space evidently being designed for the accommodation of the cattle also brought in for safety. In the inner ward of the oppidum, however, there were indications of very dense settlement, with local production of

weaponns, of glass bangles (the raw products for glassmaking
seem to have been imported), of pottery and metal-casting
workshops, on a technically high level, and a local mint.
Evidence of local minting are the finds of earthen forms for
the casting of disk-shaped semi-finished products — and of
finished gold coins. Not far from the oppidum (Steinbichl
site) is a Celtic cemetery;a second was situated within the defended area (Hundsrucken). In Irsching, a village about 6 km
north-east of the oppidum, a find was made in 1858 of over
a thousand Celtic gold coins ('*guttae iridis*'), and in the oppidum itself, in 1936, a coin-find was brought to light of Celtic
silver coins in a vessel. About 15 B. C. the oppidum was taken
by the Romans and its Celtic name was subsequently forgotten.

   The oppidum of *Kelheim* on the northern bank of the Danube,
only some 30 km north-east of Manching, (the oppidum Alki-
moennis of the geographer Ptolemy) was still larger, occupying
as it did an area of about 600 hectares, and was protected by
a transverse rampart between the two river arms of the
Altmühl and the Danube *(fig. 30)*. Here only brief mention
can be made of other Celtic oppida on German soil. *Heide-
graben*, beside Grabenstetten, north of Urach, in Württemberg, at an altitude of about 700 m, constitutes a whole system
of fortifications defending an area of about 1400 hectares and
having a circumference of about 30 km, with an inner ward
(1700 × 1800 m), well protected by a 'pincer' gateway. *Zarten*, near Freiburg in Baden, Ptolemy's Taradunon, once
a Helvetian centre, is surrounded by a rampart and a 12-metre
wide ditch, but has not so far been systematically excavated;
it occupies an area of about 200 hectares. *Donnersberg*, in the
Rhenish Pfalz, having more the character of a place of refuge,
is one of the largest strongholds in Germany. It is situated at
an altitude of about 800 m above sea-level, has a surrounding
wall about 7 $1/_2$ km long and is a site with a longer history,
finds there dating from the later phase of the Halistatt
period. The fortifications were later extended and, it would
seem, not completed; the gateway is of the 'pincer' type.
Altkönig, in the region of the Taurus Mountains, at an altitude
of 798 m, enclosed by a double rampart, also contains finds
from the Hallstatt and La Tène periods; with the outer ward,
it occupied a very large area. *Staffelberg*, on an elevation
dominating the surrounding countryside, is much smaller
(about 40 hectares, *Plate XXXIV*). *Steinsburg*, on the Klein-
Gleichberg, beside Römhild, in South-west Thuringia, at an
altitude of 600 m, encloses an area of about 65 hectares, ringed

in by a 10-kilometre-long stone-faced rampart; it played an important role in the Early La Tène period. Whether, however, Celts or Germans held it in the last century of the pre-Christian era is not possible, without systematic excavation, to decide.

A number of oppida exist, too, on Swiss soil, as at Bern (Enge-Halbinsel), in Altenburg near Schaffhausen on the Rhine, within the present-day boundaries of Lausanne, Geneva and elsewhere.

Oppida in the Czech Lands

Late Celtic oppida in the Czech Lands are mostly sited so as to be well protected from the north, either by a river or by some other topographical feature. The best known and, so far, the most notable, is *Hradiště near Stradonice*, not far from the small town of Beroun, on the right (southern) bank of the Berounka; it occupies an area of about 82 hectares and is situated at a height of about 380 m. The finds from here were exceptionally rich, but the site was not systematically excavated, digging having been carried on without plan in the second half of last century, when it was discovered. The find, in 1877, of a treasure of about 200 gold coins in the one-time stronghold, focussed attention on the place, and, within the short period of three years, self-styled archaeologists and collectors had riddled and destroyed the evidence of one of the most important and richest Celtic centres in Central Europe. Falsifications of Stradonice finds still encumber various European museums, most of them from private collections.

Hradiště near Stradonice is on a spur of land, where the Habrov Brook joins the Berounka. The system of fortifications has not been reconstructed, remains of a stone wall, in dry-walling technique and rising to a height of 2.5 m, have, however, been uncovered at certain places. The general situation indicates the ground-plan of an inner and an outer ward *(Pl. XXXV and XXXVII)*: finds point to it having been a permanently inhabited oppidum, where there was a considerable concentration of productive activity — metal casting, metalwork (including the mass production of iron brooches), enamelwork, pottery, and so on. Coins, too, were undoubtedly minted here, for, in addition to coins that had been in currency, similar evidence was found to that in Manching (earthen disc-forms,

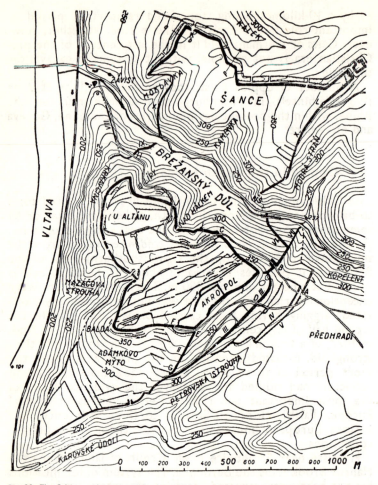

Fig. 29. The Celtic oppidum, Hradiště, above Závist, near Zbraslav. On the brows of the heights, Hradiště and Šance, are extensive fortifications. The stronghold proper, from the flat area 'U Altanu' up to the Acropolis, is laid out in a series of narrow terraces. The area, 'Adámkovo mýto' formed the outer ward or bailey. The area of the whole system of fortifications covered about 170 ha, the defended area proper about 27 ha. Only a surface investigation has been carried out so far; systematic excavation is planned for the next years. Detailed description: Prošek, Památky archeologické, Prague 1947/48.

with hollow centres, for the casting of gold standard coins). The finds from the second half of the last century B. C. clearly reflect the existence of lively trade connections with the Roman territories, from where a wide variety of goods reached the Czech Lands, including several varieties of brooches,

bronze vessels, gems and amphorae for wine; of special interest, too, are frames of wax tablets for writing and, for the
first time in the proto-history of these territories, riding spurs
and the keys of house locks. It would seem that this oppidum
lost its Celtic masters towards the end of the last century and
was, for a short time, at the beginning of the new era, under
German supremacy. Certain finds from the threshold of the
new era evidently led the archaeologist J. L. Píč, who published
a report on the Stradonice finds, to the conclusion that here
was the seat of the German leader, Marobud.

The extensive system of fortifications of *Hradiště nad Závistí* near Zbraslav occupies, along with the 'Šance' (Ger. Schan-
zen), about 170 hectares, of which the actual fort takes up
about 27 hectares. It consists of two parts, separated by the
120-metre-deep gully, Břežanský důl. The hill-fort itself de-
scends on the west to the elevation 'U altánu', about 150 m
above the water-level of the Vltava; about 50 m higher up
is the highest situated part, the 'Akropol' *(fig. 29* and *Pl. XXXVI
and XXXVII).* The whole defended area is ringed in by a rampart and ditch, in parts (beside the Akropol) still standing
6 m high and 25 m wide at the base. The space thus enclosed
contains a large number of terraces, evidently occupied by
dwellings. On the southern side, some 100 m lower, is the
outer ward (Adámkovo mýto). Of the original stone and timber
ramparts only the stone-facing remains, the timber having
rotted away, and these have not yet been thoroughly investigated. In the inner ward, evidence has been found of settlement as early as the Hallstatt period and then, mainly, in the
form of finds from the La Tène period, from the last pre-
Christian century and especially from its latter end, these
including painted ceramics. Systematic excavation of the site
is planned and will be a long-term project.

Connected with the hill-fort by means of earthworks thrown
across the Břežanský důl is the second area of the Šance,
which was also fortified, so that the whole comprises an extensive defended area. Linking up with the Šance, in the north-
east corner, is a small advanced fortlet. There are indications
that this second part of the defensive system was raised in
haste and not completed. The total defended area has a surrounding rampart about 9 km in length, with several gateways, of which some display the typical 'pincer' arrangement
of the entrance, and is one of the most imposing systems of
Celtic fortifications in Central Europe, whose future investigation will doubtless throw light on many important problems

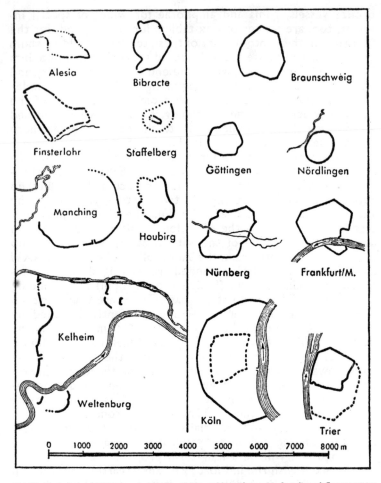

Fig. 30. The relation of the areas occupied by Celtic oppida to the areas of mediaeval German towns on the same sites and having encircling remparts (after W. Krämer).

of the period of transition on the threshold of the Christian era.

At the present time excavations are being carried out of the large oppidum in *Hrazany near Sedlčany*, on the right bank of the Vltava, about 40 km south of Prague. The oppidum is situated on a spit of land between the Vltava and the Mastník Brook, at an altitude of about 400 m above sea-level. The site is protected partly by a rocky slope rising from the river bank, but in the main by stone ramparts, the outside face of which shows gaps originally filled by upright timber-lacings, let into the ground. It is thus not a typical *murus gallicus*. The area of the hill-fort, including the southern and northern outer wards, is about 40 hectares. There seem to have been four entrances to the oppidum. The gateway on the northern side, already excavated, has in-turned ramparts, forming an entrance about 15 m long and 6 m broad *(Pl. XXXVIII)*. In the gateway and in the path leading to it there are still visible the deep ruts formed by the wheels of waggons pointing to a lively traffic. The width of the rampart varied from 5—10 m, the height from 4—5 m. Within the oppidum are traces of dwelling-place units, some in the form of individual farmsteads within a timber stockade. A whole system of sunk wells ensured an adequate supply of water for the inhabitants. It seems that the oppidum was among the last bastions of Celtic power in this region. Excavations, which have been conducted by L. Jansová for some years, are not yet completed. Another oppidum was located, as far as preliminary investigations would show, in Nevězice (Mírovice district), on a spur of land beside the Vltava; its surrounding wall was also reinforced on the outside by about 30 cm broad timber posts, inserted at about 90 cm intervals; on the inner side of the wall a ramp had been thrown up. Another stronghold in the time of Late La Tène was probably *Zvíkov*.

The most southernly situated oppidum in Bohemia, that of *Třísov* (Český Krumlov district), was founded in a countryside rich in graphite and iron ore, on a well-chosen site, at a bend of the Vltava, where it is joined by the Kremžský potok, at an altitude of about 549 m above sea-level. The inner fortified area, protected by a rampart and ditch, is reached by a gateway on the west, formed by in-turned ramparts; the stone-faced wall, has lacings of timbers about 30 cm thick, at intervals of about one metre. The total defended area covers about 21 hectares, and the finds made so far date it to the period of Early La Tène. *Lhotické hradiště* beside Nasavrky, in Eastern Bohemia, is amongst the smallest so far located, but has massive ramparts and ditches, still preserved in parts. Few finds have so far been made and these consist mainly of Late La Tène pottery sherds. Mass finds of gold coins and of iron goods in the Kolín district point to the existence there, too, of an important centre, so far not precisely ascertained.

The most important Moravian oppidum is *Staré Hradisko*, near Okluky in the Drahanská Vrchovina, with similar fortifications to those of the Czech oppida. The defended site covers an area of about 50 hectares. By the side of the main road dwellings had formerly stood, mostly wooden structures, without unified plan, some isolated, others in groups. No dwellings were erected below the ramparts, the space being probably left free for the herding of cattle. The inner fortification was also separated from the outer ward by a stone wall and ditch. The systematic excavation of the site, carried out by J. Böhm prior to the Second World War, has not been completed as yet, nor a report published. The finds, however, clearly date the oppidum to the period of Late La Tène, and it is possible that it may have survived the Stradonice oppidum for some time.

There are certain indications that *Bratislava*, in Slovakia, may also have been an important Celtic centre, possibly even an oppidum, in the Late La Tène period. From here stem treasures of Celtic coins and large pottery workshops, but more detailed investigation is not feasible, as the site is densely built-up. As regards the *Zemplín* centre, in Eastern Slovakia, it is not hitherto certain whether it still belongs to the age of Celtic supremacy or at least partly to the second half of the last century B. C., when the consequences of the Dacian incursion made themselves felt in Slovakia.

In Caesaris time, there still existed a broad belt of Celtic oppida (extending from the British Isles, across France to Southern Germany, and from as far north as the basin of the river Main to the Czech territories and to the Carpathians) with a high level of civilization. Lively trade relations were maintained among them and radiated into the neighbouring regions. The civilization of the oppida on the territories north of the Rhine continued for somewhat longer than in Gaul itself, where Romanizing influences already made themselves strongly felt towards the end of the last pre-Christian century. Gradually these percolated into the Central European oppida as well. Simultaneously, the last century saw the culmination of the influence of Celtic civilization on the native Central European environment, on which it impressed its character to a considerable extent, thus influencing the whole further course of its material and spiritual development. The growing intensity of German pressure, however, soon brought about a change in the political situation.

A peculiar feature observable in part of the Celtic world in the last century B. C. are the rectangular sites enclosed by ramparts *(Viereckschanzen)*. They occur principally in Southern

Germany, their distribution extending from the upper Neckar in the south to the foothills of the Alps, and as far east as the Inn (at Regensburg), that is, mainly in Baden, Württemberg and Bavaria. The majority are rectangular in shape (80 × 80 m and more), being enclosed by earthworks without any interior construction, with a ditch and elevated corners. Caesar makes no mention of them, although they existed in Gaul, too, in the region south of the Lower Seine to about as far as the middle reaches of the Loire. In the region at the foot of the Alps, over 250 have already been located; sometimes two such fortified places occur at no great distance one from the other (Holzhausen, Ldkr. Wolfratshausen, at a distance of 100 m, Niederleiendorf, Ldkr. Rottenburg, at a distance of 40 m). It would seem that in some cases, at least, they were the predecessors of the later rampart adaptation of a palisade structure (Holzhausen). The ground-plans of several objects are more complex than the rest and the excavated ditch-like entrance is orientated towards their centre. Most recently Kl. Schwarz, on the basis of new investigations, attributes cult character to these structures and, in his view, it was from these that the later Gallo-Roman temples developed. Formerly these buildings were held by some authorities to be farmsteads or even cattle shelters, while others suggested they might be military installations. Some are located within the oppidum (Donnersberg), others are in the vicinity of farmsteads or manors dating from Roman times.

Trade and transport

From early times the Celtic world was linked with distant regions, as important long-distance trade routes passed through France and Southern Germany. The situation as it existed in this respect in the Late Hallstatt and early La Tène periods has been described above.

The Alpine ranges ceased to be a barrier to trading relations and certain places on either side of the Alps became important reloading and transit stations for long-distance trade. The archaeological record points to this long-distance trade having been very well organized in the La Tène period, especially, in its later phase. Daily marches of about 30 km presumed regular halting-places and night shelters. Some places flourishing in the Late La Tène period are actually thought to have been toll-stations, such as La Tène itself, in Switzerland. The importance of permanent market-places increased as the result of economic and social changes and the construction of oppida. A number of them were sited at the junction of old trading routes and were famed for their trading activities. Especially favourably situated were places on the borders of tribal territories, such as Noviomagus (Nijon) near the Lingones, the border territories of certain centres of power, important later, in Roman times, arose on what had earlier been Celtic centres and markets; Forum Julii (Fréjus), Forum Neronis (Lodève), Forum Segusiavorum, Augustomagus, and others.

In Celtic markets, trade was conducted in a wide variety of commodities. In Bibracte there were large grain depots and in the market-place area large numbers of Celtic coins, issued by various tribes, have come to light. An extensive system of deep storage pits was discovered recently in the course of excavations at the Manching oppidum, and finds from Stradonice also witness to very lively trade activities. In the later phase of the La Tène period finds are increasingly frequent of parts of harness-gear, riding spurs and horse-shoes, the latter indicating that many roads already had a hard stone surface, dangerous for the horse's unprotected hoof. Trade relations were lively and communications, which employed various forms of transport, were quick. The private moveable property of individuals quickly accumulated and was protected in dwellings furnished with massive door-locks.

Celtic coinage — the oldest coinage in Central Europe

As early as the Late Hallstatt period the custom became established of regarding as standard units of value strips of unworked iron, of roughly about the same weight, broadest in the middle and with one end pinched up. These "currency bars" were exported from Celtic territories to all the neighbouring regions and, especially in Britain, long remained the unit of value. In Ireland, six heifers or three milch cows were traditionally regarded as the equivalent in value to a female slave (cumal); Celtic slaves were a welcome object of exchange in the Mediterranean regions, but Roman merchants were ready, especially in the later phase of La Tène, to accept Celtic grain, meat, bacon, pork and wool in exchange for various products of Roman or provincial Roman workshops and for southern wines, with which they supplied the oppida.

The exceptional expansion of Celtic power in the period of greatest economic and trading prosperity necessitated the minting of a coinage, the first "barbarian" coins, i uGaul and in Central Europe. Celtic warrior bands had realized the advantages of money as early as in the 4th century B. C., especially in their incursions into Greece and Italy, and Celtic mercenaries took their pay in money form. So long as the Celts were successful in their armed expeditions, they had no need for a coinage of their own. But from the 3rd century onwards, when they were increasingly dependent on their own productive activities for their economic stability and when they were already able to produce a certain surplus exceeding the local demand, a Celtic coinage became a necessary pre-condition for further development.

In the Celtic world gold and silver coins were regularly in use; much rarer were coins of other metals — copper or bronze. In the Czech Lands, the Celts minted mainly gold coins, those of silver being much less common. In the west, coins of both metals were in general circulation, the predominance of one or other being dependent on the local resources.

The earliest Celtic coins appear from about the middle of the 2nd century B. C., and in greater numbers from the second half of the century, being ultimately derived from Macedonian-Greek exemplars. Such was the stater of Alexander III. of Macedon, with the head of Pallas-Athena wearing a high Corinthian helmet on the Obverse and showing Niké, the winged goddess of Victory, holding a laurel wreath in her right hand, on the Reverse. These gold coins originally bore Greek inscriptions, weighed about 8.4 g and were about 18—20 mm in diameter. In addition to these whole staters, coins were struck having the value of a third, an eighth and a twenty-fourth of the whole. We are familiar with them from finds in Bohemia (hoards in Nechanice near Hradec Králové and in Starý Bydžov) and in many places in Moravia, especially in the neighbourhood of the oppidum of Staré Hradisko, but they turn up also as strays in Austria and in parts of Hungary. Later mints of this type, however, degenerate and depart more and more from the original exemplars.

In Central Europe, from Silesia and across the Czech Lands to Austria, gold coins appear with the head of Pallas-Athena on the Obverse, but showing the figure of a warrior with a shield, a belt round his hips and wielding a spear, that is, with motifs closely related to the native Celtic environment. They weigh about 8.16 g and vary in diameter from 15—17 mm.

Fig. 31. Celtic gold coins in Bohemia, the oldest coins struck in this country. 1. Nechanice near Hradec Králové. Derived from Macedonian staters. — 2. Hradiště near Stradonice, not far from Beroun. Coin with coiled dragon. — 3. Kopidlno near Jičín. Coin with boar symbol. — 4. Nižbor-Stradonice near Beroun. Coin with shell symbol. — 5.—6. Hradiště near Stradonice, not far from Beroun. Gold 'guttae iridis'.

These mints, too, gradually deteriorated into contoured protuberances and the figure of the warrior was represented by a purely schematic design. The purity of the gold, however, was often as much as 97 per cent. They would seem to have been in circulation at the time when the oppida were flourishing, for they have also been found at Stradonické Hradiště. Sometimes stamps of the Athena-Alcis series were used for the striking of silver coins.

In the territory of present-day France, the moneyers were strongly influenced by Massilia, which very soon made use of the coins issued by the Greek colonies of Asia Minor and then imitated them, finally (from the 4th century), issuing its own drachme, showing the head of a nymph, with a lion, later a bull, on the Reverse; bronze coins were also minted there. Subsequently Rhode, Emporion and other colonies in the northern part of the east coast of the Iberian peninsula had their own coinage. These coins percolated by way of trade into Gaul and even found their way as strays into Central Europe, for bronze imitations, with the symbol of a butting bull, have been found in Bibracte and also in Stradonice.

In Gaul itself, the main inspiration in the new art of coinage was the gold stater of Philip II. of Macedon, with the head of Apollo, and his famous four-horse chariot on the Reverse. The picture was simplified (later one horse replaced the original pair) as the typical feature of Gallic coinage. The horse on the Reverse then acquired a human head. The Greek names (that of Philip) on these coins soon became barbarized and gave way to Celtic names; later names appear only rarely on the coins, most frequently in the territory of the Treveri (Abucatos on the Biturigesian staters, Niros on the gold coins of the Nervii or Treveri, Pottina, Lucotios, Vocaran, and others — perhaps the names of tribal chieftains). Roughly cast globules, with almost unintelligible designs, appear alike in Gaul in the west, and in Bohemia, in Central Europe.

In Gaul, at a later period, silver coins were minted after the style of the Roman Republican denares of the 2nd century, with the motif of a mounted figure in the Franco-Swiss region, with a horse and the legend, Kal, Kaledu, sometimes ascribed to the Aedui (finds at the La Tène station, but also at Stradonické Hradiště), or with a human figure holding a torc.

At this time the art of coinage had also spread to the southeast, to Noricum, and to the Rumanian-Hungarian, Serbian and Bosnian territories. In these Carpathian regions, type coins for native moneyers were, among others, the tetradrachme of Philip II., of Macedon, which continued to be struck long after his death for soldiers' pay and trading relations with barbarians in the surrounding territories. Such issues, minted mainly in Amphipolis (on the Aegean seaboard, east of the peninsula of the Chalcidices) ceased soon after the collapse of Macedonian power (Battle of Pydna, 186 B. C.), and so neighbouring tribes began to mint their own imitations. Several variants of these coins were evidently minted in present-day Slovakia, probably from local raw silver; the Audoleon type (with equine Reverse and the indistinct legend "Audoleon") is found in greatest concentration round the Matra range, and a related Hont type is distributed from Burgenland as far as the Bratislava region. The silver issue of Noricum, with a horse or mounted horse on the Reverse, and the head of Apollo on the Obverse, occasionally have also a legend (Boio, Tinco, Nemet, Andamati etc.).

In Central Europe there came into circulation, at the turn of the second and last centuries B. C., a gold stater showing a boar on the Reverse, particularly common in Bohemia, quite in keeping with the cult significance of the boar in the Celtic environment. In Bohemia, too, gold staters have come to light with a barbarized representation of a head on the Obverse and with a man, running or kneeling and holding crossed sticks in his right hand, on the Reverse, as well as staters with "*Roll-tier*" motif (thought to have originated in the Scythian cultural area); they have been found in Osov and, in greater numbers, in Stradonice near Beroun and elsewhere.

Commonly current in the first half of the last pre-Christian century were two kinds of sunk-panel gold coins. The more westerly group, popularly called "*Regenbogenschüsselchen*" *(guttae iridis)* are distributed mainly throughout Bavaria, and so are usually attributed to the Vindelici; they are to be found, however, in an area stretching from Eastern France to Bohemia. On the Obverse is a Rolltier motif and, on the Reverse, a torc with six balls, later only a dragon- or bird-head, along with a wreath; in the Rhinelands, a triquental pattern is often an associated element of the design. The majority of these coins stem from hoards. At Irsching, near Manching in Bavaria, there were over a thousand, and in Gagers, south of Manching, about 1400, but others have been found in Switzerland and also in the Stradonice oppidum. The white gold from which they are minted is often less pure, sometimes falling below 70 per cent.

Heavy gold coins *(Goldknollen)*, with a high gold content (up to 90 per cent), and an average weight of 7.45 g, have not yet definitely sunk-panel form. The design is barbarized and not easily recognizable, often degenerating into indistinct protuberances. They were part of the celebrated find of coins made in 1771, not far from the village of Podmokly, near Zbiroh in the Rokycany district of South-west Bohemia. In a bronze cauldron, there were, besides a silver bracelet, close on 5,000 gold coins, comprising whole staters, thirds and eighths, that is, a treasure of several kilograms of gold. The find, however, was illegally seized and dispersed, only a part (about 1,260 coins) being recovered by the Fürstenberg Estate Office, and this part was smelted down for the minting of Fürstenberg ducats!

The other, more easterly, group of sunk-disc coins are known as "shell staters", or simply "shells"; in the literature, they are often not distinguished from *Regenbogenschüsselchen*. They, too, are of fine gold (as much as 97 %), weigh about 6.5 g and were also struck as thirds and eighths. Their execution is generally coarser. The Reverse shows a shell-like design *(figs. 31, 32)*, the Obverse, raised side, usually has a five-rayed sign, like a human hand, sometimes associated with balls or with two crescent signs. These coins are common in hoards of coins and in oppida (Podmokly near Zbiroh, the hoard of coins at the Stradonice oppidum, at Staré Hradisko in Moravia, and elsewhere). Occasionally shell coins were minted from silver.

Later on silver coins came increasingly into circulation, mainly it would seem for local transactions. A large number of types may be distinguished. The Aeduian coin, with a head looking to the left and, on the Reverse, a prancing horse also heading left, weighing about 0.45 g (the hoard of coins found at Ville-neuve-au-Roi contained 2,000 such coins out of a total of 15,000); a coin with a cruciform design, sometimes associated with ball-like excrescenses, known technically as "tectosages" (common in Württemberg, Baden and the Swiss-French region, usually weighing about 7 g); the Karlštejn sunk-panel type, with a horse symbol on the Reverse, weighing about 4 g, and many others. In the oppida these various types of coin are found in association, as, for instance, in the Stradonice coin hoard of over 500 coins. Some of them were evidently struck at Stradonice itself, especially those weighing 0.4 g, with a head on the Obverse and showing a prancing horse, with a pearly mane, on the Reverse. In Staré Hradisko, the finds so far made contain mainly gold coins, silver coins being relatively rare.

The latest Celtic coins. In the south-west tip of Slovakia finds are accumulating of large silver coins (tetradrachme) of the Biatec type, which are the latest Celtic coins in this region prior to the Dacian occupation of Pannonia and in the adjacent part of Slovakia. They were probably minted in the Bratislava region (where there is other evidence of late La Tène settlement) and may be dated to the second quarter of the last century (about 75—60 B. C.). These large silver coins, weighing on an average 16.5—17 g, are already strongly influenced by the Roman *denarii* of the last century. The front of the coin bears the simple design of a head or of two partly superimposed heads *(fig. 32);* on the Reverse is the motif of a mounted rider, a griffin, a lion, a centaur or other animal symbol, including the Rolltier motif. The lettering on these coins is in Roman capitals and is, in fact, the oldest occurrence of classical script in Czechoslovakia. The inscription on the Reverse is a patronymic, apparently that of a prince or chieftain, most commonly the name BIATEC, sometimes abbreviatted to BIAT, but many others as well, such as; NONNOS, DEVIL,

Fig. 32. Celtic Biatec silver coins from the first half of I. B. C.: 1. Gold coins, inscribed with the name Biatec. Jarovce-Jahrndorf. — 2. Reca, Slovakia. — 3. Bratislava, Slovakia (hoard of Biatec silver coins). — 4. Jarovce (Bratislava area).

BUSU, TITTO, CONVIOMARUS, FARIARIX, MACCIUS and others. Besides these large silver coins, smaller silver coins were minted of the "Simmering" type (named after the find-place of Simmering-Wien), sometimes with the legend NON-NOS.

Most of the hoards of silver coins of the BIATEC type were discovered in Slovakia, in the Bratislava region. Of those so far brought to light, 14 in all, 5 are directly from Bratislava (from the last find made in 1942, 270 coins have been preserved), and one each from Reca, Stupava, Trnava and Jarovce (formerly Deutsch Jahrndorf). In the last-named site, the hoard contained a gold shell stater, inscribed with the name BIATEC, of the same type as we find in Bohemia, only uninscribed; this would corroborate the hypothesis that part of the Celts (Boii) shifted their settlements, in the first half of the last pre-Christian century, from Bohemia to the Pannonian-Slovak region. Finds of coins of the BIATEC type extend into those parts of Austria which are topographically a continuation of the Bratislava area. The burying of these hoards of coins in the south-west tip of Slovakia is evidently a reflection of the uncertain and dangerous times of the hostilities between the Boii and the Dacians, about 60 B. C. The coin seems to have remained a short time in circulation after the defeat of the Boii, but it ends the issue of this tribe.

More complicated is the question of who had the right to mint money in the Celtic world. Many scholars hold the view that coins were issued mainly by rulers, princes and chieftains (the legends on a number of coins give credence to this view), issuing certain types of coin as tribal coinage, others incline to the opinion that the right of mintage belonged to the oppida, which are often held to be the rulers' residences. The whole development of Celtic coinage in Central Europe covers roughly a century. A reliable localization of the Celtic tribes in Central Europe is a matter of considerable difficulty, and it is an open question whether the structure of Central European Celtic tribes, at the height of Celtic power, in the period when the oppida flourished, was completely homogeneous. Celtic coinage clearly reflects the characteristic features of general Celtic development. Not even the minting shows any high degree of uniformity; we can identify a large number of mints and considerable variation in weight. And thus a fine balance (with central pivot, beam and two scales) was an essential part of trading equipment and are a common find at the excavated oppida (Bibracte, Hradiště near Stradonice, Třísov,

Staré Hradisko etc.). In certain cases, mainly in the west, it was necessary to sign or countermark the issued coin.

It would seem then that there were many minting-places and that they were not always identical with the capitals of the various tribes, for not even the centres of production at the height of Celtic development were always the same as the political tribal centre. Economic and trading interests had thus first priority and the old tribal confederacies gradually lost their original significance; the merging of parts of different tribes became quite a common occurrence. The existence of mints in certain oppida, as for instance, Manching or Hradiště near Stradonice, is reliably confirmed by finds, mainly of burnt clay disc-shaped moulds for the casting of the rough shape of the coins, which were then stamped in the mint and given their finished appearance; on some of these forms there are still traces of gold metal. We find, however, similar disc-forms in villages in the Nové Strašecí district (Tuchlovice). Evidently every larger production centre could proceed to mint its own coins and only observed the more general mintage usages. In exchange transaction, the coins were then weighed and the value determined according to weight and the purity of the metal.

In the second half of the last century B. C. Celtic coinage in Central Europe declined. Only the Celticized Eravisci in the neighbourhood of Budapest are credited with the issue of coins resembling the Roman denarii of the middle of the last pre-Christian century. They are also to be found in Slovakia and often bear the legend, IRAVISCI, RAVIS, RAVIT. Norican issues were also in circulation well into the time of Roman supremacy. In Gaul, after the Roman conquest of the country, several places retained for a short time the right to issue their own coinage, but it was all only the dying out and corruption of the once independent art of Celtic moneyers.

Celtic coins also appear in graves, as funerary gifts, sometimes placed in the mouth of the departed, and so are valuable in helping to give a more precise dating to the finds. The considerable artistic value of coin devices gives coinmaking its place within the wider framework of Celtic art, for they include many typical elements and symbols, such as the boar, the warrior, the motif of the decapitated head, torcs, triskelestriquetrum, wheel with spokes, and so on.

VIII

Celtic art and Celtic religion

The geometric style of the Early Iron Age gave place towards the end of the Hallstatt period to a more lively zoomorphic and vegetal ornament, supplemented by human head motifs, which were in favour especially in the aristocratic *milieu* of the leading circles. Rich imports from the south and south-east into the Celtic chieftains' residences introduced new patterns and new fashionable elements. Soon, however, at latest from the second half of the 5th century, native art and craft workshops arose in these centres. Native craftsmen were at work in them who combined a knowledge of foreign exemplars and motifs with independent creative talent and skill and adapted foreign impulses in a characteristically Celtic manner in the making of these original personal ornaments in which were increasingly apparent the germinal elements of the new La Tène style. The Early La Tène style penetrated to the aristocratic *milieu* of the rich chieftains' compounds mainly in the area between the Moselle, the Saar and the Rhine. This earliest purely Celtic art had several roots of origin and basic stylistic elements. Southern and south-eastern elements came from Italy and Greece, and were, perhaps, also brought later by artist-craftsmen, who entered the service of the ruling families. Early Celtic goldsmiths' workshops used almost pure gold (99 per cent). Evidence of the existence of such workshops has been provided by archaeological excavation. In Langenheim (Raunus) and Sefferweich (Eifel), we find raw materials and semi-finished goods; in the Neuwied basin near Coblenz, finds have been made in different places of what are apparently serial runs from the same workshop, and not only personal ornaments, but also fine metal-work for chariots (Waldgall-scheid, Besseringen and Kaerlich). Not monumental architecture and sculpture then, but fine handicrafts became the chief domain of Celtic manual skill and artistic perception and one which made the greatest contribution to the development of Central and Northern Europe. From the first, technical virtuosity joined to a special delight in ornament, created works of permanent artistic value. The Early La Tène style, which developed over almost a whole century, from the middle of the 5th century, has many of the traits of a native art first becoming established through the creative adaptation and modification of foreign patterns, and thus only gradually acquiring its characteristic inventory of elements and motifs.

Early La Tène style in Celtic handicrafts and Celtic ornament

Handicraft work in the Early La Tène style is still closely related to imports of the second half of the 5th century. In some features it is based on Italico-Etruscan patterns, in others on more remote elements, of Greek, and even Iranian-Persian and Central Asian origin. Already prior to the end of the 5th century the motif made its appearance in the Celtic environment of the human mask, sometimes wreathed with a kind of "leaf-crown", derived from the *Fischblasenmuster*. Such masks occur on fine relief-work of gold, and also of bronze, the core of which was often of iron. Examples are the gold plates thus decorated from Schwarzenbach (*fig. 22*), but also phalerae (horse frontlets) from Hořovičky near Podbořany, in Bohemia, on whose bronze plate with iron core are chiselled human masks, wreathed with the *Fischblasenmuster* or with other decorative elements still in a purely circular arrangement (*Pl. VIII*). The motif of masks was undoubtedly taken over from the Mediterranean art zone and passed through various phases of development in the Celtic environment, from forms with exaggerated facial grimace to those with greater equanimity of expression. In addition, the *Fischblasenmuster* had its place as a very chracteristic Celtic feature, which long remained popular and was also taken over by Celtic sculpture.

Celtic workers in gold and other metals and in metal casting soon developed other motifs. From the south they took over certain vegetal elements, especially leafy palmette forms, tendrils and lotus blooms, combining them with the S-scroll motifs, sometimes side by side, sometimes intertwined, occasionally forming a connected row of decoration; or again, two S-scroll elements form the basic lyre-scroll motif, lyres and palmettes, often in association, providing persistently recurrent and typical motifs of Early Celtic art.

Lyre-scrolls already decorate the gold ring from Rodenbach executed in early style. As a motif they had a long life, recurring in later centuries in metal-work, for example, in bronze scabbards for swords (Jenišův Újezd near Bílina, in Bohemia, *fig. 18*), or in pottery designs, either incised or stamped. Palmettes, too, however, show a certain evolution and are employed in widely varying ways; they are combined with lyres to form a single unit, or half palmettes or smaller sections are used as variants (half-palmettes etc.).

Spirals, too, increasingly dominate Celtic pattern-making. They are combined in different ways and are in a constant state of evolution, swelling and assuming trumpet, rosette and bat-winged forms with varied enrichment. Right-turned and left-turned forms evolve to make, in the culminating period of Celtic art, very complicated patterns, sometimes of flatly arabesque character, sometimes with the stress on plasticity of presentation, segmented forms and whirl designs, as well as three-way figures in what are known as triquetra and triskele. Then another feature of Celtic art makes its appearance; the turning away from strict symmetry, which was the legacy of the Hallstatt period, to a freer balance of pattern and, occasionally, to complete asymmetry. Endless variations based on a limited number of primary curvilinear forms are executed with admirable sensitiveness and inventive fertility and build up to richly elaborate compositions, concealing a symbolism which will never be fully intelligible to us.

This Early La Tène style in Celtic art makes its entry soon after the middle of the 5th century, as is apparent from the contents of the princely grave in Klein Aspergle, Württemberg. Here a Celtic artist has provided imported Attic dishes with a gold openwork mantle, combining a beaded pattern with simple leaf-like forms. The gold metal-work on a pair of drinking horns, terminating in a sheep's head, has also bead decoration and one of them has the motif of S-curved horns forming two intersecting sinuous lines. On gold plaques from the princely grave in Ferschweiler near Bollendorf (Eifel district), which are thought originally to have decorated a jewel casket, incised lotus blooms appear, still grouped stereotype fashion in a circle, as in the earlier Hallstatt period, and masks of Silenus (?), with three small horns. On a gold disc, with coral inlays, from Auvers-sur-Oise (Seine et Oise), which was originally a horse frontlet, mask motifs and S-scroll lyres, along with lobe-and-droplet forms, interwoven with beaded lines, as a supplementary decoration, already merge in a unified composition, rhythmically balanced and of considerable vitality. A small gold plaque from Weisskirchen shows a combination of four human masks grouped round a central circular motif and inset in lobe forms with beaded edging: thus arose an artistic whole which still bears traces of the old geometrical concept of ornament, but already has quite a new look. The decoration of the gold openwork mantle from the barrow-grave in Schwarzenbach (Birkenfeld) shows complete compositional mastery, in which leaf-shaped and droplet motifs are developed in innumerable variations, again with supplementary beaded *décor*, and S-scroll motifs form three-way designs, in the manner of triquetras, opposed scrolls acquiring, at the same time, the character of lyres.

The personal ornaments from the princess's grave at Reinheim in the Saar reveals Oriental taste in many of its stylistic motifs. A gold torc has plastically wrought terminal ornaments in the form of human heads and lion masks; a richly wrought penannular bracelet has a winged figure motif; a brooch terminates in a mask, and a bronze spouted flagon, with elaborate incised ornament, has an attache decorated with a plastically rendered bearded head. The grave also contained a bronze mirror, with an anthropomorphic handle.

The above-mentioned flagon is an example of independent Celtic manufacture. Celtic ornament achieved in the course of its development a remarkable degree of virtuosity, in which masks of various character, comma and lobe forms, spirals, lyres and snail-coil motifs, are combined in a carefully worked-out and unified design. At the same time other art and craft techniques show the same growing mastery, such as openwork patterns and coral inlay or enamel work. Nor is the spouted flagon of the 4th century from Basse-Yutz (Moselle), formerly often alluded to as the flagon from Bouzonville, an import, but a very perfect Celtic work, one of the finest examples of Celtic metal-work. Relief and incised ornament are here combined with coral and enamel inlay. The bottom part of the handle is of mask formation, the upper part consists of an animal, perhaps a wolf's, head. The finely curved shape is somewhat reminiscent of the beaked flagon from Hallein-Dürrnberg (Salzburg), also dating from the 4th century, richly decorated with lobe and palmette motifs, as well as with human heads and animal figures.

Works in the early style still employ archaic and sub-archaic classical forms taken over from the Greek world, which had a long life in the remote regions of civilization. They copy

Etruscan motifs (the gold finger-ring from Rodenbach), take over animal motifs from the Italian-Etruscan region (flask from Matzhausen) and Oriental impulses especially of zoomorphic character. Finds occur in greatest concentration in Southern Germany, in parts of France and Belgium, but are distributed also in Bohemia and Austria. Among them, too, are the above-mentioned mask brooches, deriving as regards construction from the Certosan-type brooches of Northern Italy. We find them in a zone extending from the middle Rhinelands east-wards as far as Central Bohemia. Their chief distinguishing feature are human and animal masks variously conceived; some faithful likenesses, others of such fantastic appearance that it is difficult to distinguish between human and animal mask motifs.

A number of Czech finds of mask brooches are particularly remarkable and artistically valuable (Panenský Týnec, Chýnov near Prague, *Plates VII, VIII*). Thus it is difficult to agree with those scholars who would presume that North-east Bavaria and the Czech Lands belonged in the Early La Tène period, to a different, eastern — Illyrian — cultural region. Mask-motif brooches occur also in Württemberg, Baden and the Rhinelands, and in association with finds of clearly Celtic character.

In the above connection it is necessary to take into account other finds in trans-Alpine territories. Besides the most recent finds in Hallein-Dürrnberg, a report on which has not yet been published, there is the sword from Hallstatt in a scabbard with figural *décor* (*fig. 18*). The figural motifs are not Celtic, but point rather to Italy (Este, Etruscan *milieu*), whereas details of dress and equipment are of native character. It is evidently the product of an armourers' workshop north of the Alps, strongly influenced by the Atestine craft-centre (Este) in North-ern Italy. From the same time, probably the 4th century, stems a sword from a barrow-grave near Dražičky, in the Tábor district of South Bohemia, the scabbard of which has leaf-form incised ornament and a medallion-decorated chape, with coral inlay (*Pl. XXVII*).

Mature La Tène style

The mature La Tène style, known also as the Waldalgesheim style, designates the second phase of Celtic art from the second half of the 4th century, and represents the mature perfection of Celtic art. Judging from the distribution of the finds, we consider the centre of this mature style to be the Rhinelands, part of Switzerland and France, but individual products are scattered all over the European continent, wherever Celtic warrior bands made their incursions. It is at the same time the style of the period of greatest Celtic expansion. The grave at Waldalgesheim, whose bronze and gold ornaments *(Pl. XIV)* gave this style its alternative name, and the graves in Filottrano, Italy, can be dated roughly to the same time, namely, the latter part of the 4th century. In both cases the ornaments represent the fully developed style. The majority of objects from the graves in Montefortino near Bologna, in Marzabotto and in other places in Northern Italy are also not earlier than from the end of the 4th and from the 3rd century B. C.; examples of the Early La Tène style of Celtic art are relatively rare in Italy. Artistically executed gold torcs in Celtic style are dispersed, however, throughout the whole Celtic world. Sometimes they are cast in precious metal, or they may have a core of another metal or be made from hollow metal plate. Some of the ornaments show considerable wear, others had evidently been placed in the burial very soon after manufacture.

In the course of the 3rd century, art and craft production entered a clearly-marked crisis. As a result of changing economic and political circumstances, the art of the princely and chieftains' halls receded somewhat into the background and its place was taken by an art and craft "industry" producing for a much wider range of consumers. There was, indeed, a certain democratization of the environment, in which, however, the warrior aristocracy still preserved its leading role. Constantly intensified production supplied the Celtic population group with a mass output of brooches and pins (articles always subject to changes of construction and fashion) from shapes with detached foot (Duchcov type) to types with foot attached to bow, a large quantity of bracelets and ankle-rings, belt chains and various articles of everyday use. Well-made bronze ornaments reached a wider range of consumers and there was a tendency to seek a market for them among non-Celtic population. Finer quality ornaments and well-executed fighting equipment still, however, continued to be made for the leading class, but the differences between the two types of goods were no longer so great.

Plastic style and Sword style

Stylistically this larger-scale production favoured relief forms, and the plastic style became widespread in the 2nd century B. C. Instead of two-dimensional ornament, there was three-dimensional relief, often supplemented by fine surface engraving. Its origins are older, but from the end of the 3rd century it flourished in richly articulated bracelets and ankle-rings, with S-scroll and "snaily coil" ornament of the individual semi-spheres *(Pl. XXIX—XXX)*, sometimes almost baroque in character, bracelets with leaf-and-tendril and rosette *décor*, rings with imitation filigree ornament, plastically articulated torcs and brooches. In Bohemia and Moravia, several workshops turned out masterpieces of the metal-casting art; in the Carpathians this type of ornament is more rare. The raw metal was mainly bronze, later also iron, the working of which into brooches or bracelets first attained a high artistic level at this time. In the west, the plastic style finds expression not only in bronze jewellery, but also in splendid gold ornaments adorned with a wealth of snaily coil and other plastic forms [cf. the rings from Aurillac (Cantal)]. Such finds, however, are less and less common. About the same time the sword style makes its *début*, named after the beautifully designed and perfectly executed scabbards, decorated on the front with incised or relief patterns incorporating vegetal and animal motifs, sometimes with diagonally aligned ornament. They occur in a zone extending from the Carpathians in the east to Switzerland in the west, where we meet with them at the name-site of La Tène itself at the turn of the second and last centuries B. C.

There is then, in the later La Tène period, especially in the West Celtic Continental region, a perceptible decline in creative artistic work in the narrower sense of the term, a certain impoverishment, if we consider the development from the standpoint of its rise and early growth. Only here and there art-and-craft workshops catering for more exacting customers survived, which specialized in granulated personal ornaments, with openwork patterns (Regöly in Hungary), late mask *décor* of the Maloměřice-Brno type *(Pl. XXIII)*, or artistically wrought cult cauldrons and other items of cult character. Altogether predominating, however, was the production of goods in a more widely accessible price range. The creative spirit still found scope to some extent in Celtic coinage.

Insular Celtic art

Quite individual in character and development is the Celtic art of the British Isles. It flourished at the time when it had already passed its zenith on the Continent and was entering the phase of larger-scale production of a more average quality. The early phase of insular art can be traced back to the middle

Fig. 33. Horned helmet from river Thames at Waterloo Bridge. Work of the 'Thames Schools' c. 30—10 B. C. After S. C. Fox.

of the 3rd century, when groups of Celtic warriors from the uplands of Champagne and the Middle Rhinelands established their overlordship in certain parts of England (mainly the chalk downlands of the south), side by side with the native population living in a peripheral Hallstatt or Iron Age "A" Culture. These armed groups first brought with them the fully-developed La Tène art, with Waldalgesheim stylistic elements. Evidence of contact with the Continent is provided by several swords and scabbards, which would fit in chronologically with the influx of Celtic settlers. It would not seem, however, that art imports in the La Tène style later reached Britain from the Continent regularly or in greater quantities.

Today British museums pride themselves on their outstanding works of Celtic art, of which the majority display the individual hallmark of native production. Very soon, namely, native workshops arose in Britain, in which native craftsmen combined high technical skill with an original gift for pattern-making, which achieved a characteristic content and a high degree of refinement. And so we can speak of insular La Tène art as a special branch of Celtic art and distinguish in it the products of various styles and schools or workshops. This older phase of Celtic insular art has been designated by Piggot the Torrs-Wandsworth style. The find-place Torrs, in South-west Scotland, is famed for the bronze pony-cap and the pair of drinking-horn mounts, formerly erroneously reconstructed as forming part of the cap.

This insular style combines free relief ornament with linear incised ornament. It makes use of palmettes, spirals, lyre motifs and tendrils, terminating in Late La Tène stylized and schema-tized bird-heads. The older style is concentrated mainly in the south-eastern part of England, and much later, towards the end of the 2nd century, penetrates to Ireland. Many finds come

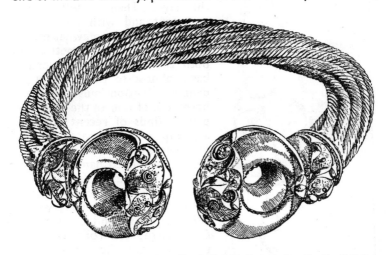

Fig. 34. Electrum torc from the Snettisham Hoard (Norfolk), England. About ²/₃. After S. C. Fox.

from river or peat beds and from bogs, from which it is often concluded that they are votive gifts. Among these finds, a fore-most place is occupied by warrior's fighting gear, by harness fittings and metal chariot *décor*. A considerable part of the finds has, however, late stylistic character, as, for instance, the round shield boss from the Thames at Wandsworth.

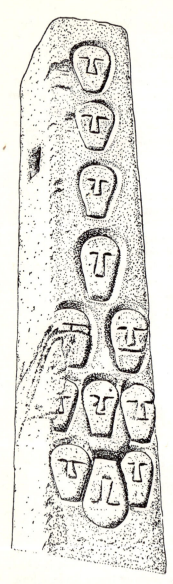

Fig. 35. Entremont (Aix-en-Provence), southern France. Originally an upright column, with 12 reliefs of heads in a Celto-Ligurian sanctuary (Hall of Heads). Height of stone column: 160 mm, width: 34—38 cm, height of heads: 15—17 cm and 23—25 cm.

In the last pre-Christian century Celtic art in Britain reached a high level and, according to Fox, at least six arts-and-crafts schools were in existence. The celebrated horned helmet *(Fig. 33)* from the river Thames at Waterloo Bridge, is the work of a'Thames Valley' school from the second half of the last century and is one of the most remarkable products of Celtic art in Britain: its *décor* is executed in fine relief, with enamel inlays, and is reminiscent of some earlier work, such as the Wandsworth shield. As compared with the frequently photographed shield from Battersea, also from the river Thames, with relief ornament and with red enamel inlays, a work of somewhat earlier date, it is strictly symmetrical on both the horizontal and vertical basis, almost to the point of pedantry. Mention must be made here, too, of one of the most surprising finds of recent years — a group of five hoards of gold ornaments and coins, from 1948—1950, at Snettisham, Norfolk, published by R. R. Clarke. Hoard E contained torcs of a gold alloy (58 % gold, 38 % silver, weight 1085 g, *fig. 34*) and coins of the Gallic Atrebates. Torcs with ring terminals are the work of the East-Central school and also date from the second half of the last century B. C. It is actually the first large group of finds of gold torcs in Britain, accompanied by coins. Beautifully designed and executed sword scabbards, decorated the whole length of the face (Bugthorpe in Yorkshire, Lisnacroghera in Ireland) date mostly from not earlier than the last century.

Several other factors, however, affected Celtic art in Britain in the last century. About 75 B. C. there was the invasion of Belgic tribes from North-eastern Gaul to South-eastern Britain. It would seem that their chieftains brought outstanding artists with them, for many of the finest works of art come from just those parts occupied by Belgic invaders or are direct from Belgic graves. To Belgic influence is attributed the more realistic modelling of animal motifs and the flowering of the art of enamelling. Bronze hoops from wooden vats are decorated in relief not only with animal (fig. 13), but also with human, masks and heads (Aylesford, Marlborough). At this time, too, the fashion of metal mirrors, with rich incised ornament spread widely, so that it is possible to speak of a special 'mirror' style.

Two expeditions by Caesar to Britain, in 55—54 B. C., initiated the first Roman influences, but in general this insular region of the Celtic world remained for another whole century cut off from direct Roman influence. And so, about the turn of the century, when Continental Celtic art had become impoverished or was in perceptible decline, insular Celtic art continued to flourish undisturbed well into the middle of the first century A. D., and, in the north, for a further three decades at least.

Celtic architecture and sculpture

The Celtic genius did not express itself in the shaping of large political units, nor in monumental architecture. Large-scale buildings had no special appeal for the Celts, but they were excellent builders of fortifications, in which they showed, time and again, their engineering ingenuity and their talent for the organizing and pooling of labour in the carrying out of such works. The system of fortifications current among the Celts had a long native tradition. Mention has already been made above of the typical 'Gallic wall' of the last pre-Christian century, described by Caesar, but limited to a certain part of the Celtic world.

Where buildings of more monumental character did, nevertheless, arise, it was always with the assistance of foreign architects and of foreign exemplars. This was true of the fort with bastions at Heuneburg, dating from the Early Hallstatt period, and applies equally to the buildings erected on the

Fig. 36. *Roquepertuse (Bouches-du-Rhône), southern France. Statue of a man (god or hero) seated in the 'Buddha' pose. From a sanctuary at the end of the 3rd or beginning of the 2nd cent. B.C.1. Limestone, traces of original polychromy. Actual height: 100—105 cm. Musée Borély, Marseille.*

southern seaboard of France in the period of La Tène. In speaking of 'Celtic' architecture and also of sculpture, it is namely necessary to differentiate between that of the southern coastal strip of France, centring round Massilia and the lower reaches of the Rhône (in the main, Celto-Ligurian territory) and the Celtic territory proper behind it, reaching from France in the west to the Czech Lands and the Carpathians in the east.

The Celto-Ligurian seaboard

In the territories into which the Celts penetrated not earlier than the latter part of the 4th century, they entered into contact with the Ligurians, and, through them, more closely for the first time with the sphere of Greek art. It is not, therefore, possible to speak of a purely Celtic art in those regions. Tradition has it that the Celts learned the art of fortification from the Greeks. This is not a generally valid assertion, but applies to just this southern French coastal strip, to Gallia Graeca, in Provence. Here oppida soon arose of a much more urban character than the Celtic oppida of Central Europe, with ramparts, regular streets and temples, in which we can clearly trace the taking over and imitation of Greek and eastern patterns, with terraces, propylaea (monumental pillared entrances) and other features, which are atypical for the "inland" area. Thus the Celtic world in the south of France enlarged its cultural horizons and contacted a material culture from which it learned much of value.

The Celto-Ligurian oppidum of *Entremont* (dep. Bouches-du-Rhône), the capital and, at the same time, the sanctuary of the Salyes, was built in the Massilian region as early as the 3rd century B. C. and was later destroyed by the Romans, in 124 B. C. Its broad rampart of stone blocks, with rounded towers, has been preserved, at places, to a height of 4 m. The rectangular houses, with stone walls, built in the dry-walling technique, are grouped to form a continuous row and broadly laid-out streets. The houses had special corner-stones and slabs to protect them from damage by cart-wheels. The storage pit or silos are valuable sources of archaeological material, being filled with supplies of native and imported goods. Nor are the basic requirements of canalization lacking, and, in places, even simple mosaic-work has been discovered. In this urban centre, where F. Benoit has been carrying out archaeological excavations for a number of years, a shrine stood on the highest ground. A path some 100 metres long led up to it, bordered on either side by statues of heroes. In the ruins of the sanctuary are preserved four-sided limestone pillars with carved human heads *(fig. 35,* 12 heads on a single pillar), part of a 'hall of heads'. In the already excavated part are numerous fragments of limestone sculptures, a child's head, a priest's head, with hair dressed to form a wreath-like diadem, a man's head, with curly hair, a woman's head, a stone with four carved heads, two male and two female, the head of a warrior and an almost intact pillar of warriors. It is, indeed, a whole gallery of sculptures, statues and torsos, but all in a desolate state, as the Romans in 124 B. C. laid waste the township and destroyed the sanctuary, as a potential centre of future resistance.

A similar situation arose elsewhere in Provence. In the op-pidum of Roquepertuse (Bouches-du-Rhône), the portal of the sanctuary consisted of three stone pillars, originally polychro-mic, also with niches for the display of human heads. On the crossbeam below the roof was installed the stone figure of a bird about to take flight, over half a metre in height, evident-ly the symbol of the journey to the world of spirits. Here, too, we find a double-headed 'Herma', and between the heads projects the beak of a bird of prey. The whole propylaeum was laid out in two terraces. Statues in the squatting cross-legged position ('Buddhist pose') represent a god or a priest or a he-roised human figure, in one case with a torc and an armlet, in another with a belted tunic, and also having traces of origi-nal polychromy.

All this points to the rise of local schools of sculpture in the south of France; stone sculptures were in demand for religious

156

Fig. 37. Monster from Noves — Tarasque de Noves (Bouches-du-Rhône). Monster devouring a human
being and with paws resting on two bearded heads. Local stone, pre-Roman. Hgt.: 112 cm. Museum
Calvet, Avignon.

and cult purposes. Here the influence of the Greek environment is clearly evident. Local artists did not, however, always interpret their patterns aright, and errors of judgement occurred in connection with the significance of individual motifs and the correctness of proportions in the general conception. Certain features of the statues of heroes in the sanctuaries of Southern France are especially characteristic; high cheekbones, a straight nose with broad bridge, eyebrows indicated by a semi-circle, hair growing close above a bulging forehead — and some of these traits then appear in purely Celtic sculpture.

The statue of the monster from Noves (Bouches-du-Rhône), the famous "Tarasque" (fig. 37), with a body like a lion, in the act of devouring a human being, and with two heavy paws resting each on a bearded head, also held to be "têtes coupées", is of native limestone from pre-Roman times. Perhaps it is meant to represent a symbol of Death, of Eternal Silence, a motif that was popular in Late La Tène; its origin and full significance are not fully comprehensible to us today. The cult of human heads must have been widespread throughout the whole territory. In the Celtic oppidum of Puig Castelar human skulls were found in which the nail from which they had hung was still present.

The Celto-Ligurian region was fortunate in having the opportunity to make contact with a wide variety of impulses from the earliest times. The road from Italy led via Nice and Olbia near Toulon westwards as far as Ampurias in Catalonia. Massilia itself, founded in 600 B.C., had an Artemedes sanctuary, with stelae in Ionian style and a seated goddess in niches, of the same type as in Ephesus in Asia Minor; the remains of the city walls also betray elements deriving from Asia Minor. Dating from a later time are Hellenist stelae (3rd-2nd cent.). Moreover, in the immediate vicinity of Massilia many other very ancient monuments are preserved. Archaeological excavations carried on by H. Rolland in Saint-Blaise over many years, and still not completed, have revealed remains of a well-preserved Greek city — Mastramele, founded prior to Massilia and not later than the 7th century. At the time of Celtic armed expansion this city was encircled by a massive rampart, with a well-protected acropolis. The Celto-Greek statue of a lion from Les Baux (Bouches-du-Rhône), from about the 3rd century, betrays Oriental patterns, but is carved from native limestone.

Several places in Provence and Languedoc have a long history

158

of human settlement, and the native environment has successively been buried beneath Oriental and Greek, then Iberian, Celtic and Roman strata. In the last phase concentrated economic and cultural influences, hand in hand with systematic Romanization, penetrated from these southern regions to the rest of France.

Ensérune (Hérault), an oppidum on the southern French coast, between Béziers and Narbonne, in Languedoc, is situated on a rocky elevation, between the mouths of the rivers Orb and Aude. Cyclopean fortifications transformed it, in the 5th century, into a first-class stronghold. Then Iberian influences infiltrated to these parts and later the site came to be an important oppidum, 750 m long by 300 m wide, capable of accommodating up to 8000 inhabitants. Settlement is documented by strata dating from the Stone Age and reaching to the Bronze Age and the Celto-Iberian period. Here we meet with Antiquity — Greek, Italian, Etruscan and Early Roman cultural streams; Hannibal, at the end of the 3rd century, documents the existence here mainly of Celts. *Glanum* (Greek-Glanon) on the Lower Rhône, in the neighbourhood of Arles (Bouches-du-Rhône), has also remains of an urban settlement, comprising at least four successive strata of settlement. The oldest monuments of the Celtic period from native sanctuaries are often reminiscent in their statuary of Entremont and

Fig. 38. Montbouy (Loiret), France. Wooden statue, found in a sacred well, in a Gaulish sacred enclosure. Hgt.: 58 cm. Musée historique de l'Orléanais, Orléans.

Roquepertuse. From Hellenistic times are preserved the remains of fortifications from the 2nd century, including among other things a peristyle or row of columns, surrounding an *impluvium* (a tank for collecting rain water), and mosaics, probably the earliest on the soil of present-day France. Later ages have also left their traces here: a large number of houses from the period of Romanization, from the mid-first century B. C., and the signs of intensive building activity from the Gallo-Roman period to the last third of the 3rd century. The town was destroyed by Germanic tribes about 270 A. D. In Glanum, too, there still stands, from about 40 B. C., the oldest city gate in Gaul, with reliefs on the side walls representing captive Gauls.

The Romanization of Gaul very soon acquired strongpoints in this southern French region. It suffices in this connection to mention Arles, with a theatre from the time of Augustus, having a stage 104 m long, with rich sculptural *décor* (statues of female dancers carved in marble); Orange (Vaucluse), where a theatre and aqueduct also date from Augustan times, Roman bridges in Apt (Apta Julia) and in Vasio Vocontiorum-Vaison-la-Romaine (Vaucluse), once an important Celtic township and, in the period of Romanization, the wealthiest town on the left bank of the Rhône, or the temple area of the sacred source in Nîmes. In the immediate neighbourhood of Entremont arose the town of Aquae Sextiae. And subject to and modified by all these influences was then the whole development in Gaul proper.

Celtic sculpture in Gaul and in Central Europe

We may consider the oldest stone figure from the La Tène period to be the statue of the warrior from Grézan (Nîmes Museum), which S. Reinach has described as Celto-Greek work from the 5th century. The war-dress, with chain-belt, and especially the Celtic armlet, is thought to form the first stage in the development of stone sculptures from Gaul and the Rhine valley. Its precise dating, however, is not easy. The earliest examples of Celtic sculpture possibly go back to the Hallstatt period, from which period date a number of small sculptures, more of handicraft character.

Celtic figure sculpture from the interior is, to judge from the finds so far, small in quantity, schematic and more or less columniform in character, with decorative features. Examples come from France, from the Rhinelands and from Bohemia. It is closely bound up with cult and religious conceptions, but the Celtic love of ornament, which finds marked expression in the small bronzes industry, is also reflected in Celtic sculpture, which seldom achieves larger dimensions. Some of them are really miniatures and obviously served only as symbols; often we sense in them survivals from a much earlier age, some, indeed, reaching back to totem conceptions.

A limestone figurine of a god, with the symbol of a wild boar carved on its breast and with a Celtic tore from Euffigneix, in the Marne valley, is only 26 cm high and is reminiscent in its technique of a woodcarving *(Pl. XVIII)*. It is Celtic in conception and is sometimes dated to earlier times, but actually it belongs to Early La Tène, from which time innumerable small sculptures of boar *(fig. 14)* have survived in all parts of the Celtic world; they are mostly small bronze statuettes, whether intended as a standard mounting or as symbols (mascots), and sometimes they are executed in relief on sculptures or incised on pottery ware. Only exceptionally are such figures of larger size. The bronze boar from Neuvy-en-Sullias (Loiret) belongs to the group of larger bronzes (hgt. 68 cm) and it seems likely that the druids buried it, in the time of the Roman occupation, on the left bank of the Loire, opposite the central sanctuary on the right bank, beside present-day St Benoît sur Loire (Floriacum, Fleury).

A bronze statuette of a god or hero from Bouray (Seine et Oise), in the Paris region, in the form of a seated figure with a deer's legs (see reference below to the god Cernunnos), is only 45 cm in height. Indicative of its origins is a Celtic torc and a typical Celtic blue-white glass inlay, preserved in the left eye; the limbs are not preserved. The sculpture is of bronze plate, having a front and back part, the inside being hollow *(Pl. XVII)*. Lantier and Hubert date it to the

Fig. 39. *Pfalzfeld (Kr. St. Goar), Celtic pillar of coarse-grained limestone; present height: 148 cm.*

2nd or 1st century B. C.; it seems to be a fairly late work.

More complicated is the problem of wooden statuettes and models. These were evidently fairly numerous in the La Tène period, but only fragmentary remains have come down to us. In the sacred well of the Gallic temple precincts in Montbouy (Loiret), a wooden statuette, 58 cm high *(fig. 38)*, and the head of another (22 cm high), have come to light. They are roughly executed figurines from the period of Gallic Romanization, which help us, at least in part, to gain an idea of what these "simulacra", as Lucan calls them, looked like.

Fig. 40. Heidelberg, Germany. Head of limestone, with typical features of Celtic art.

Several examples of Celtic sculptures come from the Rhine-lands and Württemberg. They are again mostly of menhir, columniform type. Very ancient features are incorporated in the obelisk from Pfalzfeld, in the Hunsrück *(fig. 39)*. The four-sided pillar is embellished on all four sides with relief-carved motifs, which recall the early style of Celtic art; the head is crowned with great paired lobes, the scroll-like ornaments are either intertwined or form lyre motifs. This tapering limestone monolith, 148 cm in height, perhaps originally terminated in a human head and may date from the 4th or 3rd century. Similar archaic features distinguish the fragment of a limestone head from Heidelberg, 36 cm across *(fig. 40)*, which obviously once formed part of a larger object. Belonging to the La Tène period, too, is a stone figure from Holzgerlingen in Württemberg, formerly held to be Slavonic or medieval *(fig. 41)*. The head had originally two faces *(fig. 22)*, a motif which we came across earlier in the south of France. Finally, we must mention the four-sided pillar (present height over 120 cm, *fig. 42)*, which was found in 1864, in the neighbourhood of Waldenbuch, between Tübingen and Stuttgart; the upper part is not extant. The curvilinear ornament and the decorative motifs of the belt indicate affinity with the La Tène *milieu*, although the object as a whole is not altogether typical.

Under these circumstances, the head of a hero carved in ragstone, found in Mšecké Žehrovice, in the district of Nové Strašecí, Bohemia, in what is evidently a cult centre, is a particularly valuable contribution to our knowledge of Celtic sculpture. It is the only find hitherto east of the Rhine, but is the most typically Celtic of all the works extant and dates from the culminating period of Celtic overlordship in Bohemia, most probably the 2nd century B. C. Although here, too, we may presume certain southeastern influences, the sculpture is as a whole unmistakably Celtic in spirit, with consistent stylization of the flat human face, of the mouth, beard, eyes and hair; the latter forms a kind of ornamental wreath, the rest

Fig. 41. Holzgerlingen (Kr. Böblingen), Germany. Limestone stele, with head of a god à la Janus and arm laid across the body. Hgt.: 230 cm Museum, Stuttgart. See fig. 22

of the head being plain. Round the neck is a typical Celtic torc *(fig. 44* and *Pl. XX)*. So far this head is a unique work, without any close counterparts in Gaul and is a clear proof that Celtic sculpture also took firm root in Central Europe. Further, it implies that in this region similar cult customs must have existed to those in Gaul, and, moreover, less affected by Mediterranean influences. The head had been broken off from a pedestal or from a whole statue and comes from some power-centre in Bohemia; as there were quite a number of such power centres in Bohemia and certain regions show a striking concentration of Celtic burial-grounds *(fig. 16)* and settlements, we may expect further finds of a similar kind to turn up in the future.

Celtic masks

In the cult life of the Celts, an important role fell to the mask. Celtic masks are not faithful likenesses of gods or heroes and were not always designed to cover the human face. They are rather symbols serving cult ritual, are severely stylized and often much smaller than the human face. The mask of a Celtic hero from the French Pyrenees, found as long ago as 1870 *(fig. 45)*, is of incised work on bronze sheet and was impaled on a wooden pillar, as is apparent from the carving of the neck. It is 17.2 cm high, open at the back, has holes cut out for the eyes, originally inset with enamel or semi-precious stones. The hair is arranged in spiral locks and the beard is indicated by wriggly lines; the type of nose and mouth, along with other traits, date the sculpture to the 3rd or 2nd century B. C.

The male mask (clean-shaven) from Garancières-en-Beauce (Eure et Loire), found in 1864, in the neighbourhood of Chartres, south-west of Paris, is only 9.8 cm high, is of bronze plate also open at the back *(fig. 46)*; and has, like the former work, openings for the eyes. In general it is Celtic in character, though the incised work is sharper, and belongs, it would seem, to the later group of Celtic bronzes.

From the Pyrenees to the Loire, and as far as the Marne, the masks conformed more or less to the same general principles. Towards the end of the La Tène period and in the early Roman period, we have examples of masks made of iron [mask from Allençon, (dep. Marne et Loire) from the sanctuary treasure, hgt. 12 cm]. In Bohemia, too, fragments of iron masks have been preserved and are now in museum collec-

Fig. 42. Stone figure of the La Tène period from Württemberg (Waldenbuch, south of Stuttgart). Four-sided column, the upper, damaged part is missing. Present hgt.: c. 120 cm. (R. Knorr, Germania V).

tions (Kladno district), but it is difficult to date them with precision. Celtic masks and heads were evidently sometimes set up on either side of the sacrificial table, if we are to judge from finds in St Margareten, in the valley of the Lavant, dating, however, from Roman times.

Small bronzes, as noted above, were produced in larger numbers in the Late La Tène and Early Roman periods. It is yet another type of sculpture, one presenting figural motifs in the nude, as ritually prescribed, but in movement. This is well illustrated by several bronze figures from Neuvy-en-Sullias (Loiret) or St Laurent-des-Bois (Loire et Cher, figurines of female dancers, of men walking etc.). Of a similarly divergent character are the works of Roman artists, who have left us sculptured representations of Gauls, of much greater liveliness.

The head from Prilla (Waadt, Switzerland) is the likeness of the type of Celtic inhabitant of the Swiss territories; the sculptor has carved it in bronze (eyes of copper) and imparted to it certain features of Celtic art.

Celtic sacred sites and sanctuaries

In the Celtic *hinterland* in the Rhine Basin and in Central Europe, we do not find in the La Tène period temples and sanctuaries of the kind we come across in the south of France. The evidence is rather of sacred sites of a cult character, an enclosure marked off by fence, hedge or ditch, mostly of a simple kind. Often, however, it seems to have been merely a grove with sacred trees, or a single sacred tree, or nothing more than a pole or pillar. Certain woods and hills were also sacred, being termed *loci consecrati*, or hallowed places, where the Celts sacrificed to their deities, as Caesar himself informs us.

It is necessary, in connection with the Celtic supernatural, to reckon with an old tradition, with customs and usages handed down from preceding ages. In the Kobener Wald, between Koblenz and Mayen, a circular site -Goloring-, some 200 m across, was enclosed by a bank and an inner ditch; in the middle of the central elevated area is a hole, which had held a wooden post evidently of considerable height. No evidence of burial was found, but in the central area and in the ditch silting stray potsherds of Late Hallstatt times were found. So far we have few analogues systematically excavated. In 1959 excavations conducted under the auspices of the Archaeological Institute of the Czechoslovak Academy of Sciences, in Libenice near Kolín (Central Bohemia), revealed the presence of a cult site, oval in plan, over 80 m long, enclosed by a ditch. In the eastern half of the area is a system of post-holes with a broad stone slab (stele), partly chiselled, in front of which is the base of some kind of oval sacrificial table or altar composed of larger stone blocks. As traces of wood and two wire necklaces were found in the vicinity, it is not unlikely that these were hung on a wooden post (or posts) as the central symbol of the cult. Numerous animal bones indicate that here sacrifices were offered. Sherds found in the composition of the site all belong to the Hallstatt-La Tène period of the 4th-3rd centuries. In the other half of the cult area, the skeleton was excavated of a woman, with grave furnishings of Celtic character pointing to the 3rd century B. C., along with La Tène bronze brooches with detached foot, rings and bracelets. It is the second site of cult character to be excavated in Bohemia (the first being in Mšecké Žehrovice), is evidently of later date and famed for the head of a hero *(fig. 44)*.

Fig. 43. Gaul in native dress. Gallo-Roman work, probably of the 2nd cent. A. D. Find-place: near Appoigny-Auxerre (Yonne). Limestone, hgt. 45 cm, Musée archéologique Auxerre.

It must not be forgotten that, in the La Tène period, artistically executed torcs fulfilled a similar function as symbols of supernatural power. A silver torc from Trichtingen in Germany *(Pl. XXII*, with iron core), splendid Celtic work from about the 2nd century B. C., weighs 6.75 kg, and its use as a personal ornament is very unlikely; it was much more probably hung on a wooden post or on an idol.

A cult site has also been excavated in Frilford, Berkshire, consisting of six large post-holes in two close-set lines of three each. At the foot of the central post an iron ploughshare was found which must have been placed there intentionally. It was no longer possible, unfortunately, to reconstruct the whole enclosure. To judge from the excavated burials, containing dateable brooches, the site was in use in the La Tène period, on the one hand, and in the Gallo-Roman period on the other. In Écury-le-Repos, there were four post-holes arranged to form a square, with a large post-hole in the middle; it is quite possible that it was a cult site at one time, with a sacred pole or a representation of the cult deity. The above-mentioned

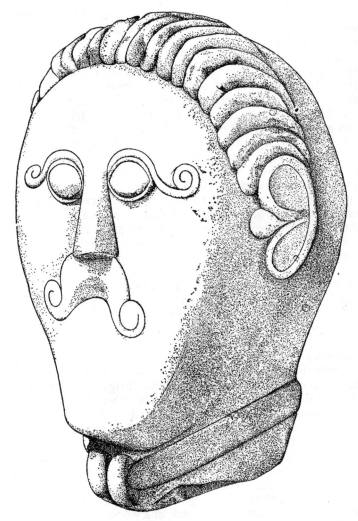

*Fig. 44. Mšecké Žehrovice (Nové Strašeci), Bohemia Head of a Celtic hero, reconstructed drawing
Ragstone, hgt.: 25 cm. See Plate XX.*

find of a Celt head with a torc, in Mšecké Žehrovice, was also
found in a pit situated in a rectangular area, 200 × 105 m,
with an embankment divided on the inner side into three
parts; in this case, too, the place was evidently a sacred enclosure.

Certain trees were believed to possess divine attributes or magic power. Evidence of such beliefs are to be found in later times, in Roman inscriptions or in Irish texts. Mention occurs in them of the gods of the oak and of the beech, of the god of the six trees, etc. According to Maximus of Tyre, the trunk of the oak served the Celts as a statue of Jupiter. In Ireland there are allusions to a sacred tree (*bile*), and certain proper and tribal names point to a similar association (Irish *Mac Ibar*, son of yew, the tribal name *Eburones*, incorporating the word for yew, the Gaulish name *Guidgen*, signifying 'son of wood', or *Guerngen*, 'son of alder'). Some Celtic sacred places were connected with burials or, perhaps, important burials were the basis for their sanctity. An early example is the stone from Stockach, Württemberg, connected with a cremation burial beneath a barrow. In North-east France, on the Marne, square ditched enclosures formed the burial-place for certain families. However, a circular raised kerb or a ditch enclosing the whole barrow is a fairly widespread feature from the Bronze Age onwards, and continued to be quite common in the Hallstatt and La Tène periods. It cannot be generally assumed that the Celtic temple was actually the enclosed grave of some hero.

A word widely distributed in place-names throughout the Celtic world is *nemeton*, which seems to have had the connotation of a sacred place, Such a place need not necessarily have been a building, but may have been a sacred wood or grove of trees. In the north-west part of the Iberian peninsula, we come across the place-name, Nemetobriga, or Nemetacum, in the territory of the Atrebates in North-eastern Gaul; Drunemeton occurs as the sanctuary and meeting-place of the Galatians in Asia Minor; there is a Vernemeton in Britain (Nottinghamshire), and Medionemeton in Southern Scotland. In Ireland, according to Powell, *fidnemed* meant a sacred wood, but a Latin gloss for *nemed* gives *sacellum*, a small shrine or enclosure. An eighth-century glossary contains a plural word '*nimidas*', explained as designating 'the holy places of the woods'. Later sources, too, speak of a wood called *Nemet*, and, according to Classical writers, the druids often performed their rites and sacrifices in woods. In Switzerland, deities of the mountains and rivers were still venerated in Roman times.

Square banked sacred enclosures were probably the forerunners of the Celtic temples which, in Roman times developed into square buildings, often surrounded by columns or by an enclosure. The Gallo-Roman sanctuaries of this kind, both square and circular, were sometimes situated on hilltops, and reference will be made to them below. Sacred sources, wells, tarns, and even peat-bogs and marshes, were held in high veneration among the Celts, as noted by the Classical writer, Poseidonius, who travelled in Gaul in the 1st century B. C.

Votive deposits and sacrifices

Another aspect of religious and cult activity were sacrifices and votive offerings connected with certain sacred places. To-day the large finds of fighting-gear from the La Tène type site and from Port (Nidau) in Switzerland are held to be, though not always quite convincingly, of this character. Of the two and a half thousand objects found at La Tène, more than a third comprised weapons: iron swords (some bearing the master-smith's punch-mark), spears, lances and shields.

As regards some of the finds, it is difficult today to determine unequivocally their character and purpose. A famous Czech deposit in the Duchcov spring (near Lahošť), discovered in 1882, contained close on 2,000 objects, the majority brooches and bracelets, most of them placed in a bronze cauldron; sometimes the find is held to be a votive deposit, sometimes a merchant's hoard.

It is known that the Celts performed great sacrifices before a battle and on its victorious conclusion, laying a part of the war booty in consecrated places. Mention is made of the custom by Caesar, as well as by Poseidonius, and Strabo refers to the great votive treasures of the Volcae-Tectosages near Tolosa (Toulouse), where was reported to be a great treasure of un-wrought gold and silver, which the Romans plundered in 106 B. C. According to Diodorus Siculus, gold was quite a common offering to the gods in Celtic sacred places and 'temples', of which the countryside was full, and no native would have dared to commit the impiety of laying hands on it.

At Llyn Cerrig Bach in Anglesey *(fig. 47)*, offerings were made from a projecting shelf of rock of weapons and equip ment, chariot metal-fittings and slaves'chains; sites of a similar kind (peat bogs and rivers) occur also in Scotland, in England and elsewhere. In Scotland, offerings were still made of whole collections of such votive objects at the beginning of our era, cauldrons often being used for the purpose (Carlingwark, Blackburn Mill, Eckford). Sometimes, however, the Celts also sacrificed old, damaged or broken objects. The splendid shields from the Thames at Battersea or from Witham, Lincolnshire are much more likely to have been lost in crossing the river than sacrificed as offerings to the gods.

In difficult situations (sickness, drought, danger), whole tribes, clans, families and individuals performed sacrifices through the intermediacy of the druids, in order to propitiate or influence in their favour the supernatural powers. Our knowledge of the nature and manner of these sacrifices is, however, very incomplete. References to the subject in Classical writers mention sacrifices of animals and of human beings. Some Gaulish tribes, according to Caesar, constructed immense wickerwork images, filled them with living beings and then set the whole alight. It was assumed that the gods would welcome most the sacrifice of persons who had committed some crime and so had lost their ritual immunity; if a sufficient number of such persons was not forthcoming, innocent persons seem also to have been offered. This is connected with the belief that certain deities could be propitiated by drowning, others by burning or hanging. Sacrifices were performed, too, to ensure good harvests, the birth of healthy children or the successful raising of cattle. The whole life of the individual and of the community was interwoven with rites and customs, in which it is not difficult to detect survivals from earlier, primitive conceptions of magic and religion.

Of considerable importance in various cults and rites were the cult cauldrons, ranging from simple forms to elaborate works of art. A splendid example of the latter group is a silver cult cauldron from Gundestrup in Jutland. It was found in 1891, in a peat bog, in the vicinity of Aalborg; it is 42 cm high, 69 cm across and weighs almost 9 kg. The walls of the piece with incised ornament have gilded silver plaques mounted on the inside and outside, with representations of gods or heroes, life-like expression being given to the eyes by the use of blue enamel. On one such plaque is the god Cerunnos, on another a god with a wheel attribute (Jupiter-Taranis?), on a third a three-headed god and, among other motifs a human sacrifice by drowning, the victims head being immersed in a tub of water. The inside plaques show warriors with standards or a mascot in the form of a boar, some figures or heads of heroes are adorned with Celtic torcs (Pl. XXIV—XXV). The place of manufacture of these sacred cauldrons has not been located with certainty. According to Drexler, they are of south-eastern provenance, coming from somewhere in the territory of the Scordistae, in the region of the Middle Danube; Hawkes and and Reinecke again do not exclude the possibility of it being

Fig. 45. Mask of a Celtic deity from the Pyrenees. Openings for the eyes, originally filled in with enamel or glass. Bronze plate. Hgt.: 17.2 cm. Tarbes Museum, France.

Celto-Ligurian work from the 2nd century, looted by the Cimbri and carried off by them to the north. Other scholars, however, hold the view that it may be a piece of later date, which arose much later under eastern cultural influences (the Mithraic cult), perhaps in North-eastern Gaul. Denmark has produced other finds of cauldrons, such as that from Rynkeby, or the most recent find made in Bra, East Jutland (a bronze cauldron with an iron hoop and figural decoration of bull's heads, about 118 cm across and 70 cm high), of which O. Klindt-Jensen is of the opinion that it may have been made in some La Tène workshop in Moravia.

Sacrifice by drowning is represented, too, on the Gundestrup cauldron. It seems possible, however, that the sacrifice or vow was sometimes made symbolically; by a weapon wound and the spurting of blood from it onto the sacred objects, altar or tree. Certain allusions in Tacitus and Lucan allow of such an interpretation.

Celtic conceptions of the supernatural

Originally the religious conceptions of the Celts exercised a strong binding influence on Celtic society and Caesar tells us that the people of Gaul were very devoted to religion. Like all other peoples, the Celts preserved certain magic ceremonies, formulas and rituals from olden times, by means of which they hoped to influence or gain the favour of various supernatural powers, or prognosticate events. There is no evidence, however, of the existence of a faith, in the sense of a body of beliefs, such as distinguish later world religions; many features survive in myth, cult and sacred terminology from an earlier stage of nature religion and magic observances. The sources containing information about Celtic ideas of the supernatural are fairly numerous, but rarely altogether reliable. They comprise the testimony of Classical writers, Gallo-Roman monuments with inscriptions, most frequently in Latin or Greek, which record at least the name of some local deity, then linguistic commentaries on the original significance of certain words, Old Irish traditions and literature, as well as archeological finds, whether connected with life in this world or the life after death. It is necessary, however, to distinguish carefully between the original conceptions of the Celts and the world of religious notions which colour the references to them in the writings of Classical authors. The latter present a picture of Celtic religion seen through Roman eyes, in the *interpretatio romana*; in order to make its essence more comprehensible to the reader they dress the Celtic deities in

Roman garb and project their own religious conceptions into the Celtic ones, with a consequent greater or lesser measure of distortion. This is true to a certain extent also of Caesar's information. It is difficult for a foreigner to grasp the full ideological content and ritual significance of a cult, without the intimate knowledge that comes only from a long first-hand acquaintance of the *milieu* in which it is practised. And it is still more difficult, if not impossible, considering the fragmentary state of our knowledge, for us who live in the 20th century and have quite a different way of thinking and a different approach to religious concepts, to enter into a proper understanding of the historical Celtic concepts of supernatural forces and modes of influencing them.

For the same reasons, it is very difficult fully to penetrate the significance of Celtic mythology. It would seem, however, that Celtic particularism was operative as much in matters of cult as in political life, so that each tribe had its local deities and cults. In these we can only guess at some aspects

Fig. 46. *Male bronze mask from Garancières-en Beauce (Eure-et-Loir). Bronze plate, hgt.: 9.8 cm. Musée de Chartres, Francie.*

common to the higher hierarchy of deities, having different local or tribal ascriptions. Considering the all-purpose character of Celtic gods, it was not difficult to approximate some aspect of the local deities to a certain Roman god, such as Mercury, Mars or others from the Roman pantheon. It was even possible for the same deity to be venerated in two distant regions, but for different attributes and functions. Vague general conceptions of such deities, however, do seem to have existed, and on these is based the view held by some scholars of the existence of a Celtic pantheon, in which tribal deities represent only regional selection from a common stock of illustration. It must, nevertheless, also be taken into account that the Celts made contact with the older native populations (especially in Central Europe) and their world of religious notions, which could not, in the course of a longer

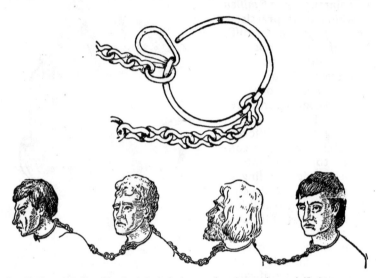

Fig. 47. Gang-chain from Llyn Cerrig Bach, Anglesey, and captives on the march (Fox's reconstruction).

period of co-existence, have been without some influence on that of their Celtic overlords. On their entry into written history, the Celts had already passed through the stage of original totemistic conceptions, from which, however, certain survivals and reminiscences remained. The earlier family totems were then replaced by the heroes of a family, clan or tribe.

In Celtic religious notions there is no definite and clear-cut line dividing gods proper from heroes. Heroes are not supernatural beings; they actually lived as human beings and only later did they become deified. In Irish legends, gods live like human beings and human beings pass into the world of gods. God and man merge, under certain circumstances, and to a greater or less degree, in one.

It seems likely that the concept of tribal gods is the one nearest the original reality. Just as in Ireland Dagda was the father of the tribe and its protector, so elsewhere the male deities were closely bound up with certain tribes. There is no evidence for the specialization of gods according to function or attribute, as, for instance, a sun god or a god of warfare or battle; these were rather linked with the concepts of various tribal gods. Such specialization among the divinities is 'something Mediterranean and urban, unknown to the Celts before, or beyond the Roman conquests'. Thus we have an explanation for the large number of names of Celtic gods, whose functions and attributes often overlap. The highly complicated symbolism of Celtic concepts prevents us from grasping its essence and all its implications. In this symbolism, an important role was played alike in the insular and in the Continental cults by the sacred cauldron. In Ireland the cauldron was the symbol of abundance and of immortality and was often set up in a sacred place or even in a building. At the feast of Gobniu, beer was brewed in a cult cauldron for the refreshment and strengthening of the gods.

Certain deities are named as being the most revered previous to the Romanization of Gaul. According to Caesar, the greatest of the gods was held to be the god of the ways and of traders (an approximation to the Roman Mercury) and the patron of the arts, crafts, skills and trades; in Ireland, Lug was the patron of all the arts and of warlike virtues, and, as we saw above, was also held in high honour in Gaul, at Lugdunum.

The god Taranis is described as the god of the heavens; in the Gallic language, this name was from ancient times linked with the symbolism of the wheel. On an inner panel of the Gundestrup cauldron is the representation of a god or hero, with outstretched arms, the right hand touching a wheel. Besides, small bronze wheels of a similar character are quite common in the inventory of Celtic oppida, as, for instance, in the Bohemian oppidum at Stradonice (Pl. XXXV), and also occur on Celtic coinage. A god with a wheel as attribute frequently appears later on numerous Gaulish monuments and is equated with the Roman Jupiter. Sometimes he holds the wheel in his hand, or again the symbol of lightning (Celtic taran signifies thunder), but the wheel in religious association also symbolized the sun.

The poet Lucan (1st cent. A. D.) names three Celtic gods — Teutates, Esus and Taranis, but not even of these gods is the essential character altogether clear. The scholiasts commenting on the above passage note that Taranis was propitiated by sacrifices by burning, whereas to Teutates victims were drowned (by immersion in a tub of water) and to Esus they were hanged. The hanging sacrifice is particularly important for an understanding of the sacred character of trees. Teutates is described by Caesar as the god of war. The name is derived from a Celtic word designating 'people' and in Roman concepts is approximated sometimes to Mars and sometimes to Mercury. Perhaps the name belonged originally to a local deity who protected his people, and that also in time of war; it must be borne in mind that a Celtic tribe also formed, in time of war, an independent unit even in common action undertaken jointly by a confederation of tribes.

Esus frequently appears later in the guise of Mars or Mercury. Lucan divides the old Celtic deities into two groups: the one comprises Esus and Teutates (Mars, Mercury), the other Taranis, in a combination of the functions of Jupiter and Dispater *(dis, pater,* from whom the Gauls claimed their descent, on the authority of druidic teaching); later this god was equated with Pluto, the god of the underworld. These names are not, however, so unambiguous as not to be applicable to almost any tribal deity.

In Provence, in the Rhinelands and in Ireland, female deities were also worshipped, and in Ireland male deities were sometimes considered subservient to them. The cult of fertility and of the underworld predominated. The cult of Mother Earth was, as we know, widespread in prehistoric Europe from the Late Stone Age, and female deities are considered to be a reflection of the older matriarchal social structure. Traces of this stage of development had a long life. Of similarly ancient origin was the veneration of the three Mothers (*Matres*, Matronae), later depicted as three seated figures bearing the attributes of fertility *(fig. 49)*. The triad was worshipped among the Treveri and elsewhere and sometimes a single goddess is substituted for the three female figures.

Representations of gods in the Buddha pose were an iconographical feature of statuary in Southern and Central France, as we saw above *(Pl. XVII, fig. 36)*. Macrobius, a Late Classical writer, holds this squatting position to be characteristic of gods of fertility and fecundity (attributes; scrip, feather, wing, basket of fruit etc.). Frequently the god holds a snake in his hand, and is represented along with a ram's head, or a Celtic torc (Gundestrup).

From the above descriptions a frequent overlapping of the functions of different gods is at once evident. The Romanization of Celtic religious concepts aimed at a selection of

apparently standardized divine representatives, but what actually took place was a change of name and the often artificial or
chance approximation to some god from the Roman pantheon.
It is then very difficult to obtain a clear notion of the character
of numerous deities known in the Celtic domain under the
names of Albiorix, King of the World, Manopos, the Eternal
Youth, Tontioris, the Ruler of the Tribe, Caturix, the King
of Battles, Ogmios, the Guide of the Dead, with club and bow,
and so on. Among the Aedui, a deity was worshipped, with
hammer and mallet as attributes, often as a a pair of gods, in
the retinue of a goddess. The sources mention something like
400 names or appellations of male and female deities. In the
Rhinelands, in Britain and in Noricum, there are numerous
dedicatory inscriptions, in which a certain name occurs no more
than once; their indicated attributes, however, are numerous
and varied. Most frequent are the attributes associated with
Mars and Mercury, less common those of Apollo, Silvan and
Minerva. The iconography of the individual deities has not
yet been worked out in detail, and there is marked overlapping of attributes among the different gods. Only a few divinities seem to have had a wider distribution. A god with a deer
symbol occurs in Central Gaul, a god with a snake symbol in
Eastern Gaul. There is evidence that Belenus was worshipped
in Gaul, in Northern Italy and in Noricum, in which territories
the mare goddess, Epona, was, also held in veneration, as well
as in Britain and in the Celto-Iberian region *(fig. 49)*. Sometimes the deities appear in pairs, a god with a female counter-
part; Sucellus and Nantosuelta in Gaul, Vidasus and Tiana
in Pannonia, to give two examples. For the Celtic domain,
however, the number three is particularly typical. We mentioned above the three Mothers, but we also come across
a three-headed or three-faced god (relief of a three-headed
god from the Reims region, a three-headed god on a vessel
from Bavai); a triple-horned bull *(tarvos trigarnos)*, animal triads
and personages having the power to triplicate themselves. The
number three was the symbol among the Celtic of strength
and perfection, a three-headed god was the most powerful of
the gods.

The divine bull Deotaros is documented in Asia Minor, the
raven, dove, ram, bull and other animals figure in sacred symbolism. The Gaulish deity Cernunnos is represented with
deer's antlers and reference has been made above to a god with
a boar symbol.

Sometimes the view is expressed in the special literature

that deities associated with certain animals had originally the form of these animals (the sacred animal of the tribe or totem), and that later, when the deities assumed more definitely human form, these animals became their mere attributes. So far, however, extant representations of gods, with associated attributes, are mostly from a later time. Large numbers of small bronze or burned clay figurines found in Gallo-Roman temples, point to the survival of Celtic religious beliefs and votive offerings deep into Roman times.

Certain objects or signs were attributed magic power, giving protection from the evil eye, plague and other misfortunes. On the ramparts of the town of Clermont, such signs, believed to have the power to protect its inhabitants from the plague, survived into Christian times.

We have referred to the role of the druids in Celtic society in another connection, and also to the Celtic minstrel-bards. *Euhags* seem to have been priests and prognosticators, and mention is made, too, of *vates*, whose function is not altogether clear.

Irish tradition has preserved a description of a very complicated ritual in connection with the inauguration of a king. The young king was held to be the mortal mate of the territorial nature goddess and entered into marriage with her in the symbolical act of receiving a goblet from her hand. He met the goddess in the form of a lovely maiden beside a well or spring. When the king grew old, the goddess assumed the aspect of a repulsive hag. It is of interest that in these kingship stories a grotesque figure appears, of great strength and appetites, clad in a short garment and wielding a huge club, sometimes drawn on wheels and with a magical cauldron having the properties of inexhaustibility, rejuvenation and inspiration. Its importance lies in the fact that bronze figurines of a man carrying a club or similar object are not uncommon in the Late La Tène period and that they have also been found at the Hradiště oppidum near Stradonice, Bohemia. In Gaul we have evidence of a similar type of deity, with the attributes of hammer and goblet or dish (Sucellus). Giraldus Cambrensis, the author of a topography of Ireland, writing about the year 1185, mentions with indignation the very archaic rite connected with the enthroning of the Kings of Ulster. The king had publicly to perform the act of generation with a mare that was then slaughtered and cooked in water, in which the king took a ritual bath, whereupon, together with his people, he partook of the flesh. This barbaric ritual is evidently of very ancient origin, for similar horse sacrifices are known in other parts of the world, as in India, for example.

The Celtic calendar counted by nights and was based on lunar observations. The year was divided into two main periods, a warm period and a cold period. In Ireland the end of the old year and the beginning of the new was marked by the *Samain* festival, which fell on the first of November, when the herds and flocks were brought together at the end of the grazing season. The preceding night was the culminating point of the festival when magic powers were liberated and magic warrior bands trooped out of caves and hillsides. The other important festival took place at the beginning of the warm season and was known as Beltane (the Celtic word for fire), or Cetsha-main (a name which it is perhaps possible to connect with the Continental deity, Belen). This festival fell round the first of May, when the cattle and sheep were driven out onto a common pasture. It was the custom during this festival to light fires through which the cattle were driven to gain them immunity from disease and ensure fertility. In Ireland there were two other festivals, *Imbolc*, on the first of February and perhaps connected with the lambing season, and *Lugnasad*, on the first of August, in 10 B. C. apparently to ensure the ripening of the crops; the latter incorporates the name of the god Lug, preserved in the names of a number of Continental towns, such as Lugdunum, present-day Lyon, once the principal town in *Gaul*. At the injuction of the Emperor Augustus, a great festival was celebrated there about the first of August, just as in Ireland, and Lug was raised to a deity of all the Gauls, as a parallel to the Roman Mercury.

Burial rites

Essential for our understanding of the religious concepts of the Celts is the information provided by Celtic burial rites. A description of burials in the preceding Hallstatt period was given above, in connection with the chieftains' graves. During the period of armed Celtic expansion the custom became established of burying the uncremated bodies in pits up to over one metre deep, in common cemeteries, known generally in archaeology as 'flat' cemeteries, as opposed to the earlier barrow graves. It must be pointed out, however, that this later burial custom was directly related to the movements of the Celtic peoples, gaining predominance in places in the old Celtic

domains, but superseding the older rite mainly in newly occupied territories. Where no larger movements of population
took place, the old manner of burial beneath mounds or barrows continued for long, some of the barrows (as in France)
becoming the burying-place of certain social units, mainly it
would seem of families. In the regions where barrow burials
long continued, La Tène Culture penetrated with a greater or
lesser time-lag, and sometimes Hallstatt-La Tène elements had
a particularly long life.

In the matter of the orientation of the individual burials in
flat cemeteries there is not complete uniformity, it being determined by tribal and regional usage. Extended burials in the
Carpathians (Slovakia) are often placed with the head pointing
south, in Moravia they have a northernly orientation; but
there are differences even between the various cemeteries in
the same region. In the Celtic flat cemeteries, it is possible to
distinguish the graves of warriors and wealthy women, then
graves with average furnishings, and, lastly, really poor graves,
without any burial gift; in some burial-grounds, these latter
comprise 10—15 per cent of the total number of burials. Besides extended burials, we also come across contracted burials,
these being most frequent in the Moravian-Austrian-Car-
pathian region. In certain Moravian cemeteries, the proportion
of such graves is relatively high and would seem to indicate
a greater degree of assimilation of the Celts to the native
environment, further documented, in the Middle Danubian
and Carpathian regions, in the living inventory, especially from
the 2nd century.

The dead were often buried in coffins or in wood-built graves.
Sometimes we may speak of true chamber graves, as, for
instance, in Brno-Maloměřice or in Velká Maňa, Slovakia. The
higher rank of the departed was often outwardly documented
by a circular or rectangular enclosure, girt by a ditch and external bank (Trnovec — Horní Jatov, Holiare, Slovakia); it was
a manner common also in the west and dated from earlier
times. In women's graves, personal ornaments sometimes made
of precious metals are often more richly represented. Ceramics
in the older phase of Central European Celtic burial-grounds
are rare, on the whole, and occur with greater frequency only
from the second century B. C. Very rich graves have been
excavated from a later period, such as the grave of the princess in Dühren, Baden, from the turn of the 2nd and 1st centuries; among the funerary furnishings were silver granulated brooches, agate and glass bracelets, gold finger-rings,

a bronze mirror with a handle, bronze vessels and silver coins.

A typical Celtic custom was the placing of part of a pig (a boar), in the grave. It was a very ancient custom, common already in the Hallstatt period and observed right through the La Tène period, being undoubtedly connected with burial customs which included a burial feast. The bones of other animals (calf, sheep, cattle) are found more rarely in graves. There is evidence, too, that the old custom of skull trepination (to relieve cranial pressure by making an oval excision in the crown) was still practised at this time.

Besides inhumation, cremation burials also occur, from the 3rd century onwards, in the flat cemeteries, especially in the occupied Central European regions, where this type of burial was the usual rite among the native population. Among the intrusive Celtic groups of population, cremation burial was adopted unevenly, in some places more quickly, in others with a greater time-lag. In certain cemeteries from the end of the 2nd century and the beginning of the last century B. C., cremation clearly predominated, inhumation, however, continuing alongside into the beginning of the new era.

IX

The civilizational and cultural heritage of the Celts

From the middle of the last century B. C. the Celtic world was caught in the press of two opposing forces. From the south the Roman Empire was quickly pushing its frontiers northwards, to the Rhine and to the Danube, while Germanic tribes were thrusting southwards, with ever increasing force and momentum. The end of the century brought a solution of the situation. On the European continent, the Celtic element had lost its dominating position and the Roman Empire had made direct contact with the regions occupied by advancing Germanic tribes. Yet, despite the fact that the power and political significance of the Celts had thus declined on the threshold of the new era, their civilizational and cultural contribution continued to operate as an important component of European civilization, alike in the domain of technical skills and in that of the arts and of literature.

The Romanization of Gaul and the Celtic heritage

For Gaul proper Caesar's conquest of the territory, concluded before the middle of the last pre-Christian century, marked the starting-point of a new development. From then on the Romanization of Gaul was energetically carried through to its logical conclusions. The men were obliged to lay down their arms and devote their energies above all to agriculture, for the Roman armies required a sufficiency of provisions.

Romanization spread from Southern Gaul, where the Romans had earlier secured a firm foothold and secure base for their further advance. The former Ligurian territory, with its rude and hardy people, where the men had the strength of wild animals and the women were their equals in bravery and fortitude, had long since undergone gradual Celtization prior to being brought under Roman domination. Provence had received a new administration under the Emperor Augustus and had become, in all respects, very similar to Northern Italy.

In the new era the whole of Gaul was mainly engaged in agricultural production for their Roman overlords. In the south there were olive groves, fig orchards and vineyards, and in the rest of Gaul grain was cultivated and animal husbandry practised. The Romans broke the power and influence of the druids, who were too dangerous a moral and intellectual force to be ignored, and introduced Roman law and legal concepts. Roman officials and traders soon filled the country. It was highly expedient for the new régime to have the support of the Celtic aristocracy, and the former "equites", who, after the loss of independence and the fall of the oppida, readily and promptly adapted themselves to the higher Roman standards of living. Builders and artisans, called in from the south, built commodious houses for them and also country residences, furnishing them with Mediterranean luxury; from the first establishment of Roman power, mortar was used as a binding material in building.

Fig. 48. Late La Tène quern. Reconstruction by E. Major, after finds in Basel.

Thus Rome was able to consolidate its power in collaboration with the landed aristocracy, who maintained a numerous body of clients or retainers on their country estates. The administration gave legal definition to the power of this class. Land-registers were drawn up, a census of people and estates was taken, and a tax assessment made. Properties thus acquired a permanent and individual character, the *fundus* became a unit, with its own woodlands, fields, vineyards, smithies and workshops; it also had its own name, which was retained even when the property changed hands.

Specially attractive for the native Celtic aristocracy were the newly founded towns, providing the opportunity for a more comfortable life, with higher living standards and often the chance to acquire Roman citizenship and the rights and privileges that went with it. In this direction, the Romans were particularly active at the close of the old and the beginning of the new era. The number of towns had increased rapidly already under Augustus and continued to do so under his successors, in Gaul, as well as in Switzerland, and, later, in the Rhine and Danube basins. Above we have already noted the rise of many new towns in the south of present-day France, with theatres,

Fig. 49. Some Gaulish deities of the Gallo-Roman period: 1. Epona, the patroness of horses (relief, Kastel Allemagne). — 2. God with hammers (bronze, Vienne, Isère). — 3. Three goddess-mothers (relief from Vertault, Côte d'Or). Musée Châtillon-sur-Seine. — 4. Four-faced Mercury (bronze, Bordeaux, Cabinet des Medailles). 5. Nantosuelta and Sucellus. Stela with dedication, from Sarrebourg. — Gallo-Roman Jupiter, with wheel and spirals. Bronze. Châtelet. Haute-Marne (P. and M. Duval, Les dieux de la Gaule).

aqueducts and other amenities. The inhabitants of Bibracte were resettled by Augustus in the newly founded town of Augustodunum (Autun), in 5 B. C. At the same time as Lugdunum (Lyon) arose, mention is made of the foundation of Raurica (later called Augusta Raurica), at the end of the road leading to the Great St Bernard pass across the Alps. Under Caesar there was founded, as a defence against the raids of the famous Helvetian cavalry, the town known as Colonia Julia Equestris, then Noviodunum and other urban centres. Between 27 and 8 B. C. the Emperor Augustus visited Gaul in person no less than four times. Cambodunum, in the area of the present-day town of Kempten, on the river Iller, is a foundation from the reign of Tiberius (the original wooden structures were replaced by stone buildings already in the 1st century A. D.), and the garrison town of Vindonissa, in present-day Switzerland, which arose in connection with the fortification works in Germania, dates from 17 A. D.

The lay-out of the towns was as a rule closely bound up with military dispositions. In the centre was the forum, the place of assembly for the townspeople and the market-square; then a temple and a basilica for the transaction of public and judicial business. The forum was also the meeting-place of the ways and round the forum were situated the business places and workshops and the spacious houses with arcades in which resided the city nobility. Roads were built with a firm surface, mostly at the expense of the towns and of the landowners. The colonizing activities of the Romans in the Rhinelands were also of great importance and played as significant a role as the urban expansion of mediaeval times. Splendid buildings arose in the country, too. Besides country residences more of a town character *(villa urbana)*, manor houses *(villa rustica)* were built with spacious living quarters and outbuildings.

The security of the Province and of the whole Empire was entrusted to *élite* bodies of Roman legionaries, later supplemented by auxiliary corps composed of native drafts. The frontiers with the Germanic world on the Rhine and on the Danube had to be defended with the strictest vigilance and garrisons of tens of thousands of men spent long years in these outposts of empire. A line of defences arose successively, with armed camps *(castra* and *castella),* the fortifications being punctuated by small forts and watch-towers. In the first two centuries this line of demarcations, the famous *limes romanus (Fig. 50)*, stabilized the frontier along the banks of the Rhine, from where lines of fortifications linked up with the Danube and continued along the Danube to the Carpathians. Garrison stations were equipped with a high measure of comfort, in order to mitigate the hardships of life in the inclement and less hospitable north. Central heating was installed below the floors *(hypocaustum)*, baths were built in *(balneum)* and other conveniences. Under the patronage of the garrison station, *canabae* grew up, settlements of vendors and tradesmen, the whole then forming a military town, with its own amphitheatre. Nearby a twin town often grew up with a civilian population, similarly equipped to provide a higher standard of living for the inhabitants. In the neighbourhood of Gaulish towns a special feature were the colonies of veterans grown old in military service. These were all far-reaching changes which deeply affected the way of life not only in Gaul, but also in the provinces of Raetia, Noricum and Pannonia, east of Gaul, and reaching as far as the area of present-day Budapest.

The Roman conquest of Gaul did not bring with it any social revolution. The majority of the inhabitants continued to live in villages, where they were more permanently bound to the soil than before, and where Romanizing influences penetrated very much more slowly than into the towns. And it was these country people who preserved their language and distinctive way of life, their customs and usages, and who now and again tried by means of revolt to hold up or retard the advance of colonization and Romanization. Moreover, these farming communities, self-sufficing in the production of food and all the necessities of life, kept alive their knowledge of skills and crafts, as well as of production methods, adapted them to changing conditions and requirements, so that the Gaulish workshops continued in operation after Roman occupation and, indeed, formed the core of Provincial-Roman production.

The high level of Celtic pottery was the pre-condition for a large and flourishing pottery industry in Roman times. *Terra sigillata*, high-quality pottery, with a brilliant reddish glaze, often decorated with figural and vegetal motifs, was originally made in the last century B. C. in Italy, the main centre of production being Arezzo (hence Arretine ware). Later, in the time of Tiberius, the centre of production shifted to Gaul, first to the south and then to Central Gaul, and, finally, had outliers in the Rhinelands. Thus workshops arose in many different places — in La Graufesenque, in the south, in Lézoux in the interior, in Reinzabern and a number of other places, some even on the far bank of the Rhine. However, the big ceramics workshops of the Arverni, in La Graufesenque and in Lézoux (Puy-de-Dôme), were centres of production prior to the coming of the Romans and had long supplied a large part of Gaul with their jugs and bowls. The production of fine ceramics was thus transferred from Italy to places in Gaul with a mature ceramics tradition and their ware was exported not only to the other Roman provinces, but were also an item of trade with the northern regions of present-day Germany,

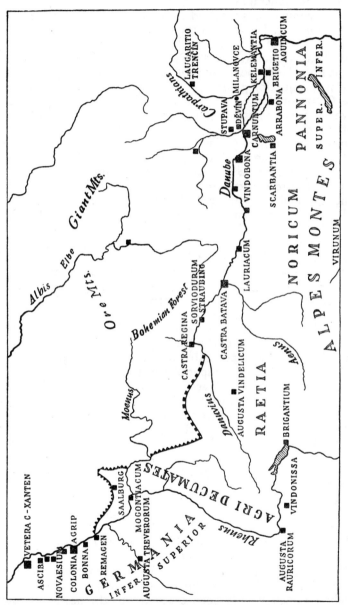

Fig. 50. Limes romanus — Roman fortified frontier on the Rhine and Danube, with main garrison stations.

Poland and Central Europe. The share of native master-potters in this production is testified to by the stamps of makers with Gaulish names. The same is true of the manufacture of bronze vessels, established somewhat later in Gaul and on the Rhine, and of the glassmaking industry, which in Gaul and especially in the Rhinelands took firm root in Roman times; the beginnings of glass production go back, as we saw above, to the time when the Celtic oppida were at their most flourishing, and these paved the way for the subsequent fame of this branch of manufacture.

In general, however, public life was strongly influenced by Italian usages. The ancient Celtic cults had become assimilated in some measure to Roman concepts, counterparts for the original Celtic deities were sought and found in the Roman pantheon and the names intermingled or interchanged. The influence of the Roman environment is also reflected in the rise of a sacred architecture of very distinctive type. From the beginnings of direct Roman influence and from the transitional period between the pre-Christian and the new era, and then in the time of the Roman Emperors, numerous temples arose with square, polygonal or circular ground-plan, usually with a surrounding portico or veranda. Today many examples are known in the territories of the Treveri and of the Mediomatrici on the Moselle and the Saar, as well as in the land of the Aedui and of the Mandubii, between the sources of the Seine and the Upper Loire and further west; they are also to be found in Britain, especially in those regions settled by Belgic tribes, and more rarely in Raetia and Pannonia. Their siting in the open countryside is a reflection of old cult concepts of sacred enclosures on hill-tops, beside river sources or at the meeting of ways. The core of the sacred structure was the shrine itself *(cella)*, usually round and 5—10 m in diameter; this was surrounded by a portico open to the outside or bounded by an arcade. In these shrines was the cult-place of the native Celtic nature or tribal deities, and their furnishings comprise a mixture of Celtic and Roman usages. Some excavations carried out, for instance, in Trier, provide grounds for the presumption that in earlier times such sacred shrines were of wood, but in the 1st century A. D. stone structures, with mortar binding, arose, whether polygonal — these being held to be the older type — or round. The sanctuary on Bibracte (Dea Bibracte) dates apparently from the time when the inhabitants had already been evacuated to the newly founded Augustodunum (Autun); this would be corroborated by the find in the shrine of 107 Gaulish crowns and only 10 Roman coins.

Roman influence made itself felt in sculpture and in other branches of the arts. More fully developed plastic forms and an increasingly realistic approach gradually pushed the old Celtic stylization and schematization, both in the representation of human and animal forms, into the background. The range of motifs was extended to include, besides the traditional native symbols of boar, dog, horse and Gallic cock, exotic animals, such as the lion, from foreign, more particularly, Oriental sources. The human statue or head, carved in stone or bronze, is much more sophisticated and realistic, but the old Celtic character is in evidence even here, whether in the typical Celtic shield with which the Gaulish warrior from Mondragon is equipped *(Pl. XIX)*, or in the Celtic weapons and symbols on the triumphal arch in Narbonne, or in the finely sculptured bronze head of the Celtic inhabitants of present-day Switzerland *(Pl. XX.)*, where there are traces of Celtic ornamental stylization in the rendering of the hair and beard. Mention has already been made of the large numbers of votive figurines of bronze in evidence at this time.

It is, on the whole difficult to distinguish what is the work of a native Gaulish artist and what the work of an artist of southern origin who has in part become assimilated to his new domicile. The spirit of the country and of its people exercised an unescapable influence on the artist from abroad. Individual elements mutually intermingled. Old Celtic reminiscences are, indeed, clearly traceable right through the succeeding Merovingian, Carolingian, Romanesque and even Gothic period styles, as, for instance, in sculpture, in the application of certain decorative motifs and in the choice of individual human heads and in the manner of their grouping (Saint-Benoît-sur-Loire). France had, however, meanwhile passed through stormy times — the invasions of Germanic tribes, the Alemanni, and then the Franks, and had repulsed the most westerly thrust of the Huns under Attila, so that the foreign impacts on the native *milieu* were many and varied.

Nevertheless, not even the strong infiltration of Roman ideas and the Roman way of life, nor the later Germanic inundations, were able altogether to blot out the distinctive Celtic tradition. It is still alive in France to this day, in the language and in geographical names. In many cases, the names of tribes survive as the names of towns, and the Celtic names of hills and rivers still retain their Celtic designations; moreover,

many agricultural terms exist which are etymologically unconnected with Late Latin. The latter provided a considerable vocabulary only in the terminology connected with Christian
ritual, when Christianity was adopted as the state religion.
In addition, many features of the feudal order of mediaeval times
are a lively reminder of the situation in which Celtic society
found itself at that time; in many ways it was a foreshad-
owing of the later development, in which were first
created the definitive pre-conditions for the victory of a new
social order.

Celtic traditions in Ireland and in Britain

The main treasury of Celtic tradition and the Celtic heritage
are the British Isles, and especially Ireland and Scotland.
Development continued undisturbed at a time when Celtic
Gaul was already being subjected to intensive Romanization,
namely practically throughout the whole 1st century A. D.
After Caligula's still-born plan to invade Britain in A. D. 40,
Claudius invaded the island with an expeditionary force,
being followed in the work of conquest by Vespasian and, in
A. D. 86, by Agricola, who began to build a line of defence
between the Clyde and the Firth of Forth, not completed,
however, till the 2nd century, under the Emperors Hadrian
and Antoninus Pius. Particularly favourable for the continuity
of the Celtic tradition was the situation in Ireland, where
neither the Roman nor, later, the Anglo-Saxon power, permanently penetrated. Thus Ireland remained the spiritual and
religious centre of the Celtic world and has preserved its
Celtic character into modern times. Scotland, too, however,
was able to maintain its Celtic mode of life. The Scots, Irish
invaders and settlers in Northern and Western Britain, began
to reach the opposite shores as early as the 2nd century A. D.,
and, in the 4th century, they are expressly named in the sources.
They founded a kingdom, Scotia, which swallowed up the
ancient Picts and Caledonians, and reinforced the Celtic
settlements in Wales, Cornwall and the Isle of Man. There the
Celtic tradition persisted for long. As late as in 1249 the
traditional inauguration of a Scottish king was still performed.
After the ecclesiastical coronation ceremony, the king was led
in procession to the Coronation Stone, where his whole
genealogy was recited in Gaelic and he received the acclama-
tions of his people.

Celtic insular art developed independently throughout the greater part of the first century of our era, and Roman influence, when it did become operative towards the end of the century, first affected the territories of Southern Britain. At this time there grew up a flourishing and highly-skilled Celto-Roman enamelling industry, which specialized in stylized brooches, akin in general conception to the Gaulish *décor* of the *terrae sigillatae*; three colours of enamel are used and the effect is to make the pattern stand out more clearly from the background. In Northern Britain, in the territory of the Brigantes, a tribe hostile to the Romans, there arose already in the 2nd century A. D. a well-developed metal-working industry. Scotland, too, contributed its share to arts-and-crafts production, with the manufacture of metal necklaces, having incised Celtic patterns representing a revival of the so-called 'Celtic' curvilinear style. For what we witness here is, indeed, a kind of revival of Celtic art, partly fertilized by southern elements belonging to the classical tradition. And once again we see documented the Celtic ability to recast foreign elements in the melting-pot of their own concepts. The abstract principle in Celtic ornament reached its culmination in the insular art of this period. It is not a mere stylization of natural forms, but a new expressive art working with forms independent of nature and of reality.

When the eastern and central part of Southern Britain was overrun by the Angles and Saxons, there were migrations of parts of the British populations from the south and south-west coasts to the opposite seaboard of the Gallo-Roman province of Armorica, which then became identified with the newcomers, from whom Brittany (Bretagne) derives its name, but a part remained. Ireland, however, remained Celtic, as did Cornwall, Wales and North-west England. The defence of Celtic positions in this period of the Anglo-Saxon Conquest is associated with the names of heroes such as Aurelius Ambrosius and King Arthur, round whom sprang up whole cycles of legends.

Very soon, already in the 4th century, Ireland accepted Christianity, which took deep and permanent root. In the 5th century a great advance in missionary work was made under Patrick, consecrated bishop in A. D. 432 for the purpose of working in Ireland. In the territories of the various tribes, monasteries and convents were established, which did not, however, form a unified network, nor were they united by a common monastic rule, so that they remained outside the centralized organization of the Roman Church, having the

Pope at its head. Thus Irish Christianity developed from the 4th century in isolation and was able to maintain various ancient customs undisturbed.

The Neo-Celtic Style and its repercussions on the Continent. Book illumination

In the 6th century a stream of Irish missionaries reached the Continent, starting their activities in Gaul and in other more distant regions of Europe. Of special significance was the missionary work of St Columcille (Columba the Younger). Thanks to him, monasteries were founded in Burgundy (Annegray) and an important monastery in Luxeuil (Haute-Saône) northwest of Belfort, in the foothills of the Vosges, which became a centre of literary activity and book illumination. Of Columba's successors, Eustasius preached Christianity in Bavaria at the beginning of the 7th century, and Gallus in Switzerland; in the second half of the 7th century Kilian went as far afield as Thuringia, being murdered in Würzburg in A. D. 688. In 782 Charlemagne called to his court Alcuin of York, probably an Irishman by birth, and entrusted to him the Abbey of Tours; his palace school *(schola palatina)* set a new, high standard of culture. Irish missionaries were also active in the dioceses of Passau and Salzburg, and in all likelihood penetrated as far as Moravia, even before the rise of the Great Moravian Empire, spreading not only Christianity, but also certain types of ecclesiastical architecture which followed in its wake.

Late Celtic art reached its full flowering in the 7th—9th centuries, alike in fine metal-working and in book illumination, which was markedly calligraphic in character. The drawings, which are executed with a pen and then delicately coloured, dispense almost entirely with the use of gold, depending for their effect on the designs and borders of intertwined ribbons, tangled knots and intricate patterns and spirals. This neo-Celtic style is, in part, a continuation of the old Celtic art, especially of Celtic ornament, but incorporates many other elements, on the one hand from Late Classicism, and, on the other, from the art of the south-east and east, including Coptic and Syrian art. Ireland became a bastion of Christianity in Western Europe and many monks from the east, under the pressure of Islamic onslaught, took refuge in the Irish-founded western monasteries. Certain features of the neo-Celtic style were unknown to the older art, such being, for instance, plaited bands and plaited patterns in general. The Celtic tradition, however, is most clearly reflected in the curvilinear decoration, which in Irish art develops into 'trumpets' or spiral whorls. Similar elements appear in fine metal-work and in manuscript illumination.

Attempts have been made to divide this neo-Celtic style into three main periods. The first, dating from the middle of the 7th century, would cover the contribution of Ireland and

Fig. 51. Detail of a drawing from old Celtic manuscripts. P. Meyer, Atlantis 1957.

Scotland and the revival of handicrafts, in which figural motifs are gradually introduced. The second period, the period of Viking aggression, would show declining interest in curvilinear ornament and the growing prominence of the plaited pattern. The third period, from the beginning of the 11th century, would be characterized by a greater concentration on church furnishings, such as reliquaries, chests for the ritual books, bells, croziers, shrines, etc. Many works of Irish artist-craftsmen are deposited in the country's museums, especially in Dublin. There are on the Continent, however, many examples of objects inspired by neo-Celtic art. One of the most famous is the Tassilo

Goblet (8th century), held by some authorities to be a copy of an Anglo-Saxon piece, by others to be the product of a workshop in Southern Britain.

Of high artistic excellence are the illuminated manuscripts of Irish origin, whether executed in Ireland itself (Scotia Major) or in Northumberland and Wales, or in some Irish-founded monastery on the Continent. Northumbria, which received Christianity from the independent Irish Church, was later (after 664) brought within the organization of the Roman Church, but in book illumination Irish influence remained strong and, from here, radiated to the Continent. The art of illumination flourished in the Hiberno-Anglian *milieu*, and many specimens of this type of decoration have come down to us. The texts of these books are religious, mainly the Gospels. Their rich *décor* is predominantly abstract and geometrical in character, even the figural motifs being greatly modified by the trend towards stylization and ornamentalization. The exact dating of the books is not easy. Some manuscripts would seem to be from as early as the 7th century. The 8th century saw the culmination of this art (Durrow, the Lindisfarne Gospels, Echternach, Lichfield, the Gospels from the St Gallen Monastery, Switzerland, and many others). In the splendidly illuminated Book of Kells, from near Dublin, dating perhaps from the end of the 8th or the beginning of the 9th century, abstract ornament is combined with animal and figural motifs, which become part of the ornamental pattern. Manuscripts of this kind were dispersed throughout the whole Celtic world, wherever Iro-Scottish influence penetrated.

The Danes and Norsemen, under the common name of Vikings, attacked, raided and effected settlement in South and North Britain, as well as in Ireland, the latter, however, offering successful resistance at the battle of Clontarf, in 1014 A. D., thus gaining a certain time for inner consolidation and the flowering of the arts, especially those dedicated to the requirements of the Church. This output must, however, be judged from the point of view of mediaeval church art, an important place in which is occupied by the Celtic stone crosses (often very richly decorated with ornamental patterns), some of which date to the 11th century (Carew in Wales).

There was a revival of the Celtic spirit when, from the 12th century, wandering minstrels spread a knowledge through France and Germany of the old Celtic tales, and poets such as Chrétien de Troyes, Gottfried of Strassburg and, most famous of all, Wolfram von Eschenbach, presented the old Celtic court epics circling round King Arthur, Parsifal, the Holy Grail and Tristan and Isolde, in new garb. In the time of the Crusades, these Old Celtic reminiscences acquired a strong admixture of eastern elements. And when the Romantic Movement of the 18th century once more focussed attention on the early history of European nations, it found, especially in the Celtic environment and in the Celtic heritage, one of the richest sources of inspiration on which drew all the foremost personalities in European culture — Herder, Goethe, Chateaubriand, Wagner, Tennyson, William Morris and others.

The Irish people is the only people to have fully retained their Celtic character. To this day there exists a Celtic literature which has as one of its mainsprings a deep love of nature. The works of some of these contemporary poets (Gruffydd in Cardiff, Roperz Er Marson in Brittany, and others) have been made at least in part accessible to European readers in translation (cf. the anthology translated and edited by J. Pokorný, published in Prague, 1944, and Bern, 1953).

The Celtic Heritage in Central and Northern Europe

In Central Europe, the Roman Empire had extended its frontiers, even before the advent of the new era, to the banks of the Danube. The regions south of the Danube became Roman provinces and included, besides Raetia and Noricum mentioned above, both Upper and Lower Pannonia, of which the Danube in its north-south course formed the eastern frontier. The Romans subdued the Dacians in the region later known as Transylvania and, in places, shifted their frontiers to positions even north of the Danube. South of the Danube new life circulated and percolated also into Southern Moravia and Slovakia, for these two regions became the immediate neighbours of the Roman Empire.

Roman power was soon able to depend on a system of military forts and garrison stations along the Danube: Vindobona (Vienna), Carnuntum, on present-day soil, opposite Slovak Devín, Scarbantia (Sopron), beside Lake Neusiedl, and Arrabona (Raab-Győr), in Brigetium, on Hungarian soil, opposite Komárno, and especially in Aquincum, in the present-day Budapest area. For a time, mainly in the 2nd century A. D., it secured a foothold further north, in Mušov, near Mikulov, Moravia, and in Stupava, Slovakia; only recently a Roman manor was discovered in Milanovce, in the Nitra district. The well-known Latin inscription on the rock in Trenčín, Slovakia, testifies to the penetration of Roman forces into this region, about A. D. 179. In the immediate proximity of present-day Moravia and Slovakia were two large centres of military power: Carnuntum, through which passed long-distance trade routes, and Aquincum, with a garrison and a civilian town, in both of which centres the inhabitants numbered several tens of thousands. On the south bank of the Danube, a Roman road was built, paved with stone, and a Roman flotilla maintained transport on the river.

Survivals of Celtic settlement and of the tribal organization of the Boii, however, undoubtedly remained in existence throughout the whole first century of our era and we have grounds for the view that the *civitas Boiorum* continued well into the second century. The Celtic names, too, on epitaphs, show that, alongside the Illyrians, the Celts represented a considerable proportion of the region's population at that time; certain symbols on these grave monuments also betray Celtic origin. Celtic reminiscences are more clearly traceable in the production of utility goods and in art-and-craft output.

About the middle of the last century B. C. the remains of Celts in the Czech Lands found themselves in a similarly unfavourable position to those already threatened with political oblivion further west. For some time strong German pressure had made itself felt from the north and smaller groups of Germanic tribes had already settled not only where the Elbe leaves Bohemia, but also in the Česká Lípa district (Jestřebí) and between Turnov and Český Dub (the *Kobyly* group of cremation burials). Hastily constructed Celtic oppida in the southern half of the country could not hold back the course of events. Some time between 10 and 8 B. C. bands of German warriors, *comitatus*, overran the whole country and brought about the fall of the remaining Celtic power, and soon, under the leadership of Marobud, the warrior chief of the Marcomanni, created a considerable military and political power on the Roman model. It cannot be ruled out that Marobud set up his residence in one of the conquered Celtic oppida. It seems likely that the oppida in Bohemia continued their existence for some time under German overlordship at the beginning of the Christian era and that a number of Celtic workshops located in them continued production.

Celtic supremacy came to an end in the Czech Lands, in Bohemia earlier than in Moravia, it would seem, and the power of the Boii had already been broken half a century earlier in Pannonia by Dacian aggression. We must, however, realize what an important contribution had been made by them to the common fund of culture and civilization in Central and Northern Europe in the form of a permanent Celtic heritage and as the starting-point for further development. The Germanic tribes, who hastened the fall of Celtic power in Bohemia

Fig. 52. Pottery from the second half of the last century B. C.: 1. Lhotice near Nasavrky (Chrudim). — 2. Kobyly near Turnov, cremation burial of the Kobyly type. Hgt.: 20.4 cm. Pardubice Museum and National Museum Prague.

and, later, in Moravia, were themselves strongly Celticized. Already in the second century B. C. they had taken over many technical achievements from the Celtic *milieu* in the field of production, in the making of personal ornaments (especially brooches) and in ceramics. It is often very difficult to distinguish what in the material culture of the Germanic tribes is original and what arose under Celtic influence. In the earliest Roman period, too, there are still evident traces of the country's Celtic past and, we may assume, of the continued existence of Celtic population groups. The making of pottery on a wheel ceased, but hand-made pottery at the turn of the era shows the undeniable influence in Bohemia and Moravia of Celtic patterns and workshops in the form, structural design and method of manufacture. The development of jewellery and especially of brooches derives in the whole basin of the Danube from Late La Tène forms, and chased, enamelled, fretted or filigree precious-metal work still employs the motifs and elements of Celtic ornament. Whole collections of Celtic iron tools and implements passed into the possession of Central European communities and practically unchanged remained a part of the artisan's and farmer's inventory, far into the Middle Ages. It is just this high technical and technological maturity of the Celts that has taken such deep root. The Celtic people withdrew from the stage of history as a military and political power factor, but their material culture formed the core of further development, experiencing in later times a kind of Renaissance in literature and in the manual arts. Many Celtic place-names have also survived, as well as the names of topographical features such as rivers and hills. Linguistic evidence points to the Celtic origin of the names of the rivers Labe (Elbe), Ohře and Jizera, and possibly of the Mže, as well as of several Slovak rivers; of the Central European ranges known as the Hercynian Forest (the 'oak' forest), the Sudeten range (the 'boar' hills?) and Gabreta, the old name for the Šumava or Bohemian Forest. Also numerous names of 'townships' mentioned by the Alexandrian scholar, Claudius Ptolemy, writing in the second century A. D., refer most probably to old Celtic trading centres in Central Europe. Celtic influence and La Tène Culture also penetrated and greatly influenced the course of development in the Polish territories north of the Carpathians and extended deep into the north-east, as far as the present-day Ukraine. On the soil of what is now the Trans-Carpathian Ukraine, Celtic power made itself felt for some time as far as the vicinity of Mukačevo; in addition, strong cultural and trading contacts were established with the Ukraine, the extent of which is reflected in the native cultures flourishing at the turn of the new era, as, for instance, as far afield as Pontus (Pontica) and in the *Zarubincy* culture, in the Kiev region; it is reflected most arrestingly in the manufacture of brooches, after Celtic patterns.

A similar situation prevailed in Northern Europe. In the period of Late La Tène, there is already evidence of trade with Denmark and Southern Scandinavia in various Celtic commodities: a variety of personal ornaments, especially brooches, artistically executed sacred cauldrons and cult chariots with elaborate metal-work fittings. These Celtic imports are valuable, too, as enabling archaeological research to work out a more precise chronology of the stages of development in Northern Europe, and trace the later survival of elements of Celtic culture in that region. When a kind of Celtic Renaissance took place in the Gallo-Roman environment, in the second and third centuries A. D., the impulse for which went out from the common people, Northern Europe benefited from it in no small measure. Individual elements of Celtic origin make their appearance again in the 7th—10th centuries, in the details of the decoration of the Oseberg ship, in the Jelling style and in other works of art; they are never, however, elements exclusively dominating the creative process, but only survivals and reminiscences, reshaped and modified by the artists of later times.

The significance of the Celts in European civilization has no parallel in the early history of Europe. In those times they rendered the service of bringing 'barbarian' Europe into contact with the advanced Mediterranean cultures and civilization of the maturing ancient world. Later the Celts turned to good purpose their organizational abilities, their technical genius and their innate aesthetic sense, and built up a remarkable economic and commercial basis, which impressed its main feature on its whole environment. They enriched European civilization with more efficient methods of production and working processes, introduced greater specialization into production and so laid the foundations for mediaeval development. With them, the pre- and proto-historical process of civilization reached its culmination in Central Europe. Eventually they lost their predominance as a political and economic power, but the Celtic heritage, with its charming reminiscences of small-scale works of art and with its mysterious world of heroic deeds, legends and tales, so persistently kept alive, especially in the west, has become a rich source of European culture, on which its greatest creative spirits have lavishly drawn. It is right that the world of today should recognize and try to gain a clearer knowledge of its debt.

Bibliography

Åberg, N.: Keltiska och orientaliska stilinflytelser i vikingatidens nordiska konst. Stockholm 1941.

d'Arbois de Jubainville, H.: Les Celtes depuis les temps les plus reculés jusqu'à l'an 100 avant notre ère. Paris 1903.

Applebaum, S.: The Agriculture of the British Early Iron Age, Proc. Prehistoric Society XX, Cambridge 1954.

Behrens, G.: Germanische und gallische Götter in römischem Gewand, Mainz 1954.

—: Kelten-Münzen in Rheingebiet. Prähist. Zeitschrift (Berlin) XXXIV/V, 1950.

Benadík, B. — Vlček, E. — Ambros, C.: Keltské pohrebiská na juhozápadnom Slovensku (Celtic Burial-Places in South-West Slovakia) Bratislava 1957.

Benoit, F.: L'art primitif mediterranéen de la Vallée du Rhône. Paris 1955.

Bieńkowski, P.: Les Celtes dans les arts mineurs gréco-romains. Cracow 1928.

Bittel, K.: Die Kelten in Württemberg. Berlin-Leipzig 1934.

Bloch, R.: The Etruscans. London 1958.

Böhm, J.: Naše nejstarší města (Our Oldest Towns), Praha 1946.

Bosch-Gimpera, P.: Les Celtes et la civilisation des urnes en Espagne. Préhistoire (Paris)8, 1941.

—: Les Mouvements Celtiques. Essai de Reconstitution. Études Celtiques 1950/51.

Břeň, J.: Černé náramky v českém laténu (Black Bracelets in the Czech La Tène), Praha 1955.

Cibulka, J.: Velkomoravský kostel v Modré (Great Moravian Church in Modrá), Praha 1958.

Clark, J. G. D.: Prehistoric Europe. The Economic Basis. London 1952. — Europa przedhistoryczna. Podstawy gospodarcze. Warszawa 1957.

Clarke, R. R.: The Early Iron Age Treasure from Snettisham. Proc. of the Prehist. Society for 1954 (1955), XX.

Dehn, W.: Die Heuneburg. Neue deutsche Ausgrabungen, Berlin 1958, 127 bis 145.

Déchelette, J.: Manuel d'archéologie IV, Paris 1927 (2nd Ed.).

Drack, W.: Wagengräber und Wagenbestandteile aus Hallstattgrabhügeln der Schweiz. Zeitschrift f. schweizer. Archäologie und Kunstgeschichte 18, 1958, 1—67.

Duval, P. — M.: Les dieux de la Gaule. Paris 1957.

Engels, F.: The Origin of the Family, of Private Property and of the State (Czech ed., Praha 1949).

Espérandieu, E.: Recueil général des bas-reliefs, statues et bustes de la Gaule Romaine, I—XIV, Paris 1907—1955.

Filip, J.: Keltové ve střední Evropě (The Celts in Central Europe), Praha 1956.
—: Pravěké Československo (Prehistoric Czechoslovakia), Praha 1948.
—: Keltská společnost v době laténské (Celtic Society in the La Tène period), Archeologické rozhledy V—1953.
—: Rod a rodina v předkeltském a keltském prostředí (Clan and Family in the Pre-Celtic and Celtic Environment), Památky archeologické (Praha) 1961.
Fox, A.: Celtic Fields and Farms on Dartmoor. Proceedings of the Prehistoric Society for 1954, XX (1955).
Fox, C.: Pattern and Purpose. Cardiff 1958.
Franz, L.: Eine keltische Niederlassung in Südböhmen, Praha 1942.
Frey, O. H.: Eine etruskische Bronzeschnabelkanne. Besançon 1955.
Goessler, P.: Der Silberring von Trichtingen. Berlin-Leipzig 1929.
Grenier, A.: La Gaule Romaine. An Economic Survey of Ancient Rome. Baltimore 1937.
—: Les Gaulois. Paris 1945.
—: La Gaule celtique. Paris 1945.
Henry, F.: Early Christian Irish Art. Dublin 1954.
Holder, A.: Alt-celtischer Sprachschatz. Leipzig 1896—1904.
Hubert, H.: Les Celtes depuis l'époque de la Tène. Paris 1950.
—: Les Celtes et l'expansion celtique. Paris 1950.
Jacobstahl, P.: Rhodische Bronzekannen. Jahrbuch des Deutschen archäol. Instituts 44—1929, 198—223.
—: Early Celtic Art. Oxford 1944.
—, *Langsdorf, A.:* Die Bronzeschnabelkannen. Berlin 1929.
Jansová, L.: Keltské oppidum u Hrazan (Celtic Oppidum near Hrazany) Archeologické rozhledy IV/1952, VIII/1956.
Jenny, W. A.: Keltische Metallarbeiten. Berlin 1935.
Joffroy, R.: Le trésor de Vix. Paris 1954.
—: Les sépultures à char du premier âge du fer en France. Paris 1958.
— et *Bretz-Mahler, D.,* Les tombes à char de la Tène dans l'Est de la France-Gallia, XVII, Paris 1959.
Jullian, C.: Histoire de la Gaule, I—III. Paris 1908—1909.
Keller, J.: Das Fürstengrab von Reinheim. Germania 33, 1955.
Kendrick, T. D.: The Druids. London 1911.
Kenner, H.: Zur Kultur und Kunst der Kelten. Carinthia I/141, 1951, 566—593.
Kimmig, W.: Zur Urnenfelderkultur in Südwestdeutschland. Goessler-Festschrift 1954 (Stuttgart), 41—98.
—, *Hell, H.:* Vorzeit am Rhein und Donau. Lindau-Konstanz 1958.
—, *Rest, W.:* Ein Fürstengrab der späten Hallstattzeit von Kappel am Rhein. Jahrbuch RGZM Mainz, I, 179—216.
Klindt-Jensen, O.: Keltisk tradition in Romersk Jernalder. Copenhagen 1952.
—: Foreign Influences in Denmark's Early Iron Age. Copenhagen 1950.
—: Bronzekedelen fra Brå. Aarhus 1953.
Knorr, R.: Eine keltische Steinfigur der Latènezeit aus Württemberg. Germania V, 1921, 11—17.
Koethe, H.: Die keltischen Rund- und Vierecktempel der Kaiserzeit. 23. Bericht RGK, Berlin 1933, 10—108.
Kossack, G.: Kammergräber der Hallstattzeit bei Grosseibstadt. Neue Deutsche Ausgrabungen, Berlin 1958, 121—126.
—: Südbayern während der Hallstattzeit, I, II. Berlin 1959.
Köves, F.: Les vates des Celtes. Acta ethnographica Academiae Scientiarum Hungaricae, IV, 1955.
Kucharenko, J. V.: Rasprostraneniye latenskich veschei na teritorii vostochnoi Evropy. Sovetskaya archeologiya 1959, (Moskva) No. 1, 31—51.

202

Lacroix, B.: Un sanctuaire de source du IVe siècle aux Fontaines-Salées Revue Archéolog. de l'Est et du Centre-Est, VII, 1956, 245—264.

Laet, S., Lambrechts, P.: Traces du culte de Mithras sur le chaudron de Gundestrup? Actes III, Session Zürich 1950, 304—306 (Congrès Inter. des sciences préhist.).

Lambrechts, P.: Contributions à l'étude des divinités celtiques, Brugge 1942.

—: L'exaltation de la tête dans la pensée et dans l'art des Celtes. Brugge 1954.

Lantier, R.: La religion celtique. Histoire générale des religions. I, 1. Paris 1948.

—: Die Kelten. Der Aufstieg Europas — Historia Mundi, München 1954, 400—458.

— *Hubert, J.:* Les origines de l'art français. Paris 1947.

Lot, F.: La Gaule. Paris 1947.

Malaquer de Motes, J.: Las culturas hallstátticas en Cataluña. Ampurias 7/8, 1945/46, 144 et seq.

Meyer, P.: Inselkeltische Handschriften. Atlantis 1957, Heft 7.

Moreau, J.: Die Welt der Kelten. Stuttgart 1958.

Müller-Karpe, H.: Das urnenfelderzeitliche Grab von Hart. Bayer. Vorgeschichtsblätter 21, 1955, 46—75.

Murphy, G.: Saga and Myth in Ancient Ireland. Dublin 1955.

Navarro, J. M. de: The Celts in Britain and their Art. The Heritage of Early Britain, London 1952.

Nejedlý, Z.: Dějiny národa českého I, (History of the Czech Nation), Praha 1953.

Oliva, P.: Pannonie a počátky krize římského imperia (Pannonia and the Beginnings of the Crisis of the Roman Empire) Praha 1959.

Ondrouch, V.: Keltské mince typu Biatec z Bratislavy (Celtic Coins of the Biatec Type from Bratislava), Bratislava 1958.

Paret, O.: Goldreichtum im hallstättischen Südwestdeutschland. IPEK 15/16, 1941/42, 76—85.

Paulsen, R.: Die Münzprägungen der Boier. Leipzig-Wein 1933.

Píč, J. L.: Starožitnosti země České II, 1, 2. (Bohemian Antiquities), Praha 1902—1903.

Piggot, S.: British Prehistory. Oxford 1949.

Pink, K.: Die Münzprägungen der Ostkelten. Budapest 1949.

Pittioni, R.: Urgeschichte des österreichischen Raumes. Wien 1954.

Pleiner, R.: Základy staroslovanského železářského hutnictví (The Foundations of Old Slavonic Iron-Working), Praha 1958.

Pobé, M., Roubier, J.: Kelten-Römer. Olten und Freiburg im Breisgau 1958.

Pokorny, J.: Keltologie. Bern 1953.

Powel, T. G. E.: The Celts. London 1958.

O'Rahilly, T. F.: Early Irish History and Mythology. Dublin 1946.

Ralegh Radford, C. A.: The Tribes of Southern Britain. Proc. of the Prehist. Soc. for 1954, 1—26.

Rice, T. Talbot: The Scythians. London 1957.

Riek, G.: Ein hallstättischer Grabhügel mit Menschendarstellung bei Stockach bei Reutlingen. Germania 25, 1941, 85—89.

Rix, H.: Zur Verbeitung und Chronologie einiger keltischen Ortsnamentypen. Goessler-Festschrift, Stuttgart 1954, 99—107.

Röder, J.: Der Goloring. Bonner Jahrbücher CXLVIII, 1948.

Sandars, N. K.: Bronze Age Cultures in France. Cambridge 1957.

Schiek, S.: Das Hallstattgrab von Vilsingen. Goessler-Festschrift, Stuttgart 1954, 150—167.

Sjoestedt, M. L.: Dieux et héros des Celtes. Paris 1940.

Stähelin, F.: Geschichte der Kleinasiatischen Galater. Berlin 1907.

Sullivan, E. Sir: The Book of Kells. The Studio 1914.

Šimek, E.: Poslední Keltové na Moravě. (The Last Celts in Moravia), Brno 1958.

Vaněček, V.: Keltská a germánsko-římská kapitola z dějin státu. (Celtic and Germano-Roman Chapter in Constitutional History). Právně-historické studie III, Praha 1957

Varagnac, E. and A.: L'art gaulois. Zodiaque, Paris 1946.

Vendryes, J.: La religion des Celtes. Paris 1948.

Vetters, H.: Zur Frage der keltischen Oppida. Carinthia I/141, 1951, 677 et seq.

Vouga, E.: La Tène. Leipzig 1923.

Wheeler, W. — Richardson, K. M.· Hill-Forts of Northern France. Oxford 1957, (with *Cotton, M. A.,* Muri Gallici).

Wyss, R.: Das Schwert des Korisios. Archaeologia Helvetica 5, Frauenfeld 1955.

Zwicker, J.: Fontes Historiae Religionis Celticae. Bonn 1934—1935.

List of the Principal Works
of Academician Jan Filip

I. Books

1. *Popelnicové pole a počátky železné doby v Čechách* (The Urnfields and the Beginnings of Early Iron Age in Bohemia). Abstract in German. Praha 1956—1957—176 pp., 90 plates and figures, 1 chart.

2. *Kulturní kapitoly z našeho pravěku* (Chapters on Prehistorical Culture). Ist and 2nd ed. Praha 1940—94 pp., 8 plates and 17 figures.

3. *Umělecké řemeslo v pravěku* (Arts and Crafts in Prehistory). Praha 1941—192 pp., 16 plates and 37 figures.

4. *Počátky slovanského osídlení v Československu* (The Beginnings of Slav Settlement in Czechoslovakia). Abstracts in Russian and English. Praha 1956—96 pp., 14 figures and 1 chart. Gained the 1947 Bohemian Land Prize for Scientific Achievement.

5. *Dějinné počátky Českého ráje* (Historical Beginnings of the Bohemian Paradise Region). Abstract in English. Praha 1947—296 pp., 72 plates, 50 figures and charts.

6. *Pravěké Československo* (Prehistoric Czechoslovakia). Praha 1948—420 pp., 48 plates and 103 figures.

7. *Praha pravěká* (Prehistoric Prague). Praha 1949—170 pp., 117 figures.

8. *Pradzieje Czechoslowacji* (Prehistory of Czechoslovakia). Poznań 1951—497 pp., 48 plates, 103 figures and 1 chart.

9. *Keltové ve Střední Evropě* (Celts in Central Europe). Abstracts in German and Russian. Praha 1956—552 pp., 132 plates and figures. Awarded a State Prize in 1957.

10. *Keltská civilizace a její dědictví* (Celtic Civilization and Its Heritage). 1st, 2nd and 3rd ed. Praha 1960—182 pp., 132 plates and 52 figures.

11. *Enzyklopädisches Handbuch zur Ur- und Frühgeschichte Europas - Manuel encyclopédique de préhistoire et protohistoire européenne.* 2 vols., about 1750, many illustrations. Published in 1966 (I) and 1969 (II) by the Publishing House of the Czechoslovak Academy of Sciences.

12. *Frühe Stufen der Kunst.* Propyläen Kunstgeschichte, Band 13, Berlin 1974 (mit M. J. Mellink).

II. Larger Studies and Articles Published in Periodicals

1. *Porost a podnebí Čech v pravěku* (The Vegetation and Climate of Bohemia in Prehistoric Times) — Památky archeologické (Archaeological Monuments) Praha XXXVI (1929—1930), pp. 196—188.

2. *Žárové pohřebiště v Březině* (Cremation Graves at Březina) — Památky archeologické (Archaeological Monuments), XXXVIII (1931), pp. 81—92. Reprinted as a separate, Praha 1932.

3. *Hallstattská kultura v Čechách* (The Hallstatt Culture in Bohemia) — Památky archeologické (Archaeological Monuments), XXXX (1934—1935), 43 pp., illustrations.

4. *Vůz pravěký a vznik vozu moderního* (The Prehistoric Chariot and Origin of the Modern Chariot.) Abstract in German. Reprinted as a separate from Věstník Československého zemědělského musea (The Journal of the Czechoslovak Agricultural Museum), IX, No. 3,14 pp.
5. *Lužická kultura v době laténské* (The Lusatian Culture in the La Tène Period). Abstract in English — Slavia Antiqua (Poznań), I (1948), pp. 166—180.
6. *Lužická kultura v Československu* (The Lusatian Culture in Czechoslovakia). Abstract in German — Památky archeologické (Archeological Monuments), XXXXI (1936—1938), pp. 14—51.
7. *Keltská společnost v době laténské* (Celtic Society in the La Tène Period). Abstract in French — Archeologické rozhledy (Archaeological Prospects) Praha, V (1953), pp. 205—208, 217—233, 276—278, 285—287.
8. *Keltské pohřebiště v Mistříně a žeh u moravských Keltů* (The Celtic Burial-Ground at Mistřina and Cremation among the Moravian Celts). Abstract in French-Archeologické rozhledy (Archaeological Prospects), V (1953), pp. 332—336, 346—361, 369—372, 422—423, 429—430.
9. *Obchodní styky Čech s Římem v době Augustově a problém mocenského střediska tehdejších Čech* (Bohemia's Trade Relations with Rome and Her Power Centre in the Age of Augustus). Abstract in French — Archeologické rozhledy (Archaeological Prospects), IV (1952), pp. 143—144, 140—154.
10. *Chronologische Probleme der Latènezeit in Europa.* Hamburg, Internationaler Kongress der ur- und frühgeschichtlichen Wissenschaften. 1958 (in print).
11. *Bibliografie československé prehistorie za roky 1929, 1930, 1931, 1932, 1933—1935, 1936—1938* (Bibliography of the Czechoslovak Prehistory for the Years 1929, 1930, 1931, 1932, 1933—1935, 1936 — 1938)—Památky archeologické (Archaeological Monuments) XXXVII (1931), XXXVIII (1932), XXXIX (1933), XXXX (1934—1935), XXXXI (1936—1938).
12. *Československá literatura o slovanských starožitnostech* — Bibliographie des travaux tchèques et slovaques relatifs aux antiquités slaves (Bibliography of the Czechoslovak Literature on Slavonic Antiquities – Slavia Antiqua (Poznań), II (1940—1950), pp. 536—562.

Index of Names

Aberg N. 200
Abucatos 137
Adria 51
Aedui 74, 75, 78, 95, 97, 110
Agnel-Pertuis 51
Aislingen 35
Akichorius 65
Albiorix 177
Alcuin of York 192
Alesia 78, 124, 125, 130
Alexander the Great 63
Alkimoensis 126
Allençon 163
Allobroges 76, 117
Almagro M. 22
Altenburg 127
Altkönig 126
Altstetten 36
Ambiani 77
Ambidravii 68
Ambigates 47, 61
Amphipolis 137
Ampurias 157
Anaxilas 54
Andamati 138
Anglo-Saxons 191
Annegray 192
Antariti 68
Antigonus Gonatas 65, 66
Antiochus Soter 65
Applebaum S. 200
Apollo 177
Appoigny 166
Apremont 43
Apt-Apta Julia 159
Aquae Sextiae 75, 78, 159
Aquileia 68
Aquincum 195, 196
Aquitania 75, 77, 79, 82, 97, 115
d'Arbois de Jubainville 200
Arezzo 186

Ariovistus 78
Arles 158
Arrabona-Rab 195
Arthur, King 85, 191, 195
Arverni 75, 78, 95, 96, 186
Atrebati 78, 80, 152, 168
Attalos I., 66
Audoleon 138
Augustodunum-Autun 125, 184, 188
Augustomagus 134
Augustus 68, 87, 125, 159, 179, 183, 184
Aurelius Ambrosius 191
Aurillac Cantal 149
Avaricum 75, 78, 122, 124
Aylesford 57, 153

Basadingen 81
Basel 183
Basse-Yutz 146
Báta 64
Battersea 152, 169
Baux 157
Bavai 177
Behrens G. 200
Belenus 177
Belgae 75, 77, 79, 82, 97, 153
Bellinzona 30, 51, 54
Bellovaci 77
Belloves 47, 61
Benadík B. 202
Benoit F. 53, 155, 202
Besançon 55
Besseringen 48, 143
Biatec 140, 142
Bibracte-Mont Beuvray 75, 78, 110, 115, 124—125, 130, 134, 137, 141, 188
Bienkowski P. 202
Bittel K. 200
Biturigi 75, 115, 125, 137

Bloch R. 200
Böhm J. 132, 200
Boii 13, 61, 63, 70—74, 75, 82, 88, 141, 196
Boio 138
Boiodurum 72
Boiohemum, Bohemia 13, 70
Bolgios 65
Bononia-Bologna 63
Bosch-Gimpera 22, 84, 200
Boudobriga 83
Bouray 160, XVII
Bouzonville 146
Brã 172
Bratislava 118, 132, 140—141
Brennus 62, 65, 116
Briganti 191
Brigetium 195
Britons 78, 79
Brno-Maloměřice 86, 102, 149, 180, XXIII, XXXI, XXXIII
Bruck a. d. Alz 30
Brütisellen 81
Břeň J. 200
Bugthorpe 152
Buchau 26
Buchheim 44
Bulliot 124
Burebista 74
Busu 141
Bussy-le Chateau 57
Bylany u Českého Brodu 35

Caesar G. J. 12, 78—79, 82, 83, 88, 93, 97, 98, 99, 102, 105, 108, 109, 110, 115, 121, 124, 132, 133, 153, 165, 169, 172, 182
Caledonians 190
Cambodunum-Kempten 185
Camp du Château à Salins 39, 53
Cantii 80
Carew, Wales 194
Carnuntum 195, 196
Carthage 54, 78
Caturix 177
Catuvelauni 80
Cenomani 62
Cernunnos 160, 170, 177
Certosa 54, 61
Charlemagne 192
Charváty by Olomouc XXVI
Chassey 17
Chateaubriand 195
Châtelet 184
Châtillon-sur-Seine 36, 38

Childe V. G. 23
Chlum by Zbiroh 55, 56, IX
Chotín by Komárno 41, 49
Chrétien de Troyes 194
Chýně by Prague 147, VIII
Cibulka J. 200
Cimbri and Teutones 71, 72, 75, 121, 171
Clark 200
Claus M. 114
Clusium 62
Colchester 57
Columba the Younger (St Columcille) 192
Colonia Julii Equestris 185
Cornovii Cotini 73
Cotton M. A. 124
Courtisois, Marne 55
Coviomarus 141
Cumae 54

Červené Pečky 102
Čínov by Žatec 58
Čížkovice by Lovosice VII

Dacians 74, 139, 141
Dagda 174
Daniel of Veleslavín 13
Déchelette J. 124, 200
Dea Bibracte 188
Deiotaros 177
Delphi 65
Devil 140
Dietikon 89
Dinnyés Puszta 76
Diodorus Siculus 13, 87, 108, 169
Dispater 186
Dobrá Voda 101
Dobuni 79
Dolany by Kolín XXXVIII
Dollhof 37
Donnersberg 126, 133
Drack W, 200
Dražičky by Tábor 147, XXVI
Drexler 170
Drunemeton 168
Dubský B. 115
Duchcov-Lahošť 169
Dühren 180
Dumnoni 79
Dürkheim 48
Durobriges 80
Durostorum-Silistria 66
Durrow 194
Duval P.-M. 184

Dvory on the Žitava 86

Eburones 77, 168
Echternach 164
Écury-le-Repos 166
Ellg 25
Emporion 77, 167
Engels B. 95
Ensérune 111, 158
Entremont 108, 117, 152, 154
Epona 111, 177, 184
Ésperandieu E. 200
Este 147
Esus 175
Etruscans 40, 53, 56, 61
Euffigneix 159, XVIII
Eustasius 192

Fabius Maximus 96
Farlarix 141
Ferschweiler 145
Filottrano 52, 55, 148
Filip J. 49, 201
Finn 85
Floriacum 160
Florus 96
Forêt des Moidons 27
Forum Julii, Neronis, Seguslavorum
    134
Fox A. 201
Fox C. 57, 150, 151, 201
Franz L. 201
Frasnes-les-Buissenal 55
Freisen 48
Frey R. 54, 201
Frilford 166

Gabréta 198
Gaels 81—85
Gaesats 88
Gallen St 192, 194
Gagers 138
Gallia 12, 63, 75—78
Galatians 12, 65—66, 168
Garancières-en-Beauce 163, 173
la Garenne 24, 41, 53
Gela in Sicily 38
Geneva 127
Gergovia 75, 78, 125
Germani 18, 25, 78, 87, 108, 182, 197
Gieshübel-Hundersingen 43
Giraldus Cambrensis 178
Glanum 158
Goethe 195
Goessler P. 201

Goidels 22, 23, 79, 81, 85
Goloring 165
Gottfried of Strassbourg 194
Grächwil-Meikirch 52, V, VI
la Graufesenque 186
Gray 36
Grenier A. 201
Grézan 159
Grosseibstadt 32, 49
Gruffydd 195
Gundestrup 92, 170, 176, XXIV, XXV
Gunzwill-Adiswil 43

Hagenau 26
Hallein-Dürrnberg 29, 63, 146, 147
Hallstatt 29, 38, 49, 76, 147
Hannibal 77, 117, 158
Hardt, Upper Bavaria 24
Hatten 56
Hawkes C., J. 19, 23, 170
Heidegraben-Grabensetten 126
Heidelberg 161
Hecataeus of Miletus 58, 61
Helvetii 74, 75, 78, 82, 97, 121
Henry F. 201
Hercynian Forest 48, 198
Herder 195
Herodotus 59
Hersart de la Villemarque 15
Heuneburg 29, 33, 36—38, 47, 49,
    51, 53, 56, 123, 153, III
Hjortspring 105
Himera 54
Hohenasperg 36
Hochmichele 33, 38, 43
Holder A. 201
Holiare 102, 106
Holubice, Moravia 101
Holzgerlingen 95, 162
Holzhausen 133
Honice 114
Horní Jatov-Trnovec on the Váh 86,
    101, 102, 111, 180
Hořovičky by Podbořany 58, 144, VIII
Hostomice by Bílina 109
Hostouň by Domažlice 58
Houbirg 130
Hradenín 31, 32, 35, 49, I, III
Hradiště above Závist 129—130,
    XXXVI, XXXVII, XXXIX
Hradiště by Písek 56, 93, IX, X, XIV
Hradiště by Stradonice 79, 93, 115,
    116, 124, 127—129, 134, 135, 136,
    137, 138, 139, 141, 142, 175, 178,
    XXXV

Hrazany by Sedlčany 130
Hrkovce 90
Hubert H. 19, 112, 160, 201
Hundersingen 36, 41, 43, 49, 76
Hügelsheim by Rastatt 44
Hunsburg 57
Hurbanovo 86, 102, 111

Ihringen 25
Illyrians 63, 65, 66, 196
Insubres 61, 63, 88
Iravisci 68, 142
Ireland 84, 98, 174—179, 190—195
Irsching 126, 138

Jacobsthal P. 56, 201
Jansová L. 201
Jarovce-Jahrendorf 140
Jegenstorf 54
Jenišův Újezd 78, 79, 102, 145
Jenny W. A. 201
Jestřebí by Česká Lípa 196
Jogasses 39, 49
Joffroy R. 24, 39, 201
Jullian C. 201
Jupiter 176, 184

Kaerlich 143
Kahrstedt 47
Kal, Kaledu 137
Karlstein near Reichenhall 110, 139
Kapell am Rhein 43, 44, 51
Kastenwalde near Colmar 54
Kbelnice by Strakonice 139
Kelheim 126, 130
Keller J. 201
Kells 194
Kendrick T. D. 201
Kenner H. 201
Kerethrios 65
Kilián 192
Kimmig W. 22, 37, 201
Kisköszeg 57
Klein Aspergle 36, 45, 46, 50, 53, 57, 145
Klein-Klein 51
Klindt-Jensen O. 172, 201
Klučov by Český Brod 103
Knorr R. 164, 201
Kobener Wald 165
Kobylnice Moravia 87
Kobyly by Turnov 196, 197
Koethe H. 201
Kopidlno 136
Korisios 81, 82, 105

Kossack G. 21, 32, 201
Kostomlaty by Nymburk 115
Košice XXVII
Köves F. 201
Kozlany, Moravia 104, XXXIII
Kraft G. 22
Kralovice by Plasy VII
Královice by Slaný 114
Krämer W. 32, 130
Křenovice, Moravia 76, 101
Kucharenko J. V. 201
Kunětická hora 119
Kuřímeny 109

Lacroix B. 202
Laet S. 202
Lahošť by Duchcov VIII
Lamboglia N. 22
Lambrechts P. 202
Langenheim 143
Lantier R. 20, 160, 202
La Tène 16, 57, 105, 133, 137, 149, 168, 172, 197
Latisco 38, 40
Lebhar on the Gabala 85
Lednice, Moravia 104, XXXI
Ledvice by Duchcov XXXII
Letky near Prague 101, 108
Lézoux 186
Lhotka by Litoměřice 32, 49
Lhotice by Nasavrky 131, 197
Libčeves by Bílina XXXIII
Lichtfield 194
Ligurians 154—159
Lindisfarne 194
Lingones 61, 75, 117, 134
Lismacroghera 153
Livy 47
Llyn Cerrig Bach 169, 174
Lot F. 202
Louis M. 22
Lovosice 32, 49, II
Lucan 161, 172, 175
Ludwigsburg 36
Lucotius 137
Luernos 96
Lug 175
Lugdunum-Lyon 76, 79, 95, 175, 179
Lysimachos 65

Maccius 141
Mac Ibar 168
Macpherson J. 15
Macrobius 176
Malaquer de Môtes 22, 202

Malpas 53
Manching 72, 106, 111, 117, 122, 124, 125, 127, 130, 134, 142
Mandach, Switz. 81
Mandubii 125, 188
Mannheim 57
Manopos 177
Mantoche 53
Marcomani 196
Marlborough 57, 153
Marobud 129, 196
Mars 173, 175, 177
Marzabotto 148
Massilia 38, 51, 52, 53, 54, 77, 78, 93, 95, 137M, 154, 155, 157
Mastramele 157
Matzhausen 147
Medimatrici 188
Medionemeton 168
Menapii 77
Melpum 61
Meyer P. 193, 202
Mercey 53, 56
Mercury 175, 176, 177 , 179, 184
Milanovce by Nitra 196
Minerva 177
Mithra 172
Modlešovice 115
Modřany near Prague 58
Mondragon 189, XIX
Montbouy, 158, 160
Montefortino 148
Mont Lassois 36, 38—39
Moravský Krumlov XXX
Moreau J. 202
Mousselots 41
Mšec 114
Mšecké Žehrovice 92, 114, 162, 167, XX
Müller-Karpe H. 202
Münsingen 89
Murphy G. 202
Mušov by Mikulov 195
Myjava 90

Narbo, Narbonne 78, 189
Navarro J. M. 22, 202
Nechanice 135, 136
Najdek, Moravia 104
Nejedlý Z. 202
Nemet 138
Nemeton 168
Nemetobriga 168
Nemilany 103
Nervii 77, 125, 137

Neuvy-en-Sullias 160, 164
Nevezice 131
Niederleiendorf 133
Nikomedes 65
Niros 137
Nitiobriges 96
Nižbor see Hradiště by Strakonice
Nonnos 140
Noricum, Noreia 61, 68, 74, 138, 195
Nová Huť by Pilsen VII
Nová Ves by Velvary 101
Noves 156, 157
Nové Strašecí 114
Noviodunum 66, 125
Noviomagus 134
Nový Bydžov 118
Numantia 78
Nyrax 61

Oberwiesenacker-Parlsberg 49
Ogmios 177
Ohnenheim 40, 44, 49
Ohrada by Kolín XXXI
Oliva P. 202
Ondrouch V. 202
O'Rahilly T. F. 202
Orange 159
Ordovices 79
Orosios 108
Oploty by Podbořany 55, 90
Osi 68
Osov 138
Ossian 15, 85
Otzenhausen 48, 123, 124

Panenský Týnec 147, VII
Pannonia 63, 68—72, 83, 177
Paret O. 42
Parsifal 195
Patrick 191
Paulsen R. 202
Pausanias 107
Pergamon, Asia Minor 117
Pernoud R. 202
Pfalzfeld 95, 160, 161
Pflugfelden 44
Philip II of Macedon 137
Píč J. L. 129, 202
Picts 190
Piggot S. 151, 202
Pink K. 202
Pipinsburg by Osterode 114
Pittioni R. 202
Plaňany 32, XXXII
Pleiner R. 202

Plešivec by Hořovice 123
Pliny 99, 109
Pluto 176
Pobé R. 202
Podbořany 115
Podmokly by Zbiroh 139
Pokorný J. 195, 202
Polybius 12, 63, 92, 105
Pompeius Trogus 63
Ponětovice 116
Port-Nidau 81, 169
Poseidonius 92, 93, 169
Pottina 137
Powell T. G. E. 23, 32, 168, 202
Prague-Podbaba XXX
Prague-Záběhlice XXVIII
Pretani 23
Prilly, Switzerland 165, XXI
Propertius 87
Přemyšlení XXXI
Ptolemy 65, 66
Pullach 44
Puig Castelar 157
Pyrrhus 65

Rajhrad XXX
Ralegh Radford 202
Ratiaria 66
Rauraci 74, 83
Raurica 184
Reca 140, 141
Regöly 149
Reinoch S. 159
Reinecke P. 20, 24, 28, 46, 170
Reinheim 50, 146
Remmsweiler 48
Rhaetians 72
Rheinzabern 186
Rhode 14, 77
Rice T. Talbot 202
Riek G. 202
Richardson K. M. 202
Rix H. 83, 202
Rodenbach 48, 145, 147
Röder J. 202
Römhild 32, 49, 126
Römerhügel 36, 44
Rolland H. 157
Roperz Er Marson 195
Roquepertuse 108, 154, 155
Rynkeby 92, 172

Saint-Benôit-sur-Loire 189
Saint-Blaise 157
Salzburg-Rainberg 64

Salyes 78, 95, 155
Sandars N. K. 202
Sarrebourg 184
Scarbantia-Sopron 195
Schiek S. 202
Schwarz K. 133
Schwarzenbach 48, 95, 144, 146
Scordistae 66, 74, 108, 170
Scotia Maior 194
Scots 190
Scythians 12, 25, 41, 49, 63, 151, 152
Sedlo by Sušice 120, XVI
Sefferweich 143
Seleukos 66
Sena Gallica 62
Senoni 61, 62, 76, 96
Sentinum 62
Sesto Calende 14
Sigmaringen 24
Sigoves 48
Silvanus 177
Simmering-Wien 141
Simmringen 41
Singidunum 66
Snettisham 151, 152
Soběsuky 109
Somme-Bionne 67
Spina, Italy 51
St Andrä by Etting 44
Staffelberg 126, 130, XXXIV
Stähelin F. 202
Staňkovice by Žatec XXXIII
Staré Hradisko by Okluky 115, 131, 135, 139, 142
Starý Bydžov 135
Steinsburg-Gleichberg 126, XXXIV
St Laurent-des-Bois 164
Stockach 140
Stonehenge 15
Strabo 65, 72, 87, 88, 95, 97, 108, 109, 169
Stradonice see Hradiště by Stradonice
Stradonice by Louny 104
Straškov 32
Stupava 141, 195
Sucellus and Nantosuelta 177, 178, 184
Sullivan E. 203
Szentes-Vekerzug 41, 49

Šárovce 113
Šimek E. 72, 203

Tábor 64

212

Tacitus 109, 172
Tajanov-Husín 26
Talian Dörögd 57
Tannheim 44
Taranis 175
Tarodunum-Zarten 83, 126
Tassilo 193
Taurisci 68, 74
Tectosages, see Volcae-Tectosages
Telamon 63, 105
Tennyson 195
Teutates 175
Theley 48
Thracians 25, 65, 66
Tinco 138
Titto 141
Tontioris 177
Torrs-Wandsworth 151
Toulouse-Tolosa 22, 65, 169
Trebeniště 40
Trenčín, Slovakia 196
Treveri 13, 76, 123, 137, 176, 188
Trishtingen 166, XXII
Trier 13, 188
Tristan and Isolda 195
Trnava 141
Třískolupy 109
Třísov 115, 131, 141
Tuchlovice 101, 115, 142

Uffing 49
Újezd u sv. Kříže 26
Ütliberg, Switzerland 36
Uttendorf, Austria 49

Vaněček V. 203
Varagnac E. 203
Vasio Vocontiorum 159
Vaucluse 51
Velká Maňa 102, 105, 180, XXIX,
   XXXI
Vendryes J. 203
Věnec-Pržmo 120
Veneti 22
Vercellae 75
Vercingetorix 78, 97, 123
Vernemeton 168

Vert-la-Gravelle 76
Vertault 184
Vetters H. 203
Vidassus and Tiana 177
Vienne 51, 184
Vikings 193
Villingen 44
Vindelici 72, 125, 138
Vindobona-Vienna 195
Vindonissa 185
Vix, France 39, 40, 42, 53, 56, XII,
   XIII
Vlkanovo-Bajč XXIX
Vocaran 137
Vocel J. E. 13
Volcae-Tectosages 66, 73, 139, 169
Vouga E. 203
Vulci 54
Vyklice 115

Wagner K. H. 122
Wagner R. 195
Waldalgesheim 50, 55, 95, 148, XIV
Waldgallshemd 143
Waldenbuch 162, 164
Wasserwald 110
Waterloo-Bridge (Thames) 150, 152
Weisskirchen 48, 146
Wellenburg 35
Weltenburg 130
Wessex 23
Wheeler W. 203
Windmill Hill 17
Winterlingen 44
Witham, Lincolnshire 76, 169
Wittnauer Horn 25
Wolfram from Eschenbach 194
Wyss R. 81, 203

Zábrdovice by Křinec 101
Zarten 83, 126
Zemplín 132
Zvíkov 132
Zwicker J. 203
Žatec XXXI
Želeč, Moravia 104

Cultural and Subject Index

Ager gallicus 62
Anthropoid swords 76, 103—104
Anthropology Celtic 86—87
Architecture 36, 153
Aristocracy 34, 97, 98, 99, 101—107, 183
Armed forces 60—63, 65, 66, 68, 70, 101—108
Art, Celtic 143—179, 188—195
Art, insular 150—153, 192—195

Bards, minstrels 93, 178, 194
Barrows, see Tumulus
Bastion 37, 38
Beer 93
Bell Beaker Folk 18—19
Battle Axe Folk 18—19
Beltine 179
Biatec see Coins
Boar 31, 64, 81, 92, 102, 105, 107, 111, 138, 160, 181
Book illumination 192—195
Bricks 37, 38
Bridle-bit, see Horse and harness-fittings
Brooches 31, 34, 38, 40, 43, 45, 52, 53, 88, 91, 116—127, 128, 147—148, 180, 198
Bull, sacrificial 99

Calendar Celtic 179
Chains, belt 89—90, 102, 104, 105
Chamber graves and chieftain burials 31—59, 102, 180—181
Canabae 185
Cantharos 50
Cashels 110
Chariots, four-wheeled 24, 30, 31, 33, 35, 40, 41, 44, 45, 48, 50, 52 two-wheeled 30, 40, 48, 67, 106
Cauldrons, cult 92, 170—172, 175, 198
Chieftain strongholds 35, 36—37

Christianity 190—194
Clientship 97, 98, 105
Clothing 34, 88—90
Coats of mail and helmets 51, 52, 105
Coffins 179—180
Coins, Celtic 105, 120, 126, 127, 134—142, 189
Corded Ware People 18
Crafts and trades 113—120, 152
Crannogs 110
Crater 40, 53
Cult of heads 108, 152, 155, 156

Dagger 34, 38, 76, 101
Diadem 39, 40, 41, 43
Dialect, Celtic 12, 13, 81—85
Dolmens 15
Drachma, see Coins
Dress, see Clothing
Druids 15, 82, 99, 100, 176, 178, 183

Enamel 89, 102, 104, 116, 127, 152—153, 160, 163, 171, 191
Enclosures, sacred 165—169
Equites 98, 99, 102, 107, 183, 185
Ethnogenesis of the Celts 23—27

Family and kin 93—95
Farming 110—113
Feasts 92—93
Fibulae, see Brooches
Field systems 112—113
Filed 100
Fine 93
Flagons 40, 45, 48, 51—52, 56—58, 146
Food 92—93
Frontlets 35, 58, 144, 145
Fundus 183

Gaulish language 82—84

Glass and glassmaking industry 89, 102, 117, 126, 188
Gods, see Religion
Gold 26, 36, 41, 42, 43, 44, 45, 48, 50, 53, 56, 68, 71, 113, 115, 136—142, 152
Graves, see Chamber graves
Groves, sacred 168—169

Hallstatt Period 28—59
Handicrafts Celtic 144—153
Heroes, see Religion
Horse and harness fittings 18, 21, 31—34, 35, 41, 42, 45, 47, 50, 107, 111, 134, 137
Horse yoke 31, 32, 33, 35
Horsemen, see Equites
House 109—110, 123—127, 132, 155
Hydria 52

Imbolc 179
Inscriptions 82, 83—84, 85, 99, 129, 140, 141
Iron 18, 25, 28, 30, 39, 51, 68, 71, 73, 113, 131
Iron bloomeries and forges 113—120
Iron smelting hearths 115

Kin, society 94
Kings 96—98
Kingship 96—96
Krater 40, 53
Kylix 40
Languages, Celtic 12, 82—84
Land ownership 93
La Tène style 144—148, 192—194
Law 94
Lead 29
Legion Roman 185—186, 195—196, XL
Limes Romanus 185—190, 195, 197
Lugnasad 179
Lužice (Lauzitz) culture 20—21
Lyre motif 144—146, 151, 161

Manor, Celtic, see House
Marriage 94
Mask 48, 58, 116, 145, 146, 147, 149, 163—164, 171, 173
Matres 176, 184
Matriarchy 94
Megalites 15, 19
Menhirs 15
Mercenaries, Celtic 66, 96, 135
Michelsberg cult 17

Mirror 5, 146, 153, 181
Murus gallicus 122, 123, 124

Nemeton 168

Oak, sacred 99, 168—169
Ogam script 84
Oppida 120—134, 141, 154—159, 184—185, 195—196
Ornament, Celtic 144—153

Palmette, 50, 56, 144—145, 151
Patriarchy 32, 94
Phalerae, see Frontlets
Pottery 117, 119, 132, 186, 197
Pottery, Black-Figure 38, 40, 48, 53, 54
        Red-Figure 48, 58
        Painted 31, 38, 119
Pottery kilns 118
Pottery workshops 111
Pyxis 54

Querns, rotary 111, 119, 183

Raths 110
Regenbogenschüsselchen 138, 139
Religion of the Celts 154—189
Romanization 79, 100, 159, 176, 182—192, 195—196
Romanticism 15, 195

Sacrifices 99, 169—172
Salt 29
Samain 179
Sanctuaries and temples 165—169, 188
Sapropelite 89, 93, 102
Sculpture, Celtic 153—174, 189
Shells, see Coins
Shield, Celtic 105
Silos 111
Slaves 58, 68, 98
Slings 106
Social differentiation and structure 31—59, 60, 86—108
Spears 34, 35, 38, 47, 105
Spirals 144—152
Stamnos 48
Swords 21, 24, 31, 33, 34, 35, 47, 76, 103—105, 117, 147, 149, 150, 152
Symbols, lunar 31, 99

Tarvos trigarnos 177
Technology, Celtic 113—120, 198
Terra sigillata 186, 191

Textiles 34, 41, 43, 88, 117
Torcs 50, 55, 90, 138, 146, 148, 152, 160, 163, 166—167
Towns, Roman 185—189, 195—196
Trade, long-distance 35, 114, 133——134
Trades, arts and crafts 113—120, 152
Transport 133—134
Trees, sacred 165—168
Trepanation 181
Tribes, Celtic 95—96, 141, 176
Trimarcisia 107
Tripod cauldron 41, 48, 56
Túath 95, 98

Tumulus 19, 23, 24, 26, 31—61, 103, 179—180

Únětice (Aunjetitz) Culture 19
Urnfields 20—23, 26, 84

Vates 99, 178
Viereckschanzen 32
Villa rustica 185
Village 109—110
Votive offerings 179—180

Wine 53, 56, 68, 77
Writing, see Inscriptions

The present state of studies in Celtic history and future prospects

Concluding remarks for the new edition of Celtic Civilization (1962).

The growing interest in the ancient history of the Celts and their influence on developments throughout Europe has been reflected in the world of scholarship; several international gatherings have been held on purely Celtic questions (Praha–Liblice international symposion 1970; the Fourth Congress of Celtic Studies, Rennes 1971; the Oxford Colloquium on Celtic Art, 1972; a conference in Székesfehérvár, 1974) and the results have been published with commendable speed (AR 23, Prague 1971; Études celtiques 13, Paris 1973; Celtic Art in Ancient Europe, London 1976). It is gratifying to see that interest in Celtic history, encouraged by such exhibitions as Early Celtic Art (the catalogue of this exhibition, edited by S. Piggott, appeared in 1971, Edinburgh and London), is also on the increase among the broader public, where there is a growing realization of the significant contribution of the Celts to the evolution of European civilization.

Much light has already been thrown⌐on⌐the difference between the eastern Hallstatt culture in a predominantly Illyrian environment, and the western Hallstatt culture which formed the basis from which Celtic culture grew. In some of the regions east of the Alps the traditional pastoral and agricultural way of life was augmented by the emergence of metalworking skills, ultimately that of iron-working, and this hastened the process of social differentiation so characteristic of the Hallstatt era, strengthening the position of the tribal aristocracy. This evolution can be traced in the great barrows of dozens of graves where rich "princely" burials can be found, complete with bronze armour, helmets, ornamented bronze vessels, belt ornaments and other objects. In the vicinity of these barrows we find fortified settlements; among the best-known Slovenian sites are Vače, Brezje, Magdalenska Gora, Stična-Sittich and the more recently excavated Novo Mesto. The social standing of the upper stratum is seen clearly in the bronze situlae, with their bands of figural ornament, human and animal, portraying scenes of everyday life as well as ceremonial occasions. This "Situlenkunst" became conservative both in form and iconography and preserved a canon of its own; it came from the Este region of Italy, moving northward to flourish from the middle of the sixth century B.C. to the fourth, when the local aristocracy was shaken by Celtic invasions and the subsequent disintegration of the socio-economic structure. There is a considerable increment of finds of ornamented situlae (new excavations of the Novo Mesto site, under *T. Knez*), supporting the hypothesis that many came from local workshops. The nature and evolution of this art has been illustrated by several European exhibitions and dealt with by *J. Kastelic* (Situlenkunst von Po bis zur Donau, Ausstellungskatalog, Wien 1962) and particularly by *J. D. H. Frey* (Die Entstehung der Situlenkunst, Berlin 1969).

In the western Hallstatt region the investigation of the Heuneburg site (pp. 36—38) has shown its importance later as well as during the early Hallstatt period (*W. Kimmig*, Heuneburg, Stuttgart 1968); the scholars concerned are preparing an assessment of the various types of finds (*H. W. Dämmer* Die bemalte Keramik; *P. Beck*, Die Wirtschaftsware); the fibulae have already been published (*G. Mansfeld*, Die Fibeln der Heuneburg 1950—1970, Berlin 1973). Revision of the results yielded by some of the great "princely barrows" has contributed further discoveries from burials in Villingen, which have been given a very personal interpretation by *K. Spindler* (Magdalenenburg, Fürstengrabhügel bei Villingen, 1, 1971).

As research proceeds, the emergence of the La Tène culture is being clarified from many angles. The typological-chronological method employed, which has already proved its worth, traces the main lines of development; the periods so distinguished are of course too simplified and too broad for the purposes of absolute chronology. Analysis of form and historical evolution as seen in the finds cannot suffice; valid conclusions to replace the hypotheses so far put forward can only be based on a complex study of all the components of the historical process, in all its aspects.

In the present state of our knowledge a clear distinction should be made between 1. the classical La Tène culture of the last centuries B.C., where the finds represent Celtic culture of a certain period only and by no means of all the Celts (e.g. it is not fully attested on the Iberian peninsula although the Celts were settled there at that time). While it represents the climax of Celtic civilization as we imagine it, it was preceded by a slow evolution both on the continent and the islands; 2. the specific features of Celtic culture in Central Europe, differing from that of Gaul or of Britain and Ireland; and 3. the Celtic La Tène culture in Europe with its marked influence on the cultures of other ethnic groups not only in the contact zones but also further afield.

The sum of the many indications for the mature Hallstatt period allows us to speak of a Celtic domain in the region stretching from north-east France, across southern Germany, to central and south-west Bohemia. The western regions of Austria and Bohemia appear to form an eastern zone of peripheral character not without significance, however, in the emergence of the new style. This is seen in the Dürrnberg finds (E. *Peninger*, Der Dürrnberg bei Hallein, I, Katalog der Grabfunde, 1972) and from the number and value of the Bohemian finds (mask fibulae, plus the unique fibula found on the Manětín–Hrádek site near Pilsen in 1967 (E. *Soudská*, AR 20, 1968), belt clasps, phalerae decorated with human masks, horse trappings and even direct Etruscan imports (*Pl. VII–XI*).

The La Tène style was born on the continent of Europe in the area we have just mapped out (Marne – Rhine – Vltava [Moldau]). This was not a case of two cultures existing side-by-side nor of the spontaneous transformation of the Hallstatt into the La Tène culture, but of a new style emerging within the existing Hallstatt culture, drawing strongly on elements and influences brought from the Mediterranean. These were arts and crafts originally developing in the service of the leading stratum of society and only later spreading to the broader population. The masterpieces of the Celtic goldsmith's art as we know them from the princely barrows of the central Rhine basin and some sites in Switzerland (the fourth century gold treasure from Erstfeld, in the Uri canton) could only be created where there were the right economic and social conditions. The flow of imports can already be seen in the sixth century, one trade route passing through Massalia and the other over the Alps from Italy; they reached their highest point in the fifth and the first half of the fourth century. We can only guess what the "upper class" could offer in return. Most scholars stress the importance of natural resources. J. *Driehaus* points out that the princely barrows and the wealthy centres have a definite geographical relationship to deposits of iron ore; *J. Pauli* (1972, 1974, Hamburger Beiträge II and Werner-Festschrift) stresses the systematic mining of salt as a source of economic prosperity not only for Hallstatt but for Dürrnberg, too, where production reached its peak in the late fifth and the fourth century. An increase in alluvial gold washing can also be observed in several places. The creative contribution of the nobles buried in the great barrows was only an indirect one; their rising standard of living made it possible for the craftsmen and their ateliers to develop their own artistic style (Formensprache) when dealing with their Mediterranean models. It cannot as yet be said with certainty whether the perfection of the new style, as seen in Jacobsthal's Waldalgesheimstyl, was the work of one or of several ateliers.

Analysis of the La Tène Early Style has shown that the early Celtic princely burials do not present a single style. According to *F. Schwappach* (Frühkeltisches Ornament zwischen Marne, Rhein und Moldau, Bonner Jahrbücher 173/1973) geometric ornament played a greater part in the eastern parts of the region and plant motifs a greater part in the west. The craftsmen who made the gold and bronze jewelry for their courtly patrons were undoubtedly acquainted with Mediterranean models when they created their own system of ornament out of the palmettes, lotus blooms and similar motifs. Pottery and the ornament used for ceramics was always more or less local in character, although outside influences were always being assimilated. British La Tène decorated pottery, for instance soon bore relationship to Armorican pottery (*M. Avery*, Études celtiques 13/1973). The mature style (Waldalgesheim, *Pl. XIV*) is not merely the continuation of the early style, and contact with the Mediterranean was maintained even later, during the Celtic migrations. The crafts were maturing at courts in the Rhine and Moselle basins when armed Celtic bands were penetrating deep into Italy as well as into Central Europe and the Carpathian plains (*J. Filip*, Le problème de la double origine des Celts en Europe centrale, Études celtiques 13/1973). These new arrivals were not acquainted with the ritual pomp of the princely burials, as still practised in the central Rhine basin in the fourth century. They formed the wide-spread Central European domain under military rule preserved for archaeology in the "flat" cemeteries (Flachgräberfelder, *fig. 16*). The mobility of these armed bands meant that their burial grounds were widely scattered, making synchronization difficult today. Large burial grounds gradually formed where there was a greater concentration of population for any length of time; the largest yet found have from 100 to 250 graves (Münsingen-Rain in Switzerland, Jenišův Újezd in Bohemia, Maňa in Slovakia, etc.). The material culture of the new Celtic arrivals in Central Europe has some parallels in the south-west, as in Switzerland and southern Germany, for example, but it is no longer a courtly art; the bronze and iron work is more mass-produced in character. In the newly conquered regions local workshops arose, each with its own area of distribution, and their work shows local characteristics alongside general Celtic features. The classical La Tène culture as we see it in the flat burial grounds assimilated some elements of the Waldalgesheim style, but made them more rustical, more suitable for mass production. As a style it has its own dynamism and is alive to new impulses, never becoming set. Precise synchronization and absolute chronology are rendered more difficult not only by the mobility of the populations but also by the numerous variations on the basic types of article from the different workshops, the fibulae, ornamented scabbards, etc. The fact that the same articles from workshops far apart are very similar is not always a guarantee that they are contemporary.

Recently a number of scholars have paid careful attention to an analysis of Celtic art, its general character and individual motifs (*W. Dehn, J. Driehaus, P. M. Duval, O. H. Frey, E. M. Jope, J. M. de Navarro, U. Osterhaus, S. Piggott, N. K. Sandars, F. Schwappach, E. Soudská, M. Szabó* and others; see also Marburger Beiträge zur Archäologie der Kelten, Bonn 1969, (Dehn-Festschrift). In his survey Art of the European Iron Age, A study of the illusive image (1970), *J. V. S. Megaw* published reproductions of most of the Celtic art of the Continent and the British Isles, and gave his own explanation of its evolution. An outline of this evolution was also given by *J. Filip* (Propyläen Kunstgeschichte, Band 13, 1974 – Frühe Stufen der Kunst). *V. Krůta* who had already published an analysis of the famous Duchcov find (Le trésor de Duchcov dans les collections tchécoslovaques, Ústí n. L. 1971) as a collection of work from a few highly specialized workshops and a small number of craftsmen, then concentrated on the ornament on metal objects from Bohemia in the 5th to 2nd centuries (L'art celtique en Bohème, Paris 1975). He brought up to date the corpus of finds published by *J. Filip* in 1956 (Die Kelten in Mitteleuropa) and distinguished not only the early style (le premier style) but also a transitional style and the first and second phases of the plastic style, giving a detailed description.

Absolute chronology presents a difficult problem, since there are few reliable criteria available. Confusion arises when the chronological systems in use for the French and Swiss regions, based on local tradition (J. Wiedmer-Stern, D. Viollier, J. Déchelette) are compared with those based on the original classification by the German scholar P. Reinecke. There is also a need for more precise analysis of the chronological relations between continental and insular art and the tracing of La Tène culture as it penetrated the British Isles from the Continent in several streams. D. Bretz-Mahler has reassessed the finds and conclusions made concerning the Marne culture in Champagne, which was originally placed very high in studies of the earliest phases of La Tène culture (La Civilisation de La Tène I en Champagne, Le facies marnien, Paris 1971). The Late Hallstatt (Jogassian) phase was followed there by skeleton burials, which the author believes reflects the arrival of another people with certain connections with the Rhine.

The most recent survey of our present state of knowledge for the determination of the chronology of the La Tène period on the Continent is that by R. Joffroy (Études celtiques 13/1973). Since few larger burial grounds have been investigated in recent years, the material on which new studies of the relative chronology have been based is taken from large burial grounds already well-known. One remarkable study is that of F. R. Hodson (The La Tène cemetery at Münsingen-Rain, Catalogue and relative chronology, Bern 1968), who has made a typological analysis and revision of the horizontal stratigraphy of the Swiss burial ground at Münsingen, originally published at the beginning of this century by Wiedmer-Stern (c. 220 graves). The general validity of Hodson's conclusions must of course be tested by confrontation with a similar analysis of large burial grounds elsewhere. In Central Europe a reliable foundation for such an approach is being laid by the gradual publication of the whole Jenišův Újezd burial ground together with finds from other sites in north-west Bohemia (P. Budinský, 1968, 1970; M. Zápotocký, AR 1973) and the results of recent research in Slovakia (B. Benadík). Under the influence of Hodson the archaeologists working in Moravia (M. Čižmář, K. Ludikovský, J. Meduna, J. Waldhauser) and publishing mainly in AR and PA, are concentrating on the more precise assessment of the earliest and the latest strata of the Celtic flat burial grounds. This provides material which can be systematically processed by mathematical methods, which help modern archaeology to understand the internal relationships between groups of material and to justify an historical interpretation.

The geographical distribution of the flat burial grounds, which correspond in the main with the limits of Celtic expansion attested in the written sources, shows the Celts in possession of the most fertile regions of present-day Czechoslovakia and Austria, and spreading into Polish Silesia and over the Carpathians into the Balkan peninsula (fig. 16). The burial grounds begin in the fourth century. As early as the Duchcov fibula stratum local workshops were already functioning in the newly-conquered lands, and the burial furniture is of the classic La Tène style, with the gradual addition of objects in the plastic style and the "beautiful scabbard" style. This culture began to acquire local features in the different regions. A new analysis of Hungarian finds (M. Szabó, Études celtiques 13/1973; see also the book Auf den Spuren der Kelten in Ungarn, Budapest 1971) attempts to define the regional features found in the Carpathian region and the influences from without, including elements of Illyrian and steppe (Scythian) cultures, all combining to produce the heterogeneous character of the culture of the "eastern" Celts. Imports or at least influences from the Greek-Hellenistic sphere also reached Moravia and Slovenia (Novo Mesto) over the Carpathians, e.g. kantharoi, pseudokantharoi, specific amphora-like forms and other types of pottery.

For at least three centuries these Celts dominated considerable areas of Europe. When they were gradually repulsed from their temporary domains on the Balkan peninsula and in Italy, they withdrew not only to Gaul but also into Central Europe, where settlement became much denser. In the third and second centuries B.C. the evolution of this Central European culture reached its climax; Celtic products were exported to the north and north-east of their Central European home, and found their imitators. This brought into being mature and late La Tène cultural groups whose complex archaeological structure makes ethnical distinctions very difficult. Some Germanic groups on the northern boundaries were particularly strongly influenced by Celtic traditions in their material culture.

Excavations have shown that in addition to the great burial grounds there were smaller cemeteries used only for shorter periods, probably because of the unsettled nature of the Celtic groups. The original predominance of earth burial later gave way to cremation burials, and cremation pits in which urns were not used (Brandschüttungsgräber) and where the funeral furniture was not rich, became a striking feature of the burial grounds. The whole of the Giengen (Württemberg) cemetery consisted only of 13 "Brandschüttungsgräber", while a small settlement close by had also been deserted early on (J. Biel, Arch. Korrespondenzblatt 4/1974).

The south German burial grounds so far examined usually consist only of a few graves, and their interpretation varies (H. Polenz, Brandgräber aus Dientzenbach, 1971). It is essential to increase the corpus of Celtic finds by systematic excavation both on the Continent and in the British Isles, for most of the earlier excavations were in the nature of rescue-work and the documentation of the finds is not complete. Of the 335 sites in Switzerland only about 2,600 burials can be dealt with in detail, almost half of them being south of the Alps (Tessin canton). In the region stretching from Bohemia to the Carpathian plain, including the Silesian-Polish area, about 1,000 flat burial grounds are known, but in some of these only an occasional burial has been preserved.

In Central Europe the use of flat burial grounds by the Celts gradually died out round the turn of the second to first century B.C. It would seem to have been typical of the Celts proper in the Central European domain. So far no burial grounds have been found in relation to the oppida; whether this reflects a profound religious and cult transformation connected with the general change in the Celtic social structure, or whether it was the outcome of the historical situation which hastened the phase of strongly fortified oppida, we cannot as yet determine with any certainty. Nor can we be sure that in this new situation cremation burial grounds without special furniture were not enclosed within the oppidum. This situation is characteristic for those Celtic groups on the Continent which did not submit to Romanization; in Gaul, the British Isles, and in mixed groups on the periphery of the Celtic oecumenium burial went on as before. This is attested by such cremation burial grounds as those of Podmokly–Bodenbach and Kobyly in north-west and north Bohemia. In the Celto-Przeworsk culture of Malopolsko, known mainly from settlements, burials seem to be much rarer than in the Przeworsk culture itself (Z. Woźniak, Celtic Settlements in Poland, in Polish with abstract, 1970). In Rumania, where there were relatively a large number of Celtic burial grounds particularly in Transylvania (Apahida is one of the great cremation burial grounds; see V. Zirra and

J. H. Crişan, AR 23/1971 and other references, and *Z. Woźniak*, Les confins orientaux de la civilisation de la Tène, in Polish with abstract, 1974), we find some Dacian features in the burials. Celtic culture influenced production throughout Dacian society, but as early as the second century the influence of the Celts was on the wane until in the last century B.C. they no longer formed an independent political force. The remnants of the Celts were lost in Dacian society and the Dacian ruler Burebista extended his power over the Carpathian plain. *Z. Woźniak* (1974) has published a survey of Bulgarian sites where cremation burial grounds of the Panagjurski Kolonii type (Pazardjik), with late finds, occupy a special position, in the Thracian context. The Celtic influence reached as far as the Ukraine and to the Black Sea, and can be seen, for instance, in the adoption of fibulae of mid to late La Tène design.

The situation was different in the Danube–Belgrade region, where the finds are attributed to the Scordisci (p. 66). Research in this area has been making good progress and large burial grounds have been found especially in the region of Belgrade (Singidunum; Karaburma, Rospi Ćuprija and others). According to *J. Todorović* (Kelti u Jugoistočnoj Europi – Kelten in Südosteuropa, Beograd 1968; Scordisci, History and Culture, 1974) the Celts did not come to this region in any great numbers until the third century, when they were withdrawing from the south-east into the Danube basin. Their culture was on general Celtic-La Tène lines, but with local variations and many non-Celtic elements. Basically this was a mixed region where the La Tène culture predominated as the outcome of a symbiosis of many elements, some autochthonic (Illyrian and Gaeto-Dacian), some from the south-east from the Graeco--Hellenist sphere. It is not impossible that this symbiosis is evidence of the emergence of a new ethnic group which took its main cultural features from the Celtic-La Tène tradition. The rich burial grounds on the southern slopes of the Alps (Tessin) and round the north Italian lakes have been known since *J. R. Ulrich* published his Die Gräberfelder in der Umgebung von Bellinzona (1914). A new analysis of the finds from these sites was used to work out a more precise chronology and check the chronological position of the different types of finds. The results have appeared in the work of *W. Stöckli* (Arch. Korrespondenzblatt 3/1973) and *J. Graue* (Die Gräberfelder von Ornavasso, Hamburg 1974). Burials were still performed here in the late La Tène and early Roman times, and the point d'appui for chronological classification of the distribution of certain types of fibula is provided by grave furniture including coins from Gaul or Rome, and imported bronze vessels (see also the article on the La Tène period by R. Wyss, Archäologie der Schweiz, Bd. IV, Eisenzeit, 1974).

English and Irish scholars have devoted many articles and books to the question of the Celts in the islands. We should briefly mention at least a few of the comprehensive studies and those accounts of prehistory which deal at least in outline with Celtic culture, and refer to further literature: Nora Chadwick, The Celts (Penguin Books 1970); Barry Cunliffe, Iron Age Communities in Britain (1974); Myles Dillon (ed.), Early Irish Society (1969); M. Dillon and N. Chadwick, The Celts' Realms (1967); I. Finlay, Celtic Art, an introduction (Noyes Press 1973); D. W. Harding, The Iron Age in Lowland Britain (1974); P. MacCana, Celtic Mythology (Hamlyn 1973); R. McNally Old Ireland (1965); D. Norton-Taylor, The Celts (New York, Time-Life Books, 1974); S. Piggott, Ancient Europe (1965); T. G. Powell, Prehistoric Art (1966); Joseph Raftery (ed.), The Celts (Mercier Press, 1967); N. K. Sanders, Prehistoric Art in Europe (Penguin Books, 1968); Anne Ross, Pagan Celtic Britain (1970).

Celtic settlements may be hamlets with a number of dwelling houses, farms which were independent economic units, or fortified centres which became very important, besides the Hallstatt-La Tène period, in the late La Tène period, the time of the Celtic oppida. The famous La Tène site by the greatest of the Swiss lakes, Neuchâtel, which gave its name to the whole era, has been variously regarded by archaeologists in the past (a battlefield, a military station, a customs post, a ritual place with sacrificial depots, and so on; the latest suggestion, from K. Raddatz, is that it was a place of sacrifice). Over 2,500 articles have been found there (weapons, at least 166 swords, spearheads, the remains of wooden shields, and also objects of a settlement nature). Similar finds were made at Port (Nidau) where the River Zihl flows out of the Bielersee (p. 169). The English expert on the La Tène culture, J. M. de Navarro, is preparing a new assessment of the finds (The Finds from the Site of La Tène, I, Scabbards and Swords, London 1972); the coins have been dealt with by D. F. Allen (The coins found at La Tène, Études celtiques 13/1973). The Swiss archaeologist H. Schwaab, working in Cornaux, only three kilometres from La Tène, discovered among other finds the remains of a wooden bridge which dendrological analysis shows to have been built about 143 B.C. This led Mme. Schwaab to reconsider the whole area of La Tène; she came to the conclusion (Germania 1974) that in the last two centuries B.C. there was a large settlement lying on both banks of the Zihl, comprising dwelling houses, workshops and warehouses so placed that goods could be loaded directly on to fairly large boats directly from the banks (which is where most of the finds were made). This settlement was destroyed by catastrophic flooding (the earlier level of the water was much lower). It should not be forgotten that a remarkable number of swords with stamped hallmarks have been found in Switzerland (Port, Basadingen, Mandach, Wangen etc.; cf. p. 81, *fig. 19*). Celtic production was at its height in the second century B.C. and seems to have been centred in places which were not fortified oppida. Articles which could be called devotional have not been found in the sites. Otherwise of course there are sacrificial and ritual sites both on the Continent and in the British Isles, as is typical of Celtic culture. Important settlement finds from the late La Tène period in France were published by *G. Chapotat* (Vienne gauloise, Le matériel de La Tène III trouvé sur la colline de Sainte–Blandine, Lyon 1970).

The evolution of independent Celtic power on the Continent and particularly in Central Europe, comes to a close with the period of the Celtic oppida in the last century B.C. (cf. pp. 120—133). The oppida did not fulfil the same function everywhere, and their duration varied according to local conditions. A survey of the present state of research into the oppida was presented at the international symposion "Die Kelten und keltische Oppida in Mitteleuropa und im Karpatenbecken" (Praha–Liblice 1970; results in AR 23/1971). The development of the oppida in Gaul was brought to an end by Caesar's victorious Gallic War, which facilitated Romanization. Systematic investigation of the oppida in France remains for the future, nor is the question of fortified centres clear in Belgium. Interest has been centred mainly on four sites: Hastedon in the province of Namur, Kesselberg (Brabant), Montauban–Buzenol (Luxembourg) and Kemmelberg (West Flanders) which is at present being excavated by *A. Van Doorselaer*. These are all smaller fortified sites and research to date does not suggest that they were of particular significance in the Late La Tène period. In contrast, many of the oppida in south Germany cover an area of 120—250 hectares (Altenburg–Rheinau near Schaffhausen, Tarodunum, Heidengraben near Grabenstetten in the Swabian Albs, where the inner area covers 153 hectares and the outer boundary encloses over 1,660 hectares, Finsterlohr, Donnersberg in Rheinland–Pfalz). Some of these sites were used as places of refuge in time of need. The only oppidum to have been systematically excavated is that at Manching near Ingolstadt (Bavaria); thanks to W. *Krämer* the rich material has already been written up and published in a series of monographs: Ausgrabungen in Manching, of which six volumes have already appeared: 1/1970, *Krämer-Schubert*, Die Ausgrabungen 1955—61; 2/1969, *I. Kappel*, Die Graphitonkeramik; 3/1970, *F. Maier*, Die bemalte Keramik; 4/1971, *V. Pingel*, Die glatte Drehscheibenkeramik; 5/1972, *G. Jacobi*, Werkzeug und Gerät; 6/1971, *J. Boessneck*, Die Tierknochenfunde. Most of the south German oppida lost their importance in the last decades of the century, perhaps around the year 15 B.C. To date it is only in Czechoslovakia that planned research into the Celtic oppida is being conducted; four are being studied in Bohemia (Závist, Třísov, Hrazany and Lhotice) and two in Moravia (Staré Hradisko, Hostýn). The information so far suggests that they all date from the last century B.C. with the possibility in some cases that they were founded at the end of the previous century. Not a single oppidum has been found, as yet, in the continuous domain of Celtic flat burial-grounds in north-west and central Bohemia, where settlement was very dense. Most are to be found in the southern half of Bohemia, to the south of Prague, mainly near the Vltava: Závist near Zbraslav, Stradonice near Beroun, Hrazany near Sedlčany, Nevězice, Třísov near Český Krumlov. The only oppidum in east Bohemia, Lhotice near Nasavrky, does not lie within the area of the flat burial grounds. This is in complete contrast to the Bavarian oppidum at Manching, where two flat burial grounds have been found dating from the time before the oppidum (Steinbichl which originally had at least 150 graves, and Hunsrucken). The distribution of the Bohemian oppida shows quite clearly that in the last century B.C. Celtic power was centred in the southern part of the country.

As a rule the oppida are found where there was a high density of population, well-developed production and changes in the socio-economic structure, and from this point of view they are sometimes compared to urban forms. This is not generally valid. So far only one Bohemian oppidum, that of Stradonice with an area of about 82 hectares, can be considered a production centre of any significance comparable with that of Bibracte (Mont Beuvray) in Gaul, regarded as the chief centre of the Aedui. The finds from both these sites are so similar that *J. Déchelette*, half a century ago, already assumed direct contact between them. The finds from Stradonice, however, come from private collections and the necessary documentation is lacking; no systematic research has been carried out there. The oppidum at Závist south of Prague has a special position; with its extensive fortifications it is one of the largest in Central Europe. Its excellent strategic position gave it importance long before the period of the oppida. Research conducted by *L. Jansová* revealed strong fortifications dating as far back as the Late Bronze Age (Knovíz culture), and others from the Late Hallstatt age and the period of late La Tène; coins of the latter period were also found. Further research is needed to determine whether Závist was of particular importance as a permanent ritual centre; a stone human head from the acropolis cannot be exactly dated. Finds of certain types of fibula are usually taken as criteria for dating the Central European oppida; this is not reliable for the absolute chronology of the stormy events of the last century B.C., for the Nauheim–Fibel and the Löffelfibel, for example, were in use for a very long time. Variations of these forms found in European oppida cannot always be regarded as proof of Celtic settlement. Certain Late La Tène types of fibula (known as J. and K. variants, after *Beltz* and *J. Kostrzewski*) are more probably evidence of Germanic penetration to the south, and it is therefore questionable whether the presence of a few Late La Tène fibulae of this type suffices to classify the Kleine Gleichberg–Steinsburg bei Römhild as a Late La Tène Celtic oppidum (*G. Neumann*, Die Fibeln vom Kleinen Gleichberge, Berlin 1973).

The Celtic oppida in Bohemia grew up in a specific historical situation, in which Stradonice and Závist played a special role. It is not possible, however, to regard all Bohemian oppida without exception as the consequence of a sudden growth in productive capacity. It is more likely that they were refuges of the Celtic people in bad times. From the third century onwards the pressures on the original Celtic domain in northwest and central Bohemia were constantly increasing. In the valley of the Elbe and surrounding regions cremation burial grounds of the Podmokly type (Bodenbach–Gruppe) are found, followed by the Kobyly type (near Turnov) which was used in the last century B.C. Analysis of the finds from both these types does not allow a single ethnic classification; from the archaeological point of view they are mixed groups with some general Celtic-La Tène types, but showing also some distinctly non-Celtic types such as are found in the more northerly Germanic regions. The Kobyly group is contemporary with the Bohemian oppida and ends towards the end of the last century B.C. It would appear that the clash between the German Cimbri and the Celtic Boii somewhere on the western borders of Bohemia about the year 113 B.C. was not only the result of pressure but had unfavourable consequences for the whole of the Celtic domain which have not been fully appreciated as yet. The area of central Bohemia settled by the Celts was already narrowing from the north-west in the second century B.C.; later, German elements can be seen penetrating the settlements in the foothills of the Ore Mountains, and in the last century B.C. new settlements finds occur on the area of the original flat burial grounds (Jenišův Újezd). At the turn of the century or in the first half of the last century B.C. some of the Boii moved eastwards into Pannonia and south-west Slovakia, where the Dacian king Burebista overthrew the power of the Boii in the middle of the century. Other groups of central Bohemian Celts (Boii) seem to have withdrawn to southern Bohemia in the course of the last century B.C., to take shelter in the oppida.

All the oppida so far investigated in Bohemia were strongly fortified and the fortifications rebuilt at least twice during the last century B.C. (Závist: L. Jansová, Vorberichte in AR 20/1968 ff. and in PA; Hrazany: L. Jansová, Hrazany, Praha 1965; Třísov: J. Břeň, Třísov, 1966, also in an English edition; Lhotice: M. Princ, AR 27/1975). The situation became critical before the middle of the last century B.C., and not only in local terms. This was the time when Boiic power in Pannonia was on the decline, when some of the Boii were looking for new places to settle, when the Helvetii were on the move and when Germanic groups under Ariovist were trying to cross the Rhine while some Belgic tribes were completing their migration across the Channel into Britain. Large hoards of gold coins were hidden in the ground in the regions under Celtic rule, around the Manching oppidum (Irsching, Gagers) as well as in Bohemia (Stradonice, two hoards; Podmokly near Hořovice, several thousand gold coins in a bronze vessel; over 300 coins in a recently found hoard in Starý Kolín, etc.). At this time, according to L. Jansová, evidence of coin minting at Závist comes to an end, and the settlement of the oppidum became less dense (PA 65/1974). During the first half of the last century B.C. it can be assumed that things were quieter and trading contact with far-away oppida in Gaul and the Roman regions was not interrupted. Around the middle of the century the prosperity of the oppida was declining and it was difficult to maintain contacts with the south. In the second half of the century the Bohemian oppida served as refuges during the withdrawal of the Celts and bear witness to their historic tragedy, as their power in Central Europe fell to pieces. The remnants of the Celts still held out in the oppida in the second half of the century; during this time the fortifications round the main gate in Závist were repaired twice, preparations were made to block the entrances to the oppida, and finds of human bones bear witness to fighting. Most of the Bohemia oppida seem to have fallen during the fighting when Germanic tribes overran the country under Marobud (Marbod) a few years before the end of the century. According to J. Břeň the oppidum of Třísov was deserted in peaceful conditions.

The distribution of the oppida in Moravia was somewhat different. The more important oppida (Staré Hradisko: J. Meduna, Germania 48/1970; Hostýn: K. Ludikovský, AR 23/1971) lie in the northern belt of flat burial grounds and thus protected the area settled by the Celts; the Germanic pressure seems to have been felt later here. Recent research has not confirmed the existence of an oppidum in Cerekwia–Bieskau (Silesia). The question of Celtic oppida in Slovakia has not yet been clarified. The oppidum in the present-day capital of Bratislava seems to have destroyed by later building on the site; the high-ground settlement of Liptovská Mara belongs to the Púchov culture, which was influenced by La Tène, while the fortified settlement of Zemplín in east Slovakia comes into the sphere of Dacian culture (B. Benadík, Germania 1965 and AR 23/1971). The late La Tène settlement of Gellerthegy–Taban in Budapest, published in 1969 by E. B. Bónis, is often considered in the context of the Eravisci, whose ethnic classification is variously determined (Celts? Celticized Illyrians?). The last century B.C. is also the date assigned to Viereckschanzen, "small square sites with a low earth rampart" which some scholars believe were ritual sites. K. Schwarz has published an atlas of these sites (1960) which are mainly known from France and southern Germany. They are now also attested for Bohemia (AR 20/1968, 22/1970, 23/1971). Apart from Mšecké Žehrovice (AR 20/1968) where a Celtic statuette was found, and some of the sites in eastern Bohemia, the Viereckschanzen are also situated mostly in southern Bohemia. Celtic ritual sites are known from various parts of the country (J. Filip, Keltische Heiligtümer und Kultplätze, in: Vorgeschichtliche Heiligtümer und Opferplätze, Göttingen 1970). Details of a ritual site in Libenice have been published (Rybová–Soudský, Libenice, Sanctuaire celtique, Praha 1962) and an attempt at reconstruction made; a stone stele and the grave of a woman were found here.

The important role of the Druids in Celtic society (p. 99) is dealt with by S. *Piggott* (The Druids, London 1968), giving a critical assessment of the written sources and the archaeological material from the time of the Megalithic sites onwards and providing an exhaustive bibliography of sources and literature. The same subject is dealt with by *N. Chadwick* (The Druids, 1966). The power of the Druids seems to have been declining in the last century B.C., at least on the Continent.

Celtic numismatics (pp. 134—142) rely on the foundations laid by earlier generations of scholars (*A. Blanchet, R. Forrer, R. Paulsen, K. Pink*), whose works are republished with the addition of later material. The present trend is not only to explain the historical context and revise the classification of different types of minted coins and their connections with known Celtic tribes, but to deal with methodology and draw up systematic lists and catalogues of all finds. In this connection the work of *W. O'Sullivan* (early Irish coins), *D. F. Allen* (early British coins and studies in Continental numismatics) should be mentioned, as well as *J. B. Colbert de Beaulieu's* survey (Études Celtiques 13/1973), *S. Scheers, K. Castelin* (Die Goldprägungen der Kelten in den Böhmischen Ländern, Graz 1965), *H. J. Kellner J. Winkler, M. König* and others.

The fall of the oppida did not of course mean that no Celts were left in Central Europe. Remnants survived both in Bohemia, where their heritage can be traced in archaeological remains, and in the Carpathian plain where written sources still refer to them in Roman times (Civitas Boiorum). The fate of the Celts after their power was broken in Central Europe was varied. In western Europe, the France of today, the Gallo-Roman period meant the gradual Romanization of the Celts while in some parts of the British Isles conditions were favourable to continued development even after the coming of the Christian era, and strong traditions were created which still influenced later centuries.

Some printer's errors in the original text of this book should be corrected (Piggott for Piggot in the Index of Names, p. 210 Hohmicele for Hachmichele etc.). Abbreviations: AR – Archeologické rozhledy, Praha; PA – Památky archeologické. For other abbreviations and details of sites and authors quoted see *J. Filip.* Enzyklopädisches Handbuch zur Ur- und Frühgeschichte Europas, Prag (Academia Verlag), Band I, 1966 (A—K), II 1969 (L—Z) and III (in preparation) bringing results up to date, probable date of publication 1977—78. The information given in this chapter is not noted in the Index, pp. 206—215.

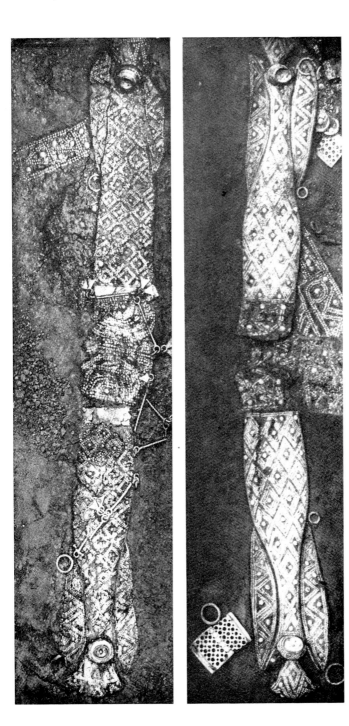

I. Splendid horse yokes from princely graves in Hradenín, near Kolín, Central Bohemia (burials on four-wheeled chariots). Grave No 46 (lgth of yoke: 124 cm) and Grave No 24 (lgth. of yoke: 126 cm). Museum Kolín.

II. Lovosice, Bohemia. Horse yoke from a Bylany Culture grave (Grave No III), discovered in 1956 (excavated by R. Pleiner and V. Moucha). General view and details of the yoke ornament.

III. Hradenín near Kolín, Bohemia. Chamber grave, No 28, with male burial on four-wheeled chariot.

IIIa. Heuneburg, not far from Sigmaringen, on the Upper Danube, in Württemberg. View from the east of the site of an Early Hallstatt stronghold (6 B.C.). Photograph: State Office for the Care of Monuments, Tübingen.

IV. Hirschlanden near Leonberg, Württemberg. Statue of a warrior, sandstone, height as preserved 150 cm. Found at the edge of a barrow in 1962. Late Hallstatt period, c. 500 B.C. Württembergisches Landesmuseum Stuttgart.

V. Grächwil–Meikirch (Canton Bern), Switzerland. Bronze vase (hydria) from a barrow with cremation burial and chariot. 6. B.C. Historical Museum Bern.

VI. Grächwil–Meikirch (Canton Bern), Switzerland. Bronze vase (hydria). 6.B.C. Detail. Decorative handle in the form of a winged goddess, with symmetrical arrangement of two pairs of lions, and other animal and bird symbols. Historical Museum Bern.

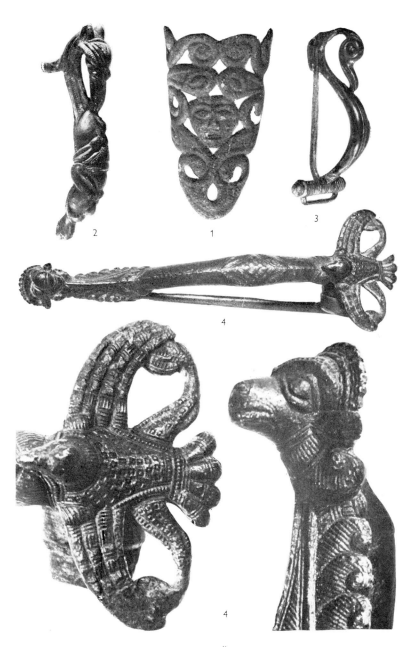

VII. Finds from the La Tène period in Bohemia: 1. Čížkovice near Lovosice. Bronze reliefwork, with mask motif from an inhumation burial (lgth.: 63 mm). Museum Třebenice. – 2. Nová Huť (Plzeň). Bronze brooch. – 3. Kralovice (Plasy). Bronze brooch (lgth.: 6,15 cm). – 4. Panenský Týnec (Louny district). Bronze mask-type brooch (lgth.: 8,1 cm). National Museum Prague.

VIII. 1. Lahošť near Duchcov, Bohemia. Bronze finger-ring (inner diameter 22 mm). Museum Ústí n. L. – Trmice. – 2. Chýnov near Prague. Bronze mask-type brooch, lgth.: 5 cm. National Museum Prague. – 3. Hořovičky near Podbořany. Horse phalera with mask décor. Bronze plate on an iron core. Diameter 12 cm. National Museum Prague.

IX. Hradiště near Písek, South Bohemia. 1. Bronze beaked jug of Etruscan provenance (with detail of the spout). Hgt. 23 cm. National Museum Prague. 2. Chlum near Zbiroh. Bronze beaked jug, 30 cm. National Museum Prague.

X. Hradiště near Písek. Bronze beaked flagon of Etruscan provenance. Cast lower attache, in the form of a four-winged siren, with human arms and the lower half ending in a bird's tail. See Pl.IX.

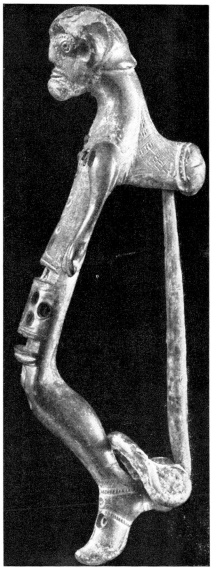

XI. Manětín – Hrádek, S. W. Bohemia. A mask fibula shaped like a human figure, originally inlaid with coral or amber. Bronze, c. 88 mm long. Second half of the fifth century B.C. Excavation by the Archaeological Institute of the Czechoslovak Academy, Prague.

XII. Vix, France. Bronze vase (krater). Greek work from about 500 B.C. From the grave of a princess with gold diadem. Detail of the decorated throat of the vase. See also fig. 8. Musée de Châtillon-sur-Seine.

XIII. Vix, France. Grave of a Celtic princess, with gold diadem. Bronze statuette decorating the lid of the bronze vase (krater), see fig. 8 and Pl. XII. Musée de Châtillon-sur-Seine.

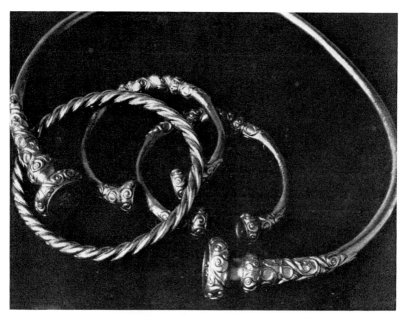

XIV. Waldalgesheim near Bingen in the Rhinelands. Gold torcs and bracelets from the princely barrow. 4th cent. – Hradiště near Písek, Bohemia. Bronze beaked flagon, detail of throat décor.

XV. Klein Aspergle near Ludwigsburg, Württemberg. Bronze vessels from a princely burial

XVI. Sedlo near Sušice in South Bohemia. Hill-fort from the Hallstatt-La Tène period.

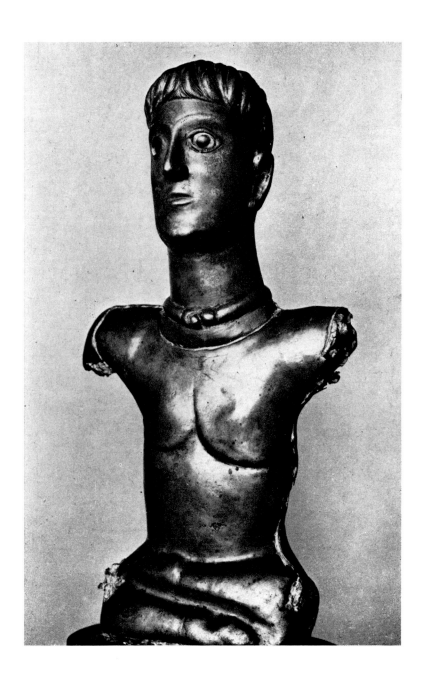

XVII. Bouray (Seine-et-Oise),France. Statuette of a god with deer's legs and Celtic torque. The left eye
is inlaid with enamel. Bronze plate. Hgt. of statuette: 45 cm. Museum Saint-Germain-en-Laye.

XVIII. Euffigneix (Haute-Marne), France. Statuette of a god, with torc and boar symbol. Quartz, hgt. : 26 cm. Museum Saint-Germain-en-Laye.

XIX. Gaulish soldier with shield. Mondragon (Vaucluse), France. Work from the Augustan Era. Musée Calvet, Avignon.

XX. Mšecké Žehrovice (Nové Strašecí district), Bohemia. Ragstone head from the La Tène period. Hgt.: 25 cm National Museum Prague.

XXI. Prilly (Waadt), Switzerland. Type of Celtic inhabitant of present-day Switzerland. Work of a Roman artist. Bronze (eyes of copper), hgt.: 27,5 cm. Historical Museum Bern.

XXII. Trichtingen, Württemberg. Celtic silver torc (with iron core), terminating in two bulls' heads. Mature La Tène. Diameter: 29,4 cm, wgt.: 6,75 kg. Museum Stuttgart.

XXIII. Brno-Maloměřice, Moravia. Bronze relief-work, with mask motifs, found in a Celtic burialground. Moravian Museum Brno.

XXIV. Gundestrup (Aalborg) in Jutland. Silver cult cauldron, found in peat bog, 1891. General view. Hgt.: 42 cm, diam. 69 cm, wgt.: 8,86 kg. National Museum Copenhagen.

XXV. Gundestrup, Jutland. Cult cauldron. Décor of one of the inside plates (lgth.: 25 cm). National Museum Copenhagen.

XXVI. Sword scabbards of the La Tène period in the Czech Lands: Dražičky near Tábor, barrow with a cremation burial. Scabbard with 'lipped' chape (with detail), lgth.: 565 mm. Early La Tène. Museum Tábor. – Charváty near Olomouc. Upper part of the scabbard (both sides), from a Celtic grave, c.100 B.C. Museum Olomouc.

XXVII. Košice. Slovakia. Celtic cremation burial, 2 B.C. Museum Košice (Pastor, AR 1954).

XXVIII. Prague–Záběhlice. Bronze torc and brooches from Celtic graves. Diameter of neckla-ce: 11 cm, lght. of brooch: 5,6—6 cm. National Museum Prague.

XXIX. Vlkanovo (Bajč, Hurbanovo district), Slovakia. Bronze anklet from a Celtic grave. Diam.: 6,7 cm. Archaeological Institute Nitra. – Velká Maňa (Nitra district). Glass bracelet from a Celtic grave. Slovak Museum Bratislava.

XXX. Bronze bracelets and anklets from Celtic graves in Central Europe: Prague–Podbaba (Nová Ju-liska), pierced ('openwork') bracelet, diam.: 6,5—7 cm. Municipal Museum Prague. – Moravský Krum-lov, bracelet with imitation filigree décor (b. 19—30 mm). Museum Moravský Krumlov. – Rajhrad near Židlochovice, Moravia. Bracelet of six semi-spherical links, with relief décor. Diameter: 10,5 cm. Mo-ravian Museum Brno.

XXXI. Artistically designed and executed bronze brooches from Celtic graves (3—2 B.C.). Top row:
Ohrada near Kolín (lgth.: 6 cm., Museum Kolín). Přemyšlení (Prague-North), lgth.: 76 mm. National
Museum Prague. – Velká Maňa, Slovakia, Grave No XIII (lgth.: 37 mm). Archaeological Institute Nitra.
Žatec, Bohemia. Museum Žatec. – Below: Brno–Maloměřice, Grave No 17 (lgth.: 76 mm). Brooch with
enamel inlays. Moravian Museum Brno.

XXXII. Bronze rosette bracelets, expanding, from women's graves (2 B.C.). Fine metal-casting from Celtic workshops in Bohemia. Ledvice near Duchcov and (below) Plaňany near Kolín. Museum Duchcov and the National Museum Prague.

XXXIII. Examples of Celtic ceramics, turned on a wheel. From burial-grounds in Bohemia and Moravia: 1. Staňkovice near Žatec, Grave No 3 (hgt.: 32,5 cm) Museum Žatec. 2. Kozlany near Bučovice, Moravia, Grave No 8 (hgt.: 18 cm). Moravian Museum Brno. 3. Libčeves near Bílina, Bohemia, Grave 8/1889 (hgt.: 17 cm). National Museum Prague. – 4.–5. Brno–Maloměřice (Cremation burial Grave No 55, hgt.: 23,3 cm. – Inhumation burial, Grave No 29, hgt.: 44 cm). Moravian Museum Brno.

XXXIV. Steinsburg near Römhild, Thuringia, hill-fort. — Staffelberg, oppidum in the basin of the Main. Air photograph.

XXXV. Celtic oppidum, Hradiště near Stradonice, not far from Beroun, Bohemia. Various finds of small bronze objects. National Museum Prague.

XXXVI. Celtic oppidum, Hradiště nad Závistí, near Zbraslav, Bohemia. View from the river Vltava of the lower part of the defended area ('U altánku'). – Rampart surrounding the acropolis, in the upper part of the oppidum. Photographs: V. Moucha, 1959.

XXXVII. *Oppidum Závist, to the south of Prague. Lower stone walling at the highest point of the acropolis, probably dating from the beginning of the La Tène period. Excavation by the Archaeological Institute of the Czechoslovak Academy, Prague.*

XXXVIII. Celtic oppidum at Hrazany near Sedlčany, in Bohemia. The in-turned entrance and the ruts formed by waggons passing in and out. Excavated in 1959, by L. Jansová.

XXXIX. Oppidum Závist, to the south of Prague. Excavation of the main gate showing remnants of the outer facing and the inner timber construction of the fortifications. Last century B.C. Excavation by the Archaeological Institute of the Czechoslovak Academy, Prague.

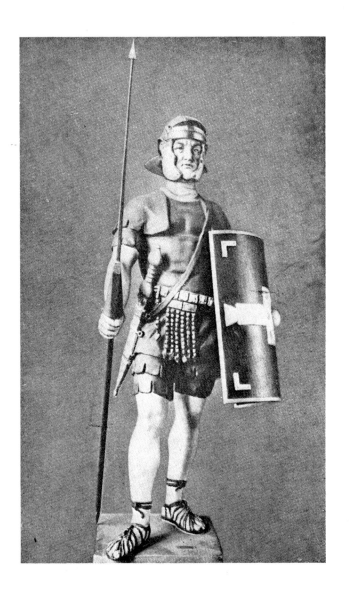

XL. Roman legionary, representative of Roman power in Gaul, after the fall of Celtic power. Central Museum Mainz (reconstruction after finds).